CHALLENGING BOUNDARIES

For the Love of Healing

Also by Audrey Murr Copland, the following audio
healing meditations:

The Temple Meditation
Meditation - A Channel for Healing
Healing Light
Relax - Release, Let Go!
Angel Power
Reiki - Pathway to the Soul
Reiki - The Sacred Shrine

Available from www.audreymurrcopland.com

CHALLENGING BOUNDARIES
For the Love of Healing

Audrey Murr Copland

Fellow NFSH The Charitable Trust Ltd.
Reiki Master Practitioner/Teacher,
Ordained Revd. Alliance of Divine Love, Healing and
Counselling Ministry, USA

This book comprises a memoir and a practical guide to healing. The events and conversations have been set down to the best of the author's ability, although some names and details have been changed to protect the privacy of individuals. The memoir reflects the author's present recollections of her experiences over time. The second part of the book comprises a practical guide to healing. The information provided in this book is designed to provide helpful information on the subjects discussed. This book is not meant to be used, nor should it be used, to diagnose or treat any medical condition. For diagnosis or treatment of any medical problem, consult your own physician. The publisher and author are not responsible for any specific health or allergy needs that may require medical supervision and are not liable for any damages or negative consequences from any treatment, action, application or preparation, to any person reading or following the information in this book. References are provided for informational purposes only and do not constitute endorsement of any websites or other sources.

ISBN: 978-1-0890-5886-1 (paperback)
This paperback edition first published in 2019
Cover painting by Doreen Davis

www.audreymurrcopland.com

DEDICATION

I have been privileged to share in and contribute to the self-healing journey of many thousands of people from all walks of life. I dedicate this book with love and blessings to these courageous and inspiring individuals, who have enriched my own self-healing journey, and also to those just beginning to develop their awareness of the healing process. I also dedicate this book to the NFSH Charitable Trust Ltd with whom I have been associated for over 40 years, wearing many different hats.

ACKNOWLEDGEMENTS

I have drawn inspiration for this book from many experiences, teachings, and people. Thank you to all those who have inspired me, both directly and indirectly. A number of people have offered me their love and support in the preparation of this book to whom I am especially grateful and indebted. Rod Gosse whose technical expertise provided invaluable support in the management of software issues and preparation of the manuscript. Anthony Ward for the practical advice he offered me at the outset. Ruth Copland, my loving and talented daughter, who believed in me with all her heart and soul, and offered extensive creative and practical support in the development of the book. Doreen Davis, my American talented artist friend who produced the art work for the book cover. Nicholas Murr for his significant and professional input and support. Lastly, Lilla Bek, with whom I have enjoyed over thirty years of friendship and professional association, and for whose unique, profound, and wondrous wisdom I have the deepest appreciation.

THE RULES FOR BEING HUMAN

You will receive a body:
You may like it or not but it will be yours for the entire period this time round.

You will learn lessons:
You are enrolled in a full-time school called life.
Each day in this school you will have the opportunity to learn lessons. You may like the lessons or think them irrelevant or stupid.

There are no mistakes. Only Lessons:
Growth is a process of trial and error: experimentation.
The 'failed' experiments are as much a part of the process as the experiments that 'ultimately' work.

A lesson is repeated until learned:
A lesson will be presented to you in various form until you have learned it. When you have learned it you can then go on to the next lesson.

Learning lessons does not end:
There is no part of life that does not contain lessons.
If you are alive there are lessons to be learned.

'There' is no better than 'here':
When your 'there' has become a 'here' you will simply obtain another 'there' that will, again, look better than 'here'.

Others are merely mirrors of you:
You cannot love or hate something about another person unless it reflects to you something you love or hate in yourself.

What you make of your life is up to you:
You have all the tools and resources you need, what you do with them is up to you. The choice is yours.

Your answers lie inside you:
The answers to life's questions lie inside you.
All you need to do is look, listen and trust.
You will forget all this.

Dr. Cherie-Carter-Scott Ph.D.

CONTENTS

Act 10

Part II
If You Want to Be a Healer

ABOUT THE AUTHOR

Audrey Murr Copland is one of the most experienced, respected, and gifted international healers and teachers in Britain in the last forty years. She has been instrumental in moving healing from the peripheries of public awareness to mainstream acceptance through her work with the charity The National Federation of Spiritual Healers (now registered as The NFSH Charitable Trust Ltd and whose working title is The Healing Trust) and via her personal workshops with people around the world. She is also a natural sensitive and intuitive counsellor, specialising in self-healing and energy renewal through creative visualisation. She has recorded a series of widely acclaimed audio Healing Meditations designed to provide personal and on-going self-healing support through guided healing journeys utilising the healing energy of her voice. In addition to being a Healer Member of The Healing Trust, Audrey is a Reiki Master Teacher and Practitioner and was ordained as a Reverend by the Alliance of Divine Love, Healing and Counselling Ministry, USA. She has appeared on radio and television in Britain and abroad, and has been a keynote speaker at major exhibitions and expos in London and the USA.

Audrey is a Fellow of The National Federation of Spiritual Healers (now called The Healing Trust) an honour she received in recognition of her unique and considerable service to the organisation. For twelve years Audrey was National Secretary managing the central office, and subsequently also served as Vice President. She was a Founding Member of the pioneering executive team which developed the first-ever professional healer development and training programme, launched in 1983. The programme established a professional standard for healers requiring two years of probationary training with oversight of practical experience as well as a study syllabus. A strong NFSH Code of Conduct was also established, which was submitted to and approved by all the Royal Colleges of Medicine, Nursing, Obstetrics and Veterinary Medicine.

Audrey was an NFSH National Tutor for the training programme for 25 years teaching throughout Britain, as well as presenting healer training workshops across Europe and North America, including in Alaska and Newfoundland, and in Israel. She helped set up permanent healer training in organisations in Madrid, North Carolina, and Toronto. In addition, Audrey implemented the NFSH's first official Distant Healing Service, which now supports many thousands of people worldwide. Audrey's work managing NFSH central office put her in constant contact with thousands of people by phone, letter, and in person, supporting the sick and dying, all of whom were looking for a lifeline from the NFSH's national referral service, the only one of its kind in Britain. Over her long career Audrey has worked with people suffering from AIDS, HIV, cancer and many other life-threatening conditions. She has initiated and led many healing and meditation groups, and also taught Spiritual Reiki at Adult Education colleges.

Audrey was fortunate to develop her skills alongside mentors such as Sir George Trevelyan, Frederic Lionel, Lilla Bek, and Dr. Brugh Joy. Throughout her career she has sought to grow and develop her skills through experience and deep study. Consequently, her work is thoroughly grounded in the teachings of the great masters and is also practically tried and tested via the hundreds of individual healing consultations she has given and through her work with groups at many conferences and courses. She first became aware of the healing power of her voice when she was presenting spiritual development groups where participants were entranced by the energy conveyed as she spoke. Students eagerly suggested that she should record her voice and she then developed her creative visualisation audio series which was an instant success.

Audrey has been married twice and is divorced. She has one daughter, Ruth, and two grandsons, Tamas and Evan, all of whom live in California. Audrey lives in mystical Glastonbury in England where amongst her many activities she finds time to work as a volunteer at the world-famous Chalice Well Peace and Healing Gardens, founded by Wellesley Tudor Pole over fifty years ago.

Audrey says "Essentially we are all Healers with wounds to heal. Inner healing is multi-dimensional and can only occur through deep relaxation and an alteration in consciousness. Practising meditation is like phoning home and keeping you in touch with the essence of who, what and why you are".

For more information visit: www.audreymurrcopland.com
where you can also purchase Audrey's audio healing meditations.

PRODUCTION NOTES

'No-one appears on our stage unless the director has placed them there for our benefit. You have come to earth to entertain and to be entertained'
- **Paramhansa Yogananda famous Yogi and author of the world best-seller 'An Autobiography of a Yogi'.**

Hello! I am the Producer and Scriptwriter of this production. It is about a personal life journey into healing and the challenging boundaries I encountered which sometimes seemed insurmountable or took my breath away at what they revealed. It is not my intention to preach to anyone or in any way convert their belief system, which I will always honour and respect. I sincerely hope though that by sharing my own healing journey with you it will encourage others to see that it is possible to be able to heal oneself. This is why I have included a practical guide to healing in the second part of the book.

In the memoir section of Challenging Boundaries I share with the reader the courage it took for me to be honest and frank about my childhood 'wounds' and not sweep them under the carpet or be in denial. I do so in the hope that it will illuminate how trauma and difficulties can pass through generations if we don't give attention to heal any chi we have inherited. My aim is to share in the book that by consciously working to heal these wounds we will experience greater personal happiness and also healthier relationships with others.

'An actor in his life-time plays many parts and wears many costumes. I don't want to be "identified" with one part let alone one costume called my "present body". I am a very different person - in body, mind and spirit - from the person I was a score of years ago. I want to be the player who has been made a better actor by every part that I have played, and I want the play to be a success, not just my acting, and Life is God's play, and - in parentheses - no one can wisely judge a play by one act' - Revd. Leslie D. Weatherhead CBE MA. Ph.D. D.Litt. DD

In 1974 I was in a persistently unhappy quandary concerning the meaning and purpose of my life and I wondered what, if anything I could do about it. Then, quite unexpectedly, something startling occurred which completely changed my life's direction when I experienced an extraordinary, deeply personal and profound spiritual awakening following the death of a beloved elderly uncle-in-law who began to create some peculiar phenomena in my home to alert my attention. He then began to make contact with me on several occasions from the 'other side'. Uncle Bert's first and subsequent messages and guidance were incredibly significant and important. For the first time in my life I received direct proof that death is only a separation on a physical level and that we can still communicate from another dimension; we never really lose touch and the journey of the soul continues on other levels of consciousness. More on this subject is revealed in Act 3 Scene 3 under Revelations From The 'Other Side'.

So profoundly meaningful were Uncle Bert's communications from the 'other side' of the veil, they were actively responsible for me commencing my own spiritual quest to discover my own Truth and the meaning and purpose of my life. In Act. 3 Scenes 6 & 7 I relate how I looked into spiritualism and psychic development and the exploration and study of the ageless wisdom and comparative religions, guided by 'Wiser Souls' in physical bodies, (plus a few who were not) who kept popping in and out of my life at various times and places. I then discovered to my complete surprise how really psychic and truly sensitive I am but seemingly had no inkling of this due, perhaps, to being spiritually asleep. Nor did I realise then how much self-healing I needed or had any idea of how this might occur or how I could ever learn to love myself which seemed to me such an alien thought.

As a five year old child I grew up during World War II within a poor army family and like so many other children then, was ill-educated and underprivileged. In addition I was insecure with dreadful feelings of abandonment due to twice being evacuated. With hindsight I can now fully understand why my mum and dad, whom I always loved unconditionally, lacked essential parenting skills due to the deep wounds they inherited from both their own acutely difficult childhood. Subsequently I had to come to terms with my own lack of confidence, low self-esteem, resentment, unconscious anger, frustration and deep and lasting feelings of abandonment. In other words I had deep wounds to heal.

In all honesty I had no idea how such a healing journey would begin or what benefit I might achieve from it. Intuitively I just knew with all of my heart and soul that if and when the opportunity presented itself I would know and I took comfort from a quote by Confucius, a Chinese Philosopher and Teacher of the Spring and Autumn period of Chinese history:

'The journey of a thousand miles has to start with the first step'.

Thus with faith and trust I decided to take a monumental leap into the Light which surprisingly manifested some profound situations; one major one being a meeting with the highly evolved Psychic Energy Researcher, Yoga Teacher and author, Lilla Bek, now a long-term friend, with whom I studied professionally for fifteen years. Lilla's loving and extraordinary spiritual guidance and support resulted in developing a channel for healing myself and then others using both my voice and the laying-on-of-hands, which I will explain more about later in the book

As part of my spiritual quest to become more enlightened I undertook one-to-one sessions in re-birthing. During the first session I experienced being in my mother's womb. Although it was dark I felt completely safe, warm and cosy even though I could hear external sounds and my movement was restricted. Then, suddenly, a great disturbance occurred when against my will I was violently squeezed and expelled through a narrow canal into what seemed at first to be a very hostile environment which extracted a piercing yell and screaming sobs from the core of my being.

Surprisingly, regression sessions revealed to me that past life experiences could have a positive affect upon my current life because of the insight I gained from them as well as the realisation that I had not always 'come down' in a female body and that I had also experienced living through many different civilisations. The cellular memory is so vast and I was completely astonished to have it unravelled and able to identify with other lives I had lived which in some cases were very supportive of my present life's potential

It's fair to say that I became consumed with the need to understand as much as possible about myself and any of the subjects connected to spiritual knowledge and insight. I attended lectures, courses, workshops and spiritual development groups in abundance. All of this was achieved while undertaking a daily working life which helped to keep everything balanced and well-grounded, under the circumstances.

In many instances the most important message that seemed endlessly to be taught by the different Teachers at these various venues was that we must first love and heal ourself before we could love or heal anyone else. This was such an alien thought to me that at first I could not take it seriously and doubted the wisdom of such a statement.

When I learnt that one of the most significant archetypal energies we possess is that of the 'child' and that throughout our lifetime this inner child can be responsible for many of the decisions we make in life and what kind of person we might become I was desperate to find out more. In Act 3 scene 14 I will share with you an extraordinary, enlightening and never-to-be-forgotten consequence of working with my inner child and the subsequent magical and healing communications that occurred between 'Little Audrey' and 'Big Audrey'.

I will always feel very blessed and forever grateful for every challenging experience I encountered during my search for the meaning of life and to all those other Teachers and students who have ultimately enriched my life with their wisdom and guidance. Sometimes it seems we have to commit to astonishing new concepts and values instead of the more comfortable ones that may have been entrenched from our childhood. We can gain so much more when we explore who, what and why we are and make ourselves available to expand our understanding of life and its ultimate purpose. Learning and practising meditation was a thrilling step forward in self-healing and such a lovely experience of being able to quieten the mind and reach another part of myself that was all knowing and being. In one early meditation I was impressed to write:

'I am my body, but I am not my body. My body is in my consciousness which is infinite. I exist simultaneously on many different levels that ultimately transcend to the divine level, the God incarnate.'

Exploring these different parts of me meant embracing the spirit within and learning about the composition and levels of consciousness, the importance of the etheric body and the energy body's chakra system and auric field and how we can, through the practice of right breathing, relaxation, visualisation, meditation, and understanding the meaning of colour and light, learn how to channel spiritual energy as a divine healing force. This proved to be as challenging as climbing Mt. Everest or swimming the English channel. The subsequent benefits of which were ultimately and unbelievably transformational.

I never dreamed that, eventually, my life would be blessed with countless opportunities to connect to and release one's own inner healer and most importantly to become acutely aware that there is a definite purpose for being born. It most certainly is not a haphazard affair. I now believe, unconditionally, that while we are here on earth we have the opportunity to learn many lessons. One thing I accept wholeheartedly is that we must put our whole heart into whatever it is we want to achieve. You cannot be half-hearted.

When I put my heart and soul into studying and practising the art and science of spiritual healing, inadvertently I began to heal the 'wounded healer' within. It is always a two-way scenario practising what you preach and teach. I consider I am still very much a 'probationer on the path' albeit now better able to understand that I am the sum total of my experiences which have been instrumental in awakening the empathy, insight and unconditional love I needed to begin to heal myself and others. Hence the reason why I am sharing my life story with you in part one of 'Challenging Boundaries'.

I know I am not unique in what I believe but in my attempt to be of service to spirit I was placed in some pretty unique situations. Constantly challenging boundaries to 'know' myself better led to some quite unprecedented developments and commitment to over thirty years of travel across the United Kingdom and many other countries in order to train and develop many hundreds of would-be healers. All in the pursuit of healing.

If this revelation touches a chord within you perhaps it might inspire you to commence or continue your own healing journey the results of which can be positively encouraging.

Undoubtedly my role in life as a healer has been an extraordinarily humbling experience particularly when listening to the doubts and fears of sick but courageous members of the public. In some instances it meant having to confront death up close and personal. I can honestly state that healing into death and dying can be one of the most challenging and privileged situations for any healer to face.

We may have to deal with challenging boundaries on a daily basis that will help us to grow spiritually in order to heal ourselves, that is why the second part of my book is entitled **'If You want To be A Healer'** and offers a simple, comprehensive healer development guide which you might be encouraged to study and to take heart from my own healing journey.

Although primarily it refers to spiritual healing through the laying-on-of-hands the information is very appropriate for practising any kind of alternative healing therapy which can only be enhanced by first attuning to the 'spiritual' level of consciousness into its delivery.

The dictionary definition of the word 'spiritual' is as follows:

Relating to or affecting the human spirit or soul as opposed to material or physical things.

Healing Blessings to one and all.

CHALLENGING BOUNDARIES

PART I

Act 1 Scene 1:

Curtain Up - An Overview

'All the world's a stage, and all the men and women merely players; they have their exits and their entrances; and one man in his time plays many parts, his acts being seven ages'
- William Shakespeare

The telephone was ringing loudly. I hesitated for a moment. Should I answer it? Then I picked it up and before I had time to speak I heard the voice of a lady urgently pleading:

"Good morning. I hope I'm through to the right number? I need help. Please can you help me? My husband's dying of cancer. His condition is terminal and he's been discharged from hospital as there's nothing medically that can be done for him. A friend has suggested that we try spiritual healing, about which we know nothing, but we are desperate and willing to try anything at this stage. I believe you keep a register of spiritual healers? Is that correct?"

As she paused for breath I could sense the real fear and anxiety in her voice and I responded as empathetically and confidently as possible.

"Yes, that's right we do keep a register of members who are practising spiritual healers so If you would be kind enough to give me your address I'll check to see who is in your area and able to do a home visit to see your husband."

"Oh! Thank God! Bless you my dear," came the relieved reply.

"I'm just at my wit's end. My husband is so ill. I suppose we are looking for a miracle but anything's worth trying at this stage."

She then gave me her details and I carefully shuffled through a card index system that had temporarily been placed in a shoe box. At last I found the name of a spiritual healer who, hopefully, lived not too far away from this lady's address.

"Hello. Yes, here we are. I've found someone for you in your area. Have you got a pen handy and I'll give you this healer's telephone number and you can call direct and make whatever arrangements are possible?"

"Thank you so much. I'm so grateful to you. Thank God that there's such an organisation for this sort of help. I'm much obliged to you. Thank you again. Goodbye."

After this initial heart-rending telephone call I knew with absolute certainty this would be no ordinary office job. With all of my heart I realised I had discovered a new role in my life which seemed to be full of meaning and service. There was a real sense of 'coming home!' Something important and quite extraordinary awakened inside of me. I absolutely knew this was part of my destiny. There could be no turning back – ever. Such was my first day of reluctantly coming out of early retirement in 1978 to temporarily assist the Administrator of the struggling National Federation of Spiritual Healers (NFSH), a registered healing charity which, due to a dire financial situation, had sold off its property in Essex and leased an attractive studio/office in Sunbury-on-Thames which my husband, Don, had fortuitously found for them not long after I had learned from an acquaintance of mine that such an organisation existed.

Being inquisitive I wanted to know what the badge my friend was wearing meant. It was the healer member's badge of the NFSH. Extremely intrigued Don left no stone unturned until he had tracked their offices down and arranged to meet the Administrator.

Having successfully given birth in October 1967 to my precious and beautiful daughter Ruth, following three failed and difficult pregnancies, the last thing I had on my mind was to return to office work. I enjoyed picking up Ruth from school each day at 4PM and I wasn't about to give up my Thursday afternoon flower-arranging classes either.

Don, however, in 1977 succeeded in persuading me to help out the Administrator for just a couple of weeks until someone else could be hired. It truly turned out to be a 'watershed' moment in all of our lives and for me personally a monumental leap forward into the art and science of spiritual healing.

It didn't take me long, therefore, to realise that 'Upstairs' had uniquely placed me at the cutting edge of what was to become the healing charity's biggest and most successful public leap forward and major transformation from being described as a 'club for healers', mainly of Spiritualist persuasion, to an exceptionally modern, progressively professional, non-denominational healing organisation.

With the subsequent appointment in 1982 of a completely new, immensely talented and inspired Executive Board of Trustees, which my husband was already a member of, and the subsequent retirement of the Administrator, I became responsible for the daily office administration and was in attendance at all Board meetings.

During the 1980s and 1990s the NFSH was considered to be the largest healing organisation in the world with a UK-registered membership of approximately 7,000, plus affiliated overseas organisations in Australia, New Zealand, Canada, America and South Africa.

Significantly, it was a period of the most forward-looking and transformational growth in the charity's history as well as in spiritual healing, which was being widely embraced and publicly accepted on a previously unimagined level, despite the fact that in the late 1960s the National Health Service granted permission for their healers to make hospital visits at a patient's request and with the knowledge of the ward manager.

Even the Orthodox Church was being stirred into seriously considering introducing healing services - hitherto lacking so far - into their congregational activities such was their concerned reaction to the immensely overwhelming public interest in what the National Federation of Spiritual Healers was publicly offering and achieving.

During this period, a strict Code of Conduct was also established for healers and duly accepted by all the Royal Colleges of Medicine, Obstetrics and Nursing. Disciplinary procedures were put into place and standards of membership for healers and probationers (now termed student healers) were upgraded, each of whom were covered by full public liability insurance for the first time.

In 1982 The NFSH became the first healing organisation in the country to launch a residential ground breaking basic healer development training course programme which, through years of previous study and dedication on my part, earned me the honour of becoming a founder member and tutor of the programme. In addition I remained employed in the daily administration of the office until 1989 when I decided to focus solely on teaching both in my own right and on the NFSH national course programme. What I learnt about the art and science of spiritual healing and the public interest in the subject during this period was incalculable.

Thus from 1982 when the residential courses began I spent ten years in the most exciting, hard working and worthwhile personal endeavour of my life. Together, Don and I, plus two other tutors, John and Jean Dreghorn, (all now deceased), taught the residential basic healer development courses/workshops to many hundreds of people across the United Kingdom until regional tutors were eventually established.

I must pay tribute here to Don Copland for his exceptional talent as a PR and events organiser for the Charity which led to the highly popular introduction of an annual conference with keynote speakers plus some seventy other events throughout the year. Don also served as President of the organisation from 1982 until 1987 and overall his twenty years of dedicated executive service to the growth and expansion of the organisation were reported to be some of the most ground-breaking years in its history.

Coincidentally during this period some kind of 'spiritual explosion' occurred within the collective consciousness of humanity bringing with it a plethora of much needed spiritual-awareness books, tapes, and national Mind-Body-Spirit exhibitions all geared up to providing everyone with more understanding and insight about who, what and why we are. It was as if all the sacred/secret wisdom over aeons of time became available overnight for our personal knowledge and spiritual transformation.

The NFSH office soon became an important 'hub of the wheel' inundated, daily, with calls from the general public, journalists and the media all seeking interviews and further information about spiritual healing. Even more so after a farewell speech by HRH The Prince of Wales to the British Medical Association (BMA) in 1983, upon his retirement as their President.

HRH The Prince of Wales had encouraged more use of complementary medicine and more understanding of the spirit within as well as just the physical body. Subsequently, the British Medical Association in 1984 set up an investigation into alternative therapies including spiritual healing. That same year, September 1983, Don and I were invited by Dr. Ann O'Brian, Programming Secretary of a local division of the BMA, to address their meeting of General Practitioners and Hospital Physicians at the Post Graduate Medical Centre, King George's hospital in Ilford, Essex, to explain to an audience of medical personnel what spiritual healing is and how it works. After Don's talk on 'The Holistic Healing Potential' we received many fascinating questions from doctors one of whom quite seriously asked:

"Could you please enlighten me as to where, in the body, the spirit is and how it could be healed?"

A rather lengthy explanation then ensued, covering the composition of consciousness, which will be referred to later in part two of this book - 'If You Want To Be A Healer'.

Paracelsus said: 'The Physician should know the invisible as well as the visible man. There is a great difference between the power which removes the invisible cause of disease and that which causes merely the external effects to disappear'.

The Temple of the Soul

Spirit taught me that the body is the temple of the soul and during meditation it is this inner sanctuary we can enter to experience solace and feel able to connect to that divine source of unconditional love and peace – the 'Christ Consciousness' – which is the consciousness of pure unconditional love.

The following is a message given to me in meditation:

'The body needs energy to feed its many systems, and exercise to keep those systems in good order and for the energy to flow well. The body responds to the thoughts we create and reflects the level of energy stored within it by putting into action harmony or disharmony. Every part of our body has seven levels of consciousness. We can operate to the highest level according to our level of awareness, sensitivity or creativity.

'It is through the human body that energies from higher levels are grounded, transmuted and used for the benefit of humanity and the planet earth. That energy is light. The more light we can reflect, the lighter we will become. If our body is heavy, sluggish, tense, then we block that light and deny its full strength. We can only become a reflection of God's light if we have a good instrument. We must not overload it, abuse it, or misuse it in any way. The body reflects the level of energy and quality of its strength so that we know when we become depleted. When we are not functioning at our optimum, the body is blocked and starved of energy. We must care, nurture, love ourselves and try to keep our body sacred so that it can truly be used as an instrument for the divine'.

In 1989 I resigned my administrative position with the NFSH charity and the Board of Trustees appointed me a Fellow of NFSH in recognition of my steadfast involvement with the organisation. The following years from 1989-2004 were spent travelling and teaching introductory healer development courses both nationally and internationally and also assisting in the development of new healing organisations in Spain, Canada and America.

My life changed significantly as did the lives of those thousands of people who, subsequently, crossed my path during my travels across the UK, Spain, Portugal, Jersey, Isle of Man, Israel, Newfoundland, Toronto, California, Florida, Atlanta, North and South Carolina, Washington, and Alaska. It was the most profoundly hardworking, uplifting and blessed period of my entire life.

This time round I had to discover my role in life and its purpose. Would I have changed anything? I will only have the answer when the final curtain falls, and at the end of any worthwhile production there is usually an encore!

Act 1 Scene 2:

Family Life

'Life is a dream for the wise, a game for the fool, a comedy for the rich, a tragedy for the poor'
- Paramhansa Yogananda

Part of why I am telling my personal story which begins with my childhood and family experiences, is to illuminate how trauma and difficulties can pass through generations if we don't give attention to trying to heal the wounds we have inherited. Mine cannot be avoided as they prepared me for adulthood and unconsciously awakened my inner healer. The sharing of my experiences is done to show that we can suffer and we can still heal and even thrive.

I must emphasise again that I always loved my mum and dad unconditionally. With the benefit of hindsight I can now fully appreciate the hardships they both suffered growing up. They had to face some very difficult and extenuating circumstances throughout their young lives which, undoubtedly, influenced their behaviour as potentially 'wounded' parents. Essentially they tried to be loving parents but sometimes misguided ones.

In all honesty, neither of them had any previous experience that would have enabled them to become good role models for myself and siblings, although I am certain they loved and cared for us as best they could. It all became much clearer and made a lot more sense after meeting my spiritual Teacher, and life-long friend Lilla Bek, who believes that we choose our parents and siblings before we reincarnate. We 'come down' to earth in a 'group soul' in order to complete unfinished business from previous lives and to act as each other's teachers and mentors.

In the summer of 1944 I was a caring, sensitive, skinny, pale faced, blonde- haired and very self-conscious girl of ten. My mum didn't want my hair to lose its blondness so, when she dyed her own hair, using a toothbrush dipped in neat peroxide, she dyed mine at the same time despite my pleading protests. The inevitable result was just awful. I hated going to school where I was bullied and taunted by the other kids calling out 'dyed hair' and 'peroxide blonde' while in the playground. Worse still, it took ages for my hair to get back to a normal colour and texture and even longer for me not to feel ashamed and humiliated. (*I am sure my Mum thought she had the best intentions doing what she did but the consequences wreaked havoc on me!*)

One day I was dreamily walking home from 'Rogers' the local sweet shop, after using up one sweet coupon - from my monthly ration book allowance of twelve - on toffees that were priced at four a penny, or a farthing each. Deep in thought, I railed one hand along the high wooden fence behind which was the Royal Army Service Corps depot where I lived with my family in army married quarters. It was a very close-knit army community and I had lots of friends who were children of other army personnel.

My dad was a regular army non-commissioned First Class Warrant Officer who, upon his return in 1928 from five years' service in India, had met my mum at an army dance when she was eighteen and in service as a parlour maid to the Colonel's wife. My dad was ten years older. They had married in November 1929 soon after they met, without really knowing one another very well, and my older brother was born in August 1930 in the army hospital at Woolwich, London. The army provided a small flat situated within the Royal Cavalry Barracks in the London Borough of Hounslow, Middlesex, where I was born on February 28th 1933 and later christened in the Royal Garrison church with a full army choir in attendance which was difficult for the congregation to hear as I screamed the place down, I am told. My mum named me Audrey after the Colonel's wife. Audrey, I understand, is a Teutonic word meaning 'noble threatener' who is wise, concerned, and very kind; and devoted to her family. 'Worth her weight in gold'. Quite something to live up to!

Not long afterwards we moved into a three bedroom army house situated near the barracks of the Royal Army Service Corp. depot just a mile away.

As I ambled along enjoying the luxury of chewing the toffee in my mouth, endeavouring to make it last as long as possible, I began wondering what I would be like when I was a grown up and how I might look and what I would be doing? Would I be a famous actress, then fall in love, marry and have children? This subject intrigued me. I had this inner knowing that one day I would look back on my life and remember this day-dream. **And know myself.**

My parents were my only role models. When I was much older I realised, sadly, just how incompatible they really were and how unstable their relationship was and why they were so unhappy. Inevitably their behaviour towards one another affected me in a negative way.

My mum, bless her, was ever resourceful and creative in how she coped with a constant shortage of money and always took great pride in her personal appearance. She was hard working and desperately in love with my dad constantly trying to make their challenging relationship work. Mum held down various jobs including a favourite one as an Announcer at the famous Waterloo Station in London. Eventually she was employed as a clerk by the Civil Service locally to where she lived.

In later life she became a doting grandmother to her ten grand children who absolutely adored her. I am full of love and admiration for all that she achieved despite the constant challenging circumstances she faced throughout her life.

My Dad's Background:

My dad was born in 1902 and lived in Kent and his mother died following the birth of her thirteenth child when he was only eleven years old. I can't imagine the effects that must have had on him. He spent thirty-three years in the army becoming a member of a Masonic Lodge while stationed in India.

He was invalided home by stretcher case from Normandy, in 1939, just three months after the army sent him there and later held the rank of First Class Warrant Office, in charge of a body of men, and awarded the MBE for services rendered in the preparation of landing craft vehicles for the invasion of Europe.

By then my dad rarely spoke about his parents but said he admired them greatly. His father was a Stoker in the Merchant Navy. A family aunt looked after them as best she could after their mother passed away. She must have been a very special person.

As soon as my dad was able to he joined the army, disguising his real age of seventeen to eighteen.

He hoped to follow some of his brothers into the Navy but failed the eyesight test.

My Mum's Background:

My mother was born in 1911 in Sunderland, part of the depressed north of England and was one of eight siblings all living in abject poverty. Always hungry, with a father out of work, who drank whenever he could afford to, my mother said she used to shovel and then haul barrow loads of coal dust from the pit head to sell at a shilling a load to buy food for the family. It hardly bears thinking about. What a strong and determined child she must have been. She was extremely attractive and intelligent and had passed the Grammar school entrance exams. Unfortunately, due to her family's impoverished situation, she was unable to attend; sadly there was no money to purchase the compulsory school uniform. Instead she was 'hired' by her paternal grandmother, who lived in the picturesque village of Whitburn, in one of the sought-after 'The Bents' attractive cottages facing the North Sea. She said she helped with the housework as well as acting as a maid, when called for, and although she had to work hard she was well fed and loved living by the sea but, surprisingly, never learnt to swim. Perhaps the sea was too cold to venture into.

Mum's grandfather was Skipper of the local lifeboat until he retired. He received a citation stating:

'John Young Purvis 78, member of the Whitburn Lifeboat for half a century, becoming Coxswain, on retirement received a purse of gold and a barometer'.

It was also acknowledged that while he was in a cob fishing boat a German U-boat suddenly surfaced and fired a torpedo at a merchant ship. My great grandfather helped to save over 300 lives.

As the depression got worse and aged only sixteen mum very courageously left the north on her own and headed down to the more affluent south into Service.

Act 1 Scene 3:

Arguments and Threats

'We can never obtain peace in the entire world until we make
   peace with ourselves'
- **Dalai Llama**

Undoubtedly, and for many reasons beyond my control, my home life was extremely stressful and unsettled. Since aged three I had often been awakened in the night and would sit shivering on the stairs in my nightdress, hugging a favourite doll, while listening anxiously to my parents, whom I loved dearly, rowing constantly and sometimes violently, over my father's drinking habit of coming home late from the Army Mess. *(Most regular soldiers spent a lot of time in the Mess, drinking, playing cards, etc., and generally enjoying 'men only' company forgetting they were married with children.)*

As the rows worsened, inevitably they began to affect me quite badly. My brothers did not seem bothered and ignored them but I was unable to. One night I ventured down the stairs to the kitchen to investigate why my mum was screaming hysterically shouting out:

"Bloody well keep away from me, or I will drink this. I mean it."

Frightened, I peered round the kitchen door and perceived that in one hand she held a bottle of disinfectant and in the other hand she was brandishing a sharp kitchen knife, while threatening to drink the disinfectant if my dad approached her. Startled by my appearance my mum immediately burst into tears as she surrendered both items to the floor and collapsed into a distressed heap. Stunned and confused I wrapped my arms lovingly around her to comfort her while my dad looked on guiltily.

When I was a little older I constantly fretted over how I could help my parents to sort out their relationship problems and prevent them from being so miserable. It really mattered to me as I cared so deeply about them so I began praying to the Lord Jesus Christ as I had been taught to do at my Sunday school. My mother's brother, my Uncle Jack, was a dedicated lay preacher at the Feltham Independent Chapel nearby and when I was five he took me along there. I loved Sunday School and found solace in 'talking to God' and spilling out all my fears and doubts and asking for His help hoping that there was something 'He' could do to change things. I looked upon 'Him' as a friendly support system and comfort. I thought of 'Him' as my 'Heavenly Father'. It was so wonderfully reassuring to trust and believe that there was a great and powerful Being, God, who could perform miracles. *(I am now utterly convinced that following my introduction to God and prayer, even as a small child, I was already learning to meditate and attune to a divine source which is what spiritual healing is all about).* Sunday school became a haven of peace for me and I loved being there and especially being taken afterwards, by my Uncle, to have tea with him and my aunt and their little daughter. My auntie, a professionally trained confectioner, made the most delicious fairy cakes decorated with coloured icing and sprinkles which, for me, were a special luxury. Their family life seemed to be a haven of calm and peace, in complete contrast to my own.

Act 1 Scene 4:

Sheltering from the German Bombing

'Mankind must put an end to war before war puts an end to humanity'
- **John F. Kennedy**

In the summer of 1939 war clouds were gathering. It was while on a family holiday that my dad received a War Office telegram instructing him to 'Return to Unit immediately'. Not long after this world war two was declared against Germany on Sunday, September 3, 1939. I was five years old and was outside my home busily introducing myself to a new neighbour's child.

"Hello! What's your name?" I asked inquisitively while, at the same time, critically eyeing her up and down. She appeared more like a boy, I concluded, dressed in shorts and a shirt. Her hair was black and cut quite severely.

"Honor." She responded shyly.

"What a funny name. How old are you?" I rudely asked.

"I'm nine years old and my name isn't funny." She remarked in an annoyed tone.

Suddenly, the peaceful Sunday morning was shattered by the wailing sound of a siren. In shock, I looked at Honor, and watched as she fled indoors. Then my mother rushed out from our house shouting:

"It's all right. Don't be scared. It is only a test run by the army to ensure the sirens are working properly. The Prime Minister

Mr Neville Chamberlain has announced on the radio that he has declared war with Germany".

A while later the 'all clear' siren sounded.

With relief I ran towards her saying:

"I don't like the siren. It's a horrible sound and makes me feel scared."

Unfortunately, I was to hear the wails of the siren far too many times over the next five years. I felt really anxious, even when it actually signified the 'all clear' after a German air raid.

At school we were fitted with ugly looking and extremely uncomfortable gas masks and instructed on how to take air raid precautions. In the sky were huge barrage balloons that looked like huge grey elephants. Not quite six years old, it all seemed rather fun, until I watched my Dad and hundreds of other soldiers all march out of the R.A.S.C. Garrison at Feltham to form part of the British Expeditionary Force on their way to France. The soldiers were singing 'South of the Border' while wives and children waved and shouted: "Good Luck. Come back soon." We all felt very sad and I wondered when I would see my dad again.

The following war years were extremely disturbing to my childhood and entirely disruptive to my education. Schools were closed down altogether for a while, due to German daytime air raids, and organised lessons at different homes took place erratically. When we were able to attend school, the Victorian building was surrounded by sand bags, and every window protected by ugly brown sticky tape criss crossing them. An inside chemical toilet was installed and curtained off from the safety area where we gathered for lessons. I dreaded having to use it and was always embarrassed when I did. Inevitably, lessons would be interrupted by the air raid siren and teachers and children would file in a 'crocodile' line and quickly make their way to the shelters. These were above ground and looked like long concrete pipes! There were wooden slatted seats inside and we sat together in a single file. A teacher would pass a packet of Horlicks tablets down the line so that each child had one to suck. The shelter was dark, cold and, to me, quite claustrophobic.

During the 1940 Blitz of London, of which Feltham was on the outskirts, nightly air raids meant sleeping down the big army shelter each night with many other families, while listening to the sound of gun fire and bombs dropping not too far away. During one particularly fearsome German raid twenty-one bombs rained down upon us locally. It was absolutely terrifying and we all clung to one another in the safety of the air raid shelter. I remember listening, in terror, to the whistling sounds of the incendiary bombs and then the explosions. My father, invalided home from France, and acting as an army air raid warden, was blown down the shelter's steep steps by the blast from the explosions, as he and a door crashed in on us. Everyone was in complete shock and so relieved that we were not going to be buried alive under a mountain of earth, that we all cheered. When the 'all clear' siren finally sounded the next morning and we emerged from the shelter everyone was shocked to the core at the huge amount of rubble and debris where once had stood three houses in close proximity to where we had all sheltered. The bombs so easily could have demolished our shelter and injured or killed outright all of the occupants. I have often wondered about this. Was this just luck or divine providence? (*In truth I just knew I would never be killed by any German bombs even though I was scared of being bombed.*)

Act 1 Scene 5:

The Power of Prayer

'Most men consider the course of events as natural and inevitable. They little know what radical changes are possible through prayer. The closer you come to God the more, surely, you will know him as Divine Love itself, the very dearest of the dear'

- Paramhansa Yogananda

Next morning it was a terrible shock when I learnt that my best friend Kathleen had sustained severe and life threatening injuries to one of her legs when she and her parents and sister had been hit by flying shrapnel while running from their home to take shelter. Kathleen's whole family were hospitalised with different kinds of minor injuries. Feeling pretty fearful and helpless I immediately commenced praying to God and continued to do so, every day, for over a year, while Kathleen was hospitalised, asking Him to save Kathleen's leg from amputation.

I wrote notes of encouragement and support to Kathleen until, finally, she came home from hospital wearing a big ugly brown leather and steel brace support on her injured leg. Though Kathleen's leg was deeply and horribly scarred, I thanked God that her leg had been saved. Not long after Kathleen left hospital and was reunited with her family, we planned our first outing together and decided to put our favourite dolls into their small prams and take a walk with them to the local park. It was such fun and such a relief, too, being able to play together again. Nevertheless, I felt saddened to observe how badly Kathleen dragged along her injured leg and remember feeling very protective towards her.

As the days and months passed by it seemed that everyone I knew longed for the war to end. Lots of my army friends were leaving the barracks. Their fathers had either been killed in action or taken prisoner of war in Germany or Japan. There were lots of empty houses and l began to feel quite dreary and lonely. Food rationing often meant feeling really hungry as there were not any of the treats that we take for granted today to cheer one up. At home there was a padlock on the pantry door, which only contained essential rations, to prevent any out-of-hours snacking by myself and two brothers. Such was the shortage of food.

Praying regularly continued to be a comforting as well as powerful method of interceding on someone's behalf. It also became a ritual which I taught and shared with other children during the long nights we spent down the air raid shelter. We prayed for peace, for our country, for our loved ones far away and so on. Retrospectively, all this praying enabled me, later in life, to sow the seeds that blossomed when, as a spiritual healer, I set up the first organised Distant Healing Group within the NFSH healing organisation. Unconsciously, the 'little healer' within me was already awakening.

Aged thirteen, I prayed really hard with tears in my eyes and in great distress, when I thought my mum might die. I remember her lying upstairs in bed bleeding profusely, while pregnant, although I didn't know that then.

As usual, my dad was at his favourite place - the Sergeant's Mess. Mum had urgently called out to me:

"Audrey, I need you to come and help me."

I rushed upstairs and was overwhelmed and in shock at the sight of wads of heavily blood stained sanitary towels in my mother's hands.

Looking very pale and in obvious discomfort my Mum quietly said:

"Here take these pads and place them in that white bucket by the side of the bed."

There was so much blood pouring out of her I was terrified that she would bleed to death.

I did as I was told and nearly vomited when I saw more heavily blood stained pads inside the bucket.

"Audrey, I want you to go and fetch your father from the Mess and tell him it's urgent."

Running as fast as I could to the Sergeant's Mess, I knocked on the side door, as usual, to get a message to my dad. The catering officer answered the door and peered menacingly at me. Before he could comment I blurted out:

"My dad is needed urgently at home. Please could you ask him to come straight away".

Within minutes my dad appeared and as we set out for home he anxiously asked:

"What has happened? Is your mother in bed?"

"Yes she is and there is blood everywhere." I answered. "What is happening? Will she be all right? Shouldn't we call the doctor or an ambulance to take her to hospital?"

Without saying a word to me my father went straight upstairs to my mum.

Waiting anxiously I spent up to an hour at the kitchen windowsill, in tears, looking out of the window up to the sky pleading over and over,

"Dear God, please, please, please, don't let my mum die. I am begging you with all my heart."

The doctor soon arrived and, thankfully, she didn't die and within a few days she was miraculously recovered from a threatened miscarriage and her pregnancy continued. And I thanked God.

The weekend I was being confirmed at a local church, where I also attended church youth club, my Dad was in Roehampton hospital undergoing stomach surgery and, while all the other confirmants had their families present who then remained afterwards to share in the cutting of the large, white, confirmation cake, I was on my own.

Arriving home, my mum said, "Your dad has had five-sixths of his stomach removed. He's stable but the pain's terrible".

Immediately I started praying for him. A few days later while sitting on a bus coming home from the cinema and thinking about the pain my dad was suffering, with tears in my eyes, I started silently praying for his recovery. My prayers were answered and he was soon able to come home and convalesce.

I had no doubt then and more than ever now, that prayer is immensely powerful and spiritually healing; also that energy follows thought and is a powerful method of being able to intercede on someone's behalf when they need spiritual healing even if they are not physically present.

(Despite these disturbing events my automatic childish response to them always led me to pray for a solution. No wonder they proved to be stepping stones towards my great love, in adult life, of distant healing as part of my development as a Spiritual Healer.)

Act 1 Scene 6:

Overcoming Stressful Situations

*'Through every trial we grow. All suffering we experience
has a meaning'*
- Paramhansa Yogananda

My older brother by two years, occasionally got into floor
wrestling incidents with my dad when he arrived home late
from the Mess for Sunday lunch, slightly the worse for drink.
Thankfully, my dad was not an aggressive man and he never
hurt my brother. It frightened me though and Sunday lunch
became an ordeal. When he finally did turn up my mum would
scream at him hysterically shouting:

"There's your bleeding dinner!"

Then, picking up the plateful of food, she would send it hurtling across the room to smash against the kitchen wall, vent-
ing her anger and frustration I guess. It was quite nerve-rack-
ing though and made me feel very anxious. Clearly though
my mum really loved my dad and so she was always trying to
make their relationship work and constantly disappointed that
despite all her efforts he spent most of his time away drinking.

Christmas Day was even worse and always spoilt by my dad
having to 'serve the troops' with their festive meal while, no
doubt, imbibing various amounts of alcohol. It saddened me
that he never sat down to lunch with us even though we waited patiently for him. On Christmas morning my two brothers

and myself always woke at the crack of dawn to view our presents that 'Father Christmas' had left at the bottom of our bed. Breakfast was the one time that day we gathered as a family and opened our gifts. Towards lunch time I would patiently sit looking out of the sitting room window waiting for my dad to show up. Eventually an army lorry would stop outside and I would call out:

"Mum, he's here. Dad's here. An army lorry has brought him home. Oh dear. He is staggering a bit. I hope he doesn't fall down."

Dad was grinning, rather stupidly, when he walked into the hall way before he collapsed on the floor and fell fast asleep.

When he woke up my exasperated mum would immediately start rowing with him instead of just ignoring him. I'm certain it just made things worse. I loved my mum and dad so just accepted the situation, which was far from ideal.

Home life was fraught and I escaped from the constant stress of it all by acting out and releasing my frustration on my numerous dolls scattered around the floor of my small bedroom. Instead of my usual 'mothering' actions I would shout and holler at them in angry frustration, accusing them of being very naughty! Therapists call it role play, or acting out one's anger. Even so, my dolls meant the world to me and most of the time I showered them with as much love as I could. I had thirteen in all and each one had been thoughtfully named by me. Belinda was my favourite china doll as she had big blue eyes and golden hair that curled. Oh how I always longed for curly hair instead of the limp, straight kind with which I had been blessed.

Being a creative, sensitive, Piscean child I also unconsciously released a lot of suppressed anger by having the ability to think up numerous imaginative games to play with my friends who, without fail, were always knocking on my door asking:

"Are you coming out to play? What exciting game are we going to play today Audrey?"

I cared about my friends so never let them down. War games were very popular. Half of us played the Germans and the rest of us played the Allies collecting and caring for the wounded. Writing and acting in simple mini-plays and choreographing dance routines and arranging garden concerts on makeshift stages was, for me, akin to acting which I fervently loved and hoped to pursue one day.

(Undoubtedly, as a child, I was a popular group leader which led later in life to me having an aptitude for leading groups.)

Quite often I imagined that I was already grown up and living peacefully somewhere else. Probably that's why at nineteen years of age it seemed a good idea at the time to get married and leave home – even if it meant only moving a short distance away.

Act 1 Scene 7:

Hospital

As a youngster, I became quite ill with severe stomach pains and vomiting and laid at home in a made-up bed in the sitting room for about a week when, finally, the visiting army doctor suspected appendicitis and I was taken into Ashford Hospital by army ambulance for observation. (*I remember seeing my best friend Kathleen looking out of the window but I was too sick even to wave.*) In hospital and with an operation imminent it transpired I had yellow jaundice so, instead of an appendix operation, I was put on a non-fat diet until I recovered.

I absolutely loved being in hospital. The nurses were so kind and attentive to me. My mum visited often bringing little treats, one of which I didn't appreciate - some shiny orange ribbon for my hair -which didn't really complement my eyes, face or skin which were a horrible, sickly shade of jaundiced yellow! While recovering I loved being able to help out in the ward, pretending to be a nurse and learning how to make a hospital bed properly with turned down corners. I easily made friends with some of the other children in the ward and enjoyed reading to those who couldn't. When the time arrived for me to leave, I was not ready to do so. I wished to remain in hospital for a while longer, which seems rather odd, as usually most people can't wait to go home. When I did I was very unsettled and it was some time before I didn't feel 'homesick' for hospital. I had experienced something rather special while there. It wasn't as if I had any aspirations to become a nurse but something akin to that was definitely stirring inside of me. I remember how good it felt to be able to assist sick people in any way possible.

Act 1 Scene 8:

Evacuation and Separation

As the blitz on London and the Home Counties relentlessly continued it was decided by my mother to take us children to North Wales to a rented cottage next door to where her army neighbour and friend, and her two girls were already installed. We arrived in the village of Deiniolen (pronounced Dennyollen) in the dead of night and I remember crossing a low, narrow bridge underneath which I could hear the gushing sound of fast flowing water. Aged seven I was really scared.

Upon awakening the next morning, tucked up warmly in bed, I gazed out of the window at the wondrous view of mini mountains and rocky terrain the like of which I had never witnessed before. It was like a dream. After breakfast we all went outside for a walk to explore the scenically beautiful countryside in North Wales full of nearby slate quarries. It could not have been more environmentally different from my home in Feltham, Middlesex.

A few weeks later we witnessed regular mass inputs of Liverpool evacuees to the area where lots of unhappy children carrying a suitcase and gas mask and their coat tagged by an ugly-looking identity label were gathered in the school playground awaiting selection by local people. I think this gave my mum an idea to place myself and my eldest brother with a local married couple and then return home to Feltham, with my younger brother, where she intended working at the army workshops with other young women who were being drafted there. It was arranged that my brother and I would share a single bed in a small box room in the council house home of a young childless couple. At our first introduction Mrs Williams was endeavouring to cuddle me while sitting me on her lap and in a strangely lilting voice asked me:

"Now then Audrey, dear, what are you going to call me? Will it be Mummy, Auntie or Mrs Williams?"

I wasn't having any of it. My immediate and positive response was:

"Mrs Williams!"

Her husband, Mr Williams, who worked at the local slate quarry, was attempting to engage my brother in conversation but he just wanted to go out and play. All too soon, my mum, who was going home to England the next day, was gone and my brother and I were put to bed. I was devastated. All I could think about was I wanted to be with my mum not these weird-talking strangers.

Wearing only my nightdress and nothing on my feet I silently crept downstairs and out the front door. It was very dark and freezing cold as I navigated my way down the steep hill, crossing over the little bridge, up an even steeper hill to where my mum was staying. I reached the cottage and banged on the door shouting:

"Mummy, it's me, Audrey. Open the door."

No one answered. She must be next door I thought.

I banged hard on that door, shivering with cold.

"It's Audrey, mum. Please let me in. I'm freezing out here."

When my mum saw me she was very upset at the way I was dressed, in a thin night dress, and bare feet. More so, because I had escaped the Williams' house undetected.

"What on earth are you up to? What are you doing here, dressed like that, you'll catch your bloody death?" she said.

"I don't like it at Mrs Williams. She talks funny. I don't want to stay there, without you, please take me home with you. Please, please" I begged.

Despite my desperate and tearful pleas she took me back to the Williams' house to an embarrassing scenario and there I stayed for six months attending a school where they spoke only Welsh and wrote on slates!

The Williams were devoutly religious so I attended a Welsh-speaking church service with them every Sunday. My brother always went missing on Sundays! After five months of continuously sending pleading letters to my mother, in which I consistently wrote: 'I don't like it here. Please come and take me home' my mum eventually arrived in Wales in a snow storm and was stranded overnight by heavy snow drifts at the local Police Station in Caernarfon. Finally, she arrived at the Williams' home, which had been partly buried under 20 foot high snow drifts. After an ecstatic reunion my brother and I were sent to bed. Later, when mum came upstairs to her room, she found the bed sheets freezing and damp so thought she would sleep with my brother and me. She jumped into what she thought was our bed saying:

"Give me a cuddle, I am so cold. I can't get warm."

To her absolute horror a freaked out Mr Williams leapt out of bed gasping:

"What do you think you are doing woman?"

Once in the correct room, we all giggled at her experience and snuggled together in the small single bed.

Act 1 Scene 9:

Home at Last

Shortly after, sporting a heavy Welsh accent, which all my friends made fun of, I was happy to be back in England sleeping down a shelter every night. As night raids eased off a little, we slept at home until the unnerving wails of the siren alerted us to dress quickly and take cover when a German air raid was imminent.

My dad would be standing by the wide open kitchen door, alertly checking the dark night sky for German planes, as we fearfully huddled together. Then, suddenly, he would shout:

"Right! It's all clear! Run! Now! As fast as you can, to the air raid shelter."

Quite terrified I have never moved so quickly in all my life, worried in case I might not reach the safety of the shelter, which was 300 yards away, before a bomb dropped from the sky and killed me.

As a natural story-teller with a vivid imagination it was very easy for me to invent joyful tales that helped us kids to forget the dreariness of the sometimes flooded shelter and the war. I also started a prayer competition to see which one of us could pray the longest prayer. It was such fun and a good distraction, too, from the exploding pom-pom guns that were strafing the night sky for enemy aircraft overhead which really unnerved me. It was difficult to sleep with such a racket. Sometimes during the daytime raids we would emerge from the safety of the shelter to watch the 'dog fights' as they were called between the German and English planes high above in the clear blue sky, not really being aware that real live pilots were flying these aircraft and being killed.

Somehow, in between all of this drama and upheaval, the army community of wives and children bonded even more closely together and supported one another, especially when the dreadful news came through that one family's husband and father had been killed in action or taken prisoner of war in Germany or Japan. In such circumstances I always tried my best to comfort my friends and used to visit their homes to read to them or make up happy-ever-after stories to help ease their sadness.

(Young as I was it was my only way of offering loving comfort and support, tantamount to healing, even though I didn't realise it at the time).

As the war progressed, my mum persuaded relatives in the North of England to accommodate us and keep us safe from the terrifying German V1 and V2 unmanned rocket planes which were creating such havoc and huge loss of life, in the south of England. We nicknamed the V1s 'buzz bombs' as they made this buzzing noise. When the buzzing stopped there was a dreadful silence and it was time to take cover wherever you could as the plane, with its bomb, exploded on the ground. On my way to school one day, such an incident occurred. I heard the loud buzzing sound and fled to the doorway of a shop, huddling down close to the ground, waiting for the explosion which, thankfully, was some distance away.

On that same occasion my mother had to dive under her work bench at the REME (Royal Electrical and Mechanical Engineers) workshops - where women helped to assemble motorcycles complete from frame until test run - when the glass roof took a direct hit from an exploding 'buzz bomb'. Fortunately nobody was killed but some were badly injured. My mother was not hurt but suffered severe shock. The V2 rocket plane did not buzz and landed like a missile, which it was, and subsequently there was no warning. Both of these unmanned planes, wreaked terror and havoc on peoples lives and property.

Act 1 Scene 10:

Leaving Home Again

'Home is where you feel at home and are treated well'
- Dalai Lama

In 1944 due to the hundreds of daily casualties in the south of England, resulting from the unmanned German 'V1' and 'V2' rocket missiles, my mother decided to take us three children to stay with relatives in the north of England, where it was relatively safe. Unhappily, my Great Aunt, whose home was on Sunderland's modern council estate, could only accommodate my two brothers so I had to join another Aunt and her five year old daughter in the home of her widowed sister and mother some five miles away. It was situated near the docks and was one of endless rows of extremely depressing old style, dreary looking terraced houses, without bathrooms and only an outside 'lavvy' down the bottom of the yard. The three of us had to share a single bed even though there was an unused room next door which had once been the bedroom of a deceased twenty year old female cousin; she had died of consumption. I frequently woke up in the middle of the night trying to crawl up the wall through either lack of bed space or having a nightmare. One day, being quite curious, I peeped into this spare room but it instantly gave me the creeps because it really felt it was occupied.

On the day before my mum was due to return home to Feltham, I caught the bus to the other side of town where she was staying with my two brothers because I desperately needed to see her one more time. We all had tea together and afterwards my mum walked me back to the bus stop and kissed me goodbye. I was eleven at the time and with a brave face I boarded the bus, hiding an unbearable feeling of abandonment, and as soon as my Mum was out of sight I broke down completely, sobbing as if my heart would break. Curled up on the dirty bus floor I was inconsolable. Fellow passengers tried their best to hug and comfort me to no avail. When the bus arrived at Norman Street I alighted, still sobbing, and walked towards my temporary home which, to my mind, was a dreary, dark place, without a scrap of comfort or loving intent. I heard my Aunt remark to a neighbour, as I approached them: "Oh dear, what is she snivelling about now"?

A keen churchgoer my Aunt attended religious services at the local Mission just along the street and sometimes took me along. Every night she would kneel by the bedside to say her prayers. Despite these rituals she never showed any real warmth or love towards me and I felt emotionally and mentally abused while living in that household. An old tin bath tub was occasionally brought out and I was the last to share the water after my Aunt and young cousin had used it. I developed scabies. My head was full of lice. I had no one to play with as other kids were all at school; I spent long, boring, depressing, days sitting outside the house on the kerbside, feeling thoroughly miserable and feeling completely abandoned. Bombs or no bombs I constantly pleaded by letter to my mother to be allowed home. To make matters worse, for some reason, in all of the nine months I was there, no-one thought to send me to school. Hence, to

my utter dismay, I failed the eleven plus grammar school entrance exam, which I had to sit soon after I arrived back home
and ended up attending the local modern secondary school, in
Bedfont, Middlesex for two years from where, aged thirteen I
attended Gregg's Secretarial College in Ealing, West London,
three months short of two years.

Act 1 Scene 11:

Family Demands and Responsibilities

*'You don't choose your family. They are God's gift to you, as
   you are to them'*
- **Desmond Tutu**

When my parents collected us from Sunderland they gleefully announced there was to be a new addition to our family
and another younger brother was born during Victory Week
on May 2nd 1945, so my mum missed all the celebrations of this
landmark occasion. It was such a shame as she had been in hospital for nearly a month with very high blood pressure, which
meant more home chores for me. I was becoming quite the little
house keeper albeit reluctantly. Much later in life I wondered
why, with so many relatives living nearby, such chores always
fell upon my shoulders. After all was said and done I was only
twelve. I remember becoming very rude and resistant when
pressed to run multiple errands and do household chores such
as picking up and shaking all the mats outside, and sweeping
and washing floors. (There was no such luxury as fitted carpeting or a vacuum cleaner).

I began to copy-cat certain swear words my mum's vocabulary constantly included as every day language. When taking
me to task many times she called me a "stupid bitch" or "stupid
cow"; it hurt. Somehow, though, she wasn't aware of how much.
In a very strange way I think my mum used these expressions

as terms of endearment. Deep down in my heart I knew that she loved me. She just had a strange way of showing it.

When I was fourteen my older cousin, Alan, was house-sitting us kids, while my mother and father attended an army function. As I was preparing to get ready for bed Alan asked:

"Why haven't you cleaned your teeth, Audrey?"

"I never bloody well do. I don't have a bloody toothbrush, do I?" Came the cheeky retort,

"You mean you never clean your teeth, ever?" he said.

"None of us do. Anyway, what's it bloody well got to do with you?"

"I am shocked at the way you swear so much and I think you should stop doing so as it is vulgar. You also need to ask your mother to buy you a toothbrush. You have good teeth and you should look after them or you will regret it later when you grow up," Alan commented.

Until that moment I did not realise I used swear words. They were a natural part of the daily vocabulary I picked up from my parents. I did become the owner of my first toothbrush not long after my cousin's talk with me and still do have very good teeth. It certainly was a watershed moment in my life and I am grateful that Alan promoted it.

Act 1 Scene 12:

Celebrating Victory

'Peace is always beautiful'
- Walt Whitman

On Victory in Europe Day 5th May 1944 aged eleven, myself and practically everyone in Feltham (except my mum who had just given birth to my baby brother) seemed to be out on the town and headed for the War Memorial situated near the village green and pond, so my friends and I decided to join in. My dad was at his favourite place, the Sergeant's Mess, and my mum was in hospital. There were ten of us kids in all and, with great excitement, we scooped up the youngest ones and placed them in a big old pram which, unfortunately, due to only having three wheels made our progress rather slow. The streets were filled with throngs of people, young and old, all singing, dancing and hugging one another and generally expressing their intense joy and happiness. My friends and I were having such fun, too, shouting and screaming with everyone else:

"The war is over! We have beaten the Germans! Long Live the King!"

As dusk fell the most amazing event occurred. Suddenly, it seemed as if every light, in every shop and house was switched on. After five years of complete blackout it was a most dazzling sight to behold. Some people were shining torches up to the sky and strangers offered us treats. I couldn't believe it! No more air raids, no more separations, no more darkness. At last, I could put the light on in my bedroom, without drawing the ugly blackout curtains ever again.

Upon returning home, I remembered the prayer I had said every day, (and still do), which I realise now, had sustained me through some difficult periods. It was suggested by the Archbishop of Canterbury, Cosmo Gordon Lang, at the outset of the war:

LIGHTEN OUR DARKNESS,
WE BESEECH THEE O' LORD
AND BY THY GREAT MERCY
DEFEND US FROM ALL THE PERILS AND
DANGERS OF THIS NIGHT.

Act 1 Scene 13:

A Distressing Incident

'Abuse is never deserved, it is an exploitation of innocence and physical disadvantage'
- Lorraine Nilon

One of my really pleasant and favourite distractions towards the end of the war was visiting the local picture house. There was no such entertainment then such as television. On one sickening occasion, seriously engrossed in the film I was watching, I was hardly aware of a man arriving and sitting down next to me. After a few minutes and, to my absolute horror, he suddenly placed his hand up between my legs and then into my knickers. I squirmed in terror, speechless and frozen to the seat, before being able to pluck up enough courage to push his hand away. Still terrified I left my seat and moved as far away from him as I could.

Never having received any kind of sexual education, and being totally naïve, I related the incident to my friends as we travelled home on the bus and then worried myself sick in case, somehow, the man had made me pregnant! I didn't dare tell my mum. Nowadays that incident would be described as sexual abuse and I should have reported him to someone. It was just too embarrassing for me to do so and too much of a personal violation of my most intimate area.

Act 1 Scene 14:

Still Stagestruck

'Love is the absence of judgement'
- Dalai Lama

Watching so many films at the local 'flea pit' which we named the cinema, I soon became convinced that I could act as well, if not better, than some of the child actors on screen. Totally starstruck I sent off for film star photos and autographs, writing mini-plays, organising and participating in concerts, choreographing dance routines, all of which were held in the gardens of friends, where we acted out different routines to an audience of children who paid a penny entrance fee to watch the show and another penny for lemonade refreshments. It was such fun.

Youth club beckoned when I was thirteen where I learnt ballroom dancing, played table tennis and absolutely loved the drama classes. Recognising my talent for acting and after winning drama festival awards the drama teacher arranged for me to have an audition at The Guildhall Academy of Dramatic Art. Sadly my parents were having none of it as they felt an acting career was precarious. Office work was much more stable.

Regretfully, the rows between my parents continued unabated. Thankfully, we had survived World War II and, regrettably, World War III was taking place in my home! I began to develop terrible headaches and my monthly menstrual periods were intensely agonising for hours on end and, eventually, I ended up having to undergo some surgical procedures. (*Amazingly when I was married and expecting a baby the labour pains were not as intense as my period pains had been. They just lasted longer*).

Although office work did not attract me in any way, I 'soldiered' on at Gregg's Secretarial College where I went aged thirteen, in 1946, which was quite a journey each day by bus and underground from Feltham to Ealing, a busy borough of West London, making the most of this opportunity for further education. And I wore the college blazer with pride. Learning shorthand was a joy and I easily attained some very high speeds. A highlight for me though was being able to visit one of the big sound stages at Ealing Film Studios which backed onto a nearby park which I visited every lunchtime. In awe I watched actors, some famous, as they walked on and off the set wishing with all my heart I could be one of them.

Then my mum became pregnant with my baby sister and, unfortunately, was hospitalised with high blood pressure for a month before her delivery date. For me this meant leaving college prematurely to take care of my two-year-old baby brother. This was a terrible blow. I was only three months away from graduation which I would miss. Fortunately, though, I was able to return to perform in the school's variety show, in whose production I had been heavily involved, and played a major role. This was such a memorable occasion for another reason as one of my classmates, Keith Williams, gave me my first kiss backstage as he congratulated me. I was thrilled and embarrassed at the same time. I did look quite attractive though as I was wearing a beautiful green satin evening dress which had circular panels of black lace inserted into the full skirt. It belonged to my mother and had been altered for me to wear.

I adored my new baby sister but not the extra household chores and having to frequently take her out in her pram. By then as a well developed fifteen year old I worried in case people thought the baby was mine, especially as I was then becoming very interested in boys at the local youth club, which I loved to attend because for a few hours I could escape the battleground situation at home and it became for me a complete 'life saver'.

Meanwhile, unbeknown to me, my mother had written to a national newspaper column running a feature about low paid wages for talented teenagers, in which she drew attention to the fact that her fifteen year old daughter had just left secretarial college with a shorthand speed of 180 wpm and would that ensure a better salary for her when she started looking for work?

The first I knew about this article was when a dozen letters arrived from prospective employers with job offers and interviews. Completely mortified by her actions and too embarrassed to follow up on any of the offers for employment, I applied to various other organisations and found my own job myself.

Act 2 Scene 1:

Working in the Big City

In 1948, inexperienced and not yet sixteen, I started my first job in London working in Wimpole Street as a junior secretary to a psychiatric social worker at the National Association for Mental Health, now known as MENCAP. It was extremely interesting work taking down in shorthand and typing back dictated case histories of schizophrenic and other psychiatric patients; it was subject matter I had never given a thought to before and initiated an empathetic reaction from me towards the mentally afflicted. Fleetingly, I even considered studying psychology but there seemed to be so many other diversions at the time to distract me.

I absolutely loved working in the 'big city' and, even though I had to follow an early daytime regime, walking in all weathers the two miles from my home to Feltham station, it was a ritual I coveted. This was my special time of peace and reflection. Joining fellow travellers we boarded the workman's train which left at 7.45AM into Waterloo, London's famous station, from where I travelled by underground to Oxford Street. After having lived in suburbia all my life, London seemed like another world to me. Everywhere seemed so much larger and I was completely dazzled by the plethora of big fancy stores with their amazing shop window displays. I couldn't wait to explore them all. Once a month, after work, with my precious pay packet in hand, I headed for my favourite budget store C&A Fashions, to browse for bargains and possibly a new outfit. My salary didn't go very far after I paid my mum something towards my keep and put aside my travel expenses. I was so happy though as I loved to look fashionable and managed, eventually, to save up enough money to purchase a new item of clothing when I saw something I really fancied.

Oxford Street sported a huge F W Woolworth & Co, the famous worldwide chain of stores, sadly now defunct. I will never forget Feb 5th 1953 as being the day that sweet rationing finally ended and during my lunch break I dashed down to Woolworth's and nearly lost my eyesight when greeted by all the sweet counters inside the store filled to capacity with colourfully wrapped chocolate bars and delicious looking sweets of all descriptions. It was like fairyland; unbelievably, there wasn't any limit to what one could purchase. Remembering the war years' monthly meagre three-quarters-of-a-pound sweet coupon allowance and no choice of candy to spend it on, such a sight was quite overwhelming to behold. Every spare penny I had with me on this occasion was cheerfully spent on purchasing whatever treats I could to share with my family.

As my social worker boss and I became better acquainted, she informed me that her husband was an actor with the National Theatre so I shared with her my love of acting. One day she mentioned that there was a vacancy at the National Theatre for a call girl and that her husband had said he could arrange an interview for me if I was interested. I knew it to be a marvellous opportunity to pick up all kinds of experience in acting and stage craft. I was really excited. Unfortunately, my parents were totally unimpressed and cited all kinds of reasons to completely discourage me from taking the matter any further. My father said:

"It is a ridiculous idea. Do you think we have paid out all these college fees to have you end up working as a lackey in a theatre? And what about your safety? You would be travelling late at night. God knows what might happen to you."

My mother then intervened:

"Your father's right. It is far too risky. You would have to get lodgings, which will be costly. Anyway, what would be the point of it all? It's not as if you will be able to act. You will just be a lackey, the money is terrible, and it will be a complete waste of your time at secretarial college."

Reluctantly, with a heavy heart, I had to agree. I knew, in all honesty, I did not have the confidence to leave home and find digs near the National Theatre. I was too young and insecure to take it any further. Extremely disappointed and frustrated with myself I felt thwarted having to miss what, in my opinion, was such a great opportunity for me.

My headaches were troubling me a great deal and after several weeks, with no real respite, the doctor ordered tests which proved negative. Not surprisingly, given my home situation, he said they were probably caused by tension.

Act 2 Scene 2:

Dating, Mating and Marriage

Aged sixteen, ballroom dancing was a past time I adored and on most Saturday evenings I attended dance functions at either the Hanworth Village Hall or Feltham Hotel, where live bands played all the latest hit tunes. My girl friends and I spent time before the cloakroom mirror attempting to make ourselves appear as glamorous and fetching as possible to the opposite sex. Our chief objective was to have a good time and, perhaps, find a boy friend; preferably someone who could also dance! Our one ambition in life, at that time, was to become engaged and married before the age of twenty-one. Otherwise you were considered to be 'on the shelf'. It was a very serious business for teenagers. What a strange priority when, nowadays, marriage seems to be the last commitment anyone wants to make. None of the girls, without a partner, ever danced with other girls, even if you waited all night for a male partner.

Attending a dance when I was seventeen, a good-looking young soldier whom I already had my eye on, walked towards me from across the other side of the dance floor.

"Hello, my name is Ken. Would you like to do this quick step?"

With great joy in my heart I immediately responded:

"Yes, thank you".

As we spun around the dance floor, keeping in step to the music, I felt immediately attracted to Ken; he was a good dancer, too, which was a bonus.

"I'm home on leave from army National Service," he commented.

"Do you come here often"? he enquired.

I nodded in the affirmative. We danced some more and Ken asked if he could walk me home? I readily agreed.

Aged eighteen, and after a year's courtship, which included going to the cinema and taking cycle rides to various countryside venues, Ken and I were deeply in love with one another and became engaged. Even though nearly nineteen, I was extremely naïve about sexual matters, never having received any education on the subject and I dared not risk having pre-marital sex in case I became pregnant.

Walking me home one evening from the cinema Ken looked at me and said:

"Why don't we get married as soon as I finish my National Service? I love you and I don't want to wait."

"I love you too but there's just one slight problem, we don't have any money. We should save up first." I replied.

Ken thought about this suggestion for a moment before wrinkling up his nose, hugging me close to him and commented:

"Oh! We can save up after we get married. I don't want to wait. Let's set a date and see what happens."

So we decided to 'take the plunge' and make plans to be husband and wife. Ken spoke to my father and asked for permission to marry me. After asking Ken how he was intending to support me and satisfied with Ken's intention of serving an apprenticeship to become a qualified electrician, my father gave his consent.

My mother was horrified. Taking me aside she spoke very seriously to me.

"Please, Audrey, don't get married. You are far too bloody young to throw your life away, like I did, when you can really make something of yourself. Join the WRNS instead, where you can use your secretarial skills and make a worthwhile career with lots of opportunities. What's here for you? What kind of a life will you have? I bloody well want more for you." Her words fell on deaf ears, as did Ken's parents, who also tried to change his mind, saying he was too young, even though is twin sister, Iris, was already wed.

Ken became an apprenticed electrician once he was out of the army. He was only twenty-two, and I had just celebrated my 19th birthday on 28th February when, on 23rd March 1952 (the year King George VI passed away) on Mothering Sunday, after morning Service, we were married in St Catherine's Church in Feltham. Proudly, I wore the wedding dress I had designed myself: The skirt of which was made from stiff, white French spotted net over a full underskirt of taffeta, which was given to me by the Mayfair textile company I was then employed by. The bodice was of silk with long pointed sleeves and a mandarin neckline. My best friend, Kathleen, agreed to be my chief bridesmaid, together with my ten year old cousin, Elizabeth, daughter of my favourite Aunt Daisy and my four year old sister. Their dresses were in gold and white taffeta material and each carried a matching muff.

My trousseau, consisting of pretty underwear and nightwear using dyed parachute silk, was generously made for me by Mrs Madams, a long-time family friend, as a wedding present. It made me feel very special and awfully glamorous too.

Somehow, much to my appreciation, my parents scraped together enough money to pay for a wedding reception in an adjoining hall to the Sergeant's Mess - my dad's favourite haunt. All the guests enjoyed a sit -down hot luncheon, followed later by afternoon tea. We danced to the music provided by a small band, until I went home to change into my 'going away' clothes which were bought, of course from C&A my favourite low budget store.

Tired and excited Ken and I spent our wedding night at a small hotel in London not far from Waterloo station. I nervously donned one of the night dresses from my trousseau, in black parachute silk, with rose pink trimmings, while Ken was undressing in the bathroom. Both tired and exhausted our love making did not go terribly well. The next day we caught the train to Clacton-on-Sea Essex, to stay for a week in a seaside chalet my mother had booked for us through a friend. Upon our arrival there we both looked in complete horror at the state the chalet was in. We couldn't even reach the front door as the garden was awash with water and mud. Shocked and bitterly disappointed we looked at one another.

"Oh dear what on earth are we going to do?" I wailed as I looked, miserably, at my new husband.

"I have no idea. We can't go back home." Ken replied, looking equally dejected.

Then, to our utter relief, as if an Angel from heaven had descended, a kind lady, passing by, stopped and asked:

"Oh my goodness. I hope you were not expecting to stay in this chalet? This side of the park has really suffered this winter from flooding due to the amount of rain we have experienced recently."

Recognising we were newlyweds and instantly summing up our situation, this merciful Angel offered to let us stay in one of her warm and cosy chalets situated away from the flooded area. The weather was freezing cold and wet. Ken and I were so grateful to her; this was our honeymoon after all. We just wanted to be on our own and to enjoy being married and to be able, at last, to make love properly for the first time especially as Ken said I was as passionate as a young greyhound.

Act 2 Scene 3:

Home Making

In 1952, without savings of any kind and only our joint income from our jobs, with great enthusiasm I wholeheartedly started married life in two upstairs rooms in Ken's parent's house, making a tiny box room into a kitchen in which we added a cooking stove, kitchen cabinet with a fold-down table and two chairs. The bathroom sink was used for washing up and for running water. Ingeniously, my father-in-law, a sheet metal worker, made us a stainless steel draining board that clipped over the bath. Our bedroom had a fire place and on cold evenings Ken would build a fire making the room very cosy. We used hire purchase to furnish the room with a double bed and a wardrobe. I couldn't have been happier.

One year later Ken's parents moved their bedroom downstairs, providing us with an extra room. Thrilled, I set about purchasing a sofa, two armchairs and a carpet for our new-sitting room, which had been freshly painted and wall papered. I was so proud of the end result and loved being a caring wife to Ken and playing host to particular workmates and their partners. Food rationing still existed in 1954 but I always shopped carefully on Friday's, after work, at the privately owned local grocery store. I remember introducing Ken to fried mushrooms, which he had never tasted before, adding them to his breakfast of egg and bacon. They became a firm favourite.

Ken's parents, had been bombed out of their original home in Bermondsey, East London, and had been re-housed in Feltham. Their rooms were sparsely furnished from charity donations and lacked any floor carpeting, only linoleum. By contrast our rooms upstairs must have seemed luxurious to them as Flo seemed quite envious of the lovely comfortable home I had created for her son and myself and especially when we purchased a small refrigerator and a vacuum cleaner. Sadly, they were luxury items which she had never had and neither had my parents while I lived at home.

On my afternoon off I did our weekly wash downstairs in my mother-in-law's kitchen, using her gas copper, which I filled up with cold water and our dirty laundry. When the water came to the boil, I used the big wooden tongs to shift the sheets, towels, and personal items, around in the soapy liquid for about fifteen minutes. Then everything had to be lifted out and put into the sink to rinse. I used the antiquated mangle with its large rollers, to squeeze out as much water as possible and with great satisfaction hung everything on the line outside to dry. A neighbour once commented she had never seen sheets so white which made me feel quite proud of myself.

Act 2 Scene 4:

The Coronation of Queen Elizabeth II

'Therefore I am sure that this my coronation is not the symbol of power and splendour that are gone but a declaration of our hopes in the future and for the years I may, by God's Grace and Mercy, be given to reign and serve you as your Queen'
- Coronation 1953

Having secured in 1953, a new secretarial position at London Heathrow Airport, with Philippine Airlines, working for the American Operations & Engineering Manager and the Station Manager, I cycled the five miles from my home in all weathers to their office situated in one of the many prefabricated buildings. The position was well paid which enabled me to save money from my salary each month towards a home of our own when we planned to start a family.

One of the highlights while working there was the upcoming coronation of HM Queen Elizabeth II on 2nd June 1953. Philippine Airlines' head office was in a prime position in Pall Mall and was directly overlooking the coronation route from Buckingham Palace to Westminster Abbey. In preparation for this historical event, builders erected tiered seating behind the London office's large plate glass windows. VIPs from overseas stations and local personnel, including myself and husband, all received gold embossed invitations to celebrate and view this spectacular event. On that day in June we observed the young and beautiful Queen seated inside the golden coronation coach, with her husband HRH Prince Phillip by her side, accompanied by an endless, colourful parade of Commonwealth forces, all marching in the torrential rain on that June day, in 1954, without a hint of discomfort.

Afterwards, we mingled with the huge crowds, as we made our way to the station to catch the train home. The rain had, finally, stopped and the sun shone brightly. I felt very blessed to have been able to witness such a unique and historic occasion in the history of our country and became a life long admirer of HM the Queen Elizabeth II and all that she stood for.

Act 2 Scene 5:

A Tragic Event

On 24th January 1954 while preparing our evening meal before Ken came home from work, I turned on the radio to listen to my favourite programme, 'The Archers', a serial about country folk, only to hear a shocking news announcement that a Philippine Airlines' plane had crashed at Rome airport with the loss of everyone on board. I immediately telephoned my boss for more information and he informed me he was flying to Rome that night to assist in the accident enquiry. Regrettably, my job ended not long after the accident, when PAL terminated their flights into London Heathrow Airport.

Only a few months later I secured another secretarial position in the engineering department with BOAC – later renamed British Airways - when it amalgamated with British European Airways.

The airport in the late 1950s was nowhere near the size it is today and there was a total absence of any real security. Anyone could wander out on to the Apron area where aircraft maintenance work or passenger loading was taking place. Nissen huts and one storey pre-fabricated buildings became temporary offices and were scattered all around the airport perimeter.

I continued saving my salary towards the deposit on a house which was something I still longed for and dreamed about. As fortunate as Ken and I were to have the accommodation we did there was a constant invasion of our privacy. My mother-in-law would call up:

"Ken, do you want to come down and sample some of the bread pudding I have just made. I know it's your favourite." Or his dad would call up and ask:

"Ken there is a 'footie' match on in a minute, are you coming down to watch it, son?"

It became embarrassing and intrusive upon whatever plans we may have made. Ken was in an impossible situation and, unfortunately, I became more and more irritated by it. Perhaps it was my own feelings of insecurity but I resented his parent's frequent interruptions and I longed to have our own space and freedom from what seemed to me to be my in-laws overbearing interference in our lives. In retrospect I realise my behaviour was immature and petty and must have been terribly awkward for Ken. I needed and demanded his unconditional loyalty to me - his wife - without considering his loyalty to his parents. Was it one of those 'catch twenty-two' situations or another challenge for me to become more tolerant and understanding? With hindsight I believe I needed to grow up.

Act 2 Scene 6:

Motorcycle Accident

About two years into our marriage, while still living at his parent's address, Ken decided to buy a motorbike and sidecar so we could get around more easily. One day, after a pleasant visit to have tea with my brother and his wife at their home in Kew, we said our farewells at their front door and I climbed into the sidecar of our motorcycle as Ken prepared to drive off down the road at about 12 mph. I had just finished waving goodbye to my brother as we approached a small crossroad on the estate; just as we made our way to the middle of the road a speeding sports car came round a blind bend crashing into us. All I remember was seeing bright lights hurtling towards me. Then, in a flash, I was coming round on the ground having been flung upwards out of the sidecar. I have often thought about how completely disassociated I was when the car hit us. There was no sensation of fear or pain while it was occurring. It was as if I was 'out' of my body. Completely not there.

Minutes later I came to lying flat on my back on the ground, with blood pouring down my face; my brother was leaning over me. He had rushed from his house having heard the crash and was attempting to reassure me.

"It's okay Audrey. You're in safe hands."

"What's happened to my face? I can't see properly and why is there all this blood?" I sobbed.

"Where is Ken? Is he all right?"

"The ambulance will soon be here. Try not to worry," my brother replied.

Ken had taken the full blast from the car that hit us and his leg was badly fractured. He was lucky to be alive. I couldn't see him or speak to him. The car driver was okay. An ambulance took both of us to Richmond hospital and Ken was immediately taken into surgery. Considering I had been ejected upwards from the side car, losing my stockings and shoes in the process, the emergency staff mainly ignored me, except to put stitches in my injured nose before sending me home, by ambulance, with instructions to return to outpatient's the next day for a check up!

Ken's parents were anxiously waiting for us to return home and were beside themselves with worry when I explained to them what had happened. I never slept a wink and spent the night in the bathroom processing the symptoms of extreme shock! To my amusement when I went back to the hospital the next day, accompanied by my mother-in-law, I was placed into a wheelchair and taken by a nurse into the outpatient's section for a cursory examination. I had aches and pains all over my body which was black and blue like my face but the doctor seemed satisfied and discharged me. Thankfully, Ken was comfortably settled in a ward with his leg completely in plaster and seemed to be taking everything in his stride, probably to calm his mother down who was fussing all over him. (Tragically for me, I had major difficulty in being able to take a pregnancy to full term, due to an undiagnosed lower back and pelvic injury at the time of the accident and lost three babies as a result.)

Ken remained in hospital for two weeks and recuperated at home for six more with me taking him out in a wheel chair until he could manage crutches. Happily, he made a full recovery and bought another motor cycle as the other one was a write off.

Continuing to live under the same roof with Ken's parents, particularly his doting mother's constant fussing over her son, began to have quite a resentful affect upon me. I didn't understand them, they didn't understand me, and I didn't understand myself.

Act 2 Scene 7:

A Home of our Own

'The course of true love never did run smooth'
- William Shakespeare

In 1957 after five years of working and saving for a deposit on a house, it was with some relief and much excitement that Ken and I finally moved into a new, modern, centrally heated house of our own, in the picturesque village of Thorpe, near Egham, Surrey. Ken's mother was terribly upset on the day we moved out. She kept on asking:

"When will I see you again, Ken?"

I tried to reassure her.

"We are only a few miles away. Why don't you come and have tea with us tomorrow? It is not going to take us very long to unpack." She declined saying:

"It's Sunday tomorrow and dad and I always visit your twin sister every Sunday."

Ken said: "Don't worry so much mum. I will pop round to see you at lunch times, when I am able." His place of work was really near to where his parents lived.

Once installed in our new home we quickly made friends with our neighbours who, like us, were also young, first-time home buyers. Most of our spare time was spent in homemaking, planning and planting the garden, entertaining both mine and Ken's parents and, sometimes, friends and colleagues from work. Everything seemed perfect and to be everything I had ever dreamed of. Or so it seemed.

One year later I was absolutely horrified to discover that, unbelievably, my darling husband had embarked on an affair with a young woman in the factory where he worked. I knew her briefly from my youth club days. Extremely distressed by Ken's unbelievable behaviour I pleaded with him for months on end to help me to understand why he was doing this? What on earth had gone wrong? I reasoned that we had a beautiful home at last, were ready to start our own family and nothing made any sense because not once had he ever indicated he was unhappy. I truly believed that our marriage was rock solid for life. Of course we had encountered some not too serious 'ups and downs' from time to time, and I knew that I could be a little possessive on occasion, due to my inherent insecurity, but he had never given me the slightest hint that anything was wrong with our relationship. My heart felt completely and utterly broken. Ken wouldn't or couldn't explain why he was sabotaging what I truly felt was a good marriage. It was worse than a bereavement. I was totally bereft.

We were committed to visit close friends in New York using my new employer's (BOAC) airline concession for the first time. I begged Ken not to disappoint them, or me, because he said he didn't want to go. He finally gave in to my pleas and I had every reason to believe all would be well. Our friends, delighted by our visit, were great hosts and took us on several wonderful sightseeing trips to Niagara Falls, Connecticut and New York. Ken and I relaxed and began to enjoy our visit and amazingly were even making love again. I was certain the hiccup in our marriage was being healed and everything would be all right.

This turned out to be wishful thinking on my part. Ken seemed determined to continue his affair.

A few weeks after returning home from America I began to feel quite unwell and had bouts of sickness most afternoons. I was confused as I was still having a monthly period so did not think I could be pregnant. The doctor, however, confirmed I was about eight weeks pregnant.

Cautioning me he said:

"Due to the medical situation I am concerned there is a possibility that you may miscarry so I am advising you to bed rest for two weeks."

I was thrilled and excited about the baby news although a little concerned there might be a problem. Surely, now, I reasoned, Ken would end his affair and focus on becoming a father.

When I arrived home from the doctor's surgery, Ken was sitting by the fire in the living room; he looked up at me with a quizzical expression upon perceiving my happy, smiling face.

"Darling, I have just been to see the doctor and I have some wonderful news. I am two month's pregnant. We are going to become parents." I announced.

My heart sank as I watched his face reflect shock, horror and anger. I desperately tried to ignore his response and to hold back tears.

"There is a slight problem and the doctor has recommended bed rest for a couple of weeks," I said, looking hopefully at him.

"This is not going to make any difference Audrey to our situation. Forget about the bed rest and just carry on as normal and go back to work."

He sounded so heartless. I couldn't believe he could be so callous. Where, I wondered, was the lovely man I had fallen in love with? What was happening to us?

I ignored Ken's advice and I did rest up for one week before deciding to return to work as I was feeling so depressed and so abandoned.

Ken's problem, in having a pregnant wife and a lady friend he wouldn't stop seeing, was solved for him a month later, after I was rushed into hospital one night when, tragically, I miscarried our baby. Afterwards, I felt extremely fragile by this loss and acutely wounded by Ken's lack of concern. In the hospital, the following morning, sitting by my bedside Ken, unbelievably, and without any compassion remarked:

"Thank goodness that problem is solved."

Once home again and feeling thoroughly miserable I managed somehow to struggle on for a few weeks more until it became obvious that Ken was not going to change his mind and stop the affair. In 1959 we separated when I asked him to move out and he went back to live with his parents. It was the bleakest and most traumatic period of my life. I had lost both the baby I had longed for and the husband I still loved with all my heart. I was grief stricken. My heart felt as if it had been ripped open. What on earth had gone so badly wrong I wondered? I knew I wasn't perfect but I was unable to imagine what could have made him do such a thing. Then everything became even worse. Weeks later my mother informed me by telephone that I needed to hear what she had to say.

"I have some shocking news for you Audrey." My heart sank in anticipation of what she had heard.

"Ken's lady friend has announced to work colleagues, after returning from the Easter recess, that she and Ken have married and she has been showing everyone her wedding ring." For a moment my heart stopped beating. I couldn't breathe and I felt sick to my stomach. Then, taking a deep breath, I reasoned with my mother and adamantly retorted:

"Don't be so silly. How could they be married? We are not even divorced."

"I'm telling you this is what I have heard from people who work with her. Why would I make it up? What are you going to do about it? Evidently she is about five months pregnant."

That extra piece of information pierced like an arrow, deeply into my heart, which already felt like an open wound.

There now seemed no way back from this appalling news if it were true. My solicitor hired an inquiry agent who, subsequently, followed Ken and his mistress one evening to a restaurant and served divorce papers on them, having first ascertained from them that this lady was, indeed, very pregnant and that Ken was the father!

Anyone unhappy in a marriage can seek a divorce. They don't have to betray you and have an affair. At the age of twenty-seven, and eight years after we had married, I attended the High Court in London when I cited Ken with adultery and his lady friend as co-respondent and was granted a divorce in 1961

After some negotiation with Ken, I remained in the house for which I had saved so hard and I joined the local Thorpe Players of which Frank Muir, the celebrated radio and TV writer and performer, (now deceased), was President.

Don entered my life at this time and we became friendly neighbours.

Happily, for the next sixteen years with the Thorpe Players I acted every kind of character and stage role imaginable: comedy, drama, farce, etc. With tremendous enthusiasm I tackled everything. 'Treading the boards' so to speak was unbelievably magical, creatively therapeutic and, finally, a fulfilment of my acting dreams. I also formed wonderful friendships. The Thorpe Players were highly esteemed for their professionalism and we were encouraged to enter a one act play ('Fumed Oak' by Noel Coward) in a very prestigious drama festival competing against ten other Societies. Acting the role of a frustrated, brow-beaten housewife, with a husband fond of his drink and a dysfunctional family was, as they say, 'a piece of cake' for me. The play won best production and I won the outstanding actress award! I was often asked how I was able to get inside the character I was portraying on stage so deeply that my own self disappeared completely? During rehearsals I learnt all my stage moves, spoke the dialogue with as much feeling as possible, and made certain I became word perfect. I would earnestly heed the director's guidance until, technically, I felt competent but anxious as the first night of the production drew closer.

Nervously waiting in the wings for my cue, to go on stage in front of a paying audience, I would feel slightly faint and insecure. Stepping into the footlights, and speaking my first lines, elicited an instant transformational change of consciousness. I lived and breathed the character I was portraying, experiencing the illusion of her emotional fear, pain, joy and jealousy as if it was a reality. I was totally in another state of being and it would take some time to become myself again after the production was over.

Act 2 Scene 8:

Relationships

'Good night, good night! Parting is such sweet sorrow that I shall say goodnight till it be tomorrow'
- **William Shakespeare**

Newly divorced at the age of twenty-eight and seeking more income to support myself I succeeded in obtaining a more responsible and better paid position within BOAC in 1961 where I was already employed. My new boss was the Technical Manager of Flight Operations. As a pilot and engineer, he was responsible for all the cockpit layout of new aircraft coming into service with the airline. He was assisted by two test pilots. I had to sign the Official Secrets Act and was responsible for recording the minutes of technical meetings and securing the typed-up information and other documents in a locked cabinet. My boss was away a lot attending overseas meetings and, in all honesty, apart from holding a prestigious position which was sometimes viewed, enviously, by other female members of staff, who may have been candidates for the post, the job was extremely boring. The only exciting development, while I was in office, was being part of the fifteen strong Secretariat at an IATA week long conference held in Lucerne, Switzerland, which was attended by some hundred airline delegates, including my boss.

Usually, when he attended overseas conferences, I used his spacious office to rehearse my next acting role with the Thorpe

Players. I was in my element having such an opportunity to seriously study the character I was to portray in the next production.

The Flight Planning Section, just down the corridor from my office, consisted completely of male staff. One day a tall, curly headed, good looking male – whom I had already clocked with interest – introduced himself to me. I felt an immediate rush of chemistry and a strong attraction to Kit (which turned out to be mutual) so it was a big disappointment to learn he was already married which seemed to rule out any kind of romantic involvement. Then Christmas came along and it was 'open house' for anyone from other offices to attend the planning department's famous party. I changed into a rather fetching black, off-the-shoulder cocktail dress, which I had brought with me to the office. As soon as I entered the party room a beaming Kit immediately targeted me:

"Hello! Please, let me get you a drink. What would you like?" he kindly enquired.

"Thank you," I replied, "I fancy a small vodka with lime juice".

"Right! Stay exactly where you are," he instructed. "Don't move. I will be back in a moment."

He then disappeared into the throng of party goers.

Incredibly, in that instant, I experienced a quite overwhelming feeling that, somehow, we 'belonged' together. Inexplicably, I believe I fell 'in love' with Kit there and then. The chemistry between us was tangible!

At that time I was in a developing relationship with Don so it was all rather confusing.

As the weeks passed by and Kit and I got to know one another much better, mostly in work time. It would have been so easy and completely natural for us to have become intimately involved but something held me back from such an adulteress involvement. We spent occasional lunch hours together, sharing our thoughts and feelings. Kit told me his marriage was difficult but as he had two children he couldn't leave. He was very honest; and he was not looking to compromise me. Life can be very tantalising at times. In truth I wanted to be compromised. We were drawn to each other like magnets and I am convinced, now, we must have had some strong past life connection as we kept in touch, as best we could, for a number of years. The following Christmas I was thrilled when Kit presented me with a bottle of Chanel No. 5 perfume with a card in which he wrote: 'Here's to another year of clean living!' I have never been able to romantically discard Kit from my thoughts which constantly tormented me, because of my involvement with Don. I have often wondered, even now, what point there was in Kit and I meeting as, despite our deep feelings for each other, we both had other commitments and there was no way we could have a life together, without wrecking the lives of others.

Some twenty-five years later, I was at the bank in my home town of Camberley, feeling rather irritated at the delay in being served, when a gentleman approached me and enquired:

"Excuse me but are you by any chance Mrs Copland"?

Puzzled, I looked at this man for a moment or two not sure of who it was addressing me. Then, suddenly, it dawned on me. It was Kit. A blast from the past, standing in front of me. Surprised, excited and stunned by his totally unexpected appearance, I blurted out:

"Oh! My God! Is that really you, Kit? I don't believe it!" Then our eyes met and we gazed at one another in complete silence.

Leaving the queue and moving to a less public place, we talked animatedly for about fifteen minutes.

"Would you like to join me for a coffee"? I ventured.

"Sorry, I can't. My wife is just down the road waiting for me at the hairdressers. Do you live here locally? Perhaps I could call round and see you one day?" he enquired.

"I would like that; and yes, I do live nearby I replied. "Do you live locally?"

"Yes, I moved here about ten years ago." Kit responded and then asked: "What is your address?"

When I provided it we were both amazed to learn that for the past ten years, unbelievably, he had lived less than one mile from my home and our paths had never crossed. Kit had to leave to meet his wife but before doing so pocketed my address and telephone number.

A few days later Kit turned up, unexpectedly, at my home one morning, for a 'catch up' chat to discover how the past twenty-five years had worked out for us. He admitted he had fallen deeply in love with me after that party night but it was a good thing he had stayed in his unhappy marriage due to some sad circumstances which eventually occurred.

We could have talked for hours. There was so much to share. Kit was keenly interested and surprised to hear about my extensive travels as a Spiritual Healer/Teacher. I realised, of course, I was a changed person from when we first met. My perspective on life was so different. When it was time for Kit to leave, he stood up and looked at me intently. Then he asked:

"Would you mind terribly if I kissed you?"

Somewhat taken aback, I bashfully replied:

"No. I don't mind."

I stepped forward and our lips locked together.

During this kiss I suddenly became aware of an unhealthy, rather stale and sickly smell emanating upwards from his stomach area. Immediately I sensed he had cancer. When we parted company I felt very sad indeed as I knew, intuitively, Kit had not long to live and that I would never see him again in this life time. Some nine months later I read of his passing, which was announced in the British Airways staff magazine. Kit had reached Board level and been awarded an OBE. I felt really blessed and grateful to have been given this unsolicited opportunity to talk to Kit one last time before he made his transition to the 'other side'.

I now fully understand and wholeheartedly agree that all spiritual growth comes through relationships.

Act 2 Scene 9:

New Beginnings

'What do I want? My heart knows the answer'
- **Deepak Chopra**

My second husband, Donald Frank Copland, was born in the City of Lincoln in November 1930 and experienced a completely different childhood to mine. His father was a company director and the family lived comfortably in a detached house on prestigious Yarborough Crescent. Don had a sister, Margaret, who was eight years older than him, who was extremely academic. As a child Don suffered badly from asthma resulting in his mother over protecting him to the point, he told me, she would wrap him up in an overcoat, scarf and woolly hat, while playing on the beach with other children who were wearing only bathing costumes.

He had a grammar school education and also acted as a junior Server at Lincoln Cathedral. There couldn't have been a bigger contrast in our backgrounds.

Don studied architecture and building construction and, when we first met, was a successful sales representative for Taylor Woodrow Homes. Coincidentally, we had both bought one of their homes, on the same estate in Thorpe, Surrey, when previously married to other partners.

Following the distressing breakdown of both our marriages Don and I met, casually, at another neighbour's marriage break-up party and drifted into a comfortable, friendly, relationship, participating in a busy round of social events. To my surprise, Don joined the Thorpe Players, showing a rare talent for the design and construction of the sets which were extremely professional and drew much acclaim.

Though not a tennis player myself, due to lower back problems, I loved the sport and would accompany Don to many of his matches. I tried so hard to play tennis but my back pain always defeated me. Instead I took my turn to organise the club teas, making sandwiches and cakes, and was co-opted on to the tennis club's committee, as Minutes Secretary.

Don and I were somewhat sceptical about what 'falling in love' meant anymore, having both experienced such distressing episodes in our previous marriages. Don had confided in me that while he was away from home, at an annual territorial training camp, he received a letter from his wife informing him she had 'gone to America' and would not be returning. Upon arriving back home Don said he was contacted by his ex-neighbour, an American Air Force Colonel, who was some twenty-five years older than him, who volunteered that he was having an affair with Don's wife, who was leaving him, and that he had planned her trip to America like a military operation. Initially, he had shipped his own wife and daughter back to the States. The Colonel stated that it was never intended that Don's nearly two-year-old son would accompany his wife, but contingency plans to have him taken care of by Don's mother, went awry. As it was illegal, then, for a mother to take a child out of the country without the father's permission, the Colonel insisted that if Don went to the American Embassy or Passport Office, then he would never hear from his wife again. I can only imagine the shock and emotional pain Don would have expe-rienced. He did not see his little son for near on twelve years.

Don was a really good looking man who was kind and con-sistently attentive about my welfare, which resulted in making me feel comfortable, safe and secure. A most important and practical deciding factor in continuing our relationship - if not a totally romantic one.

After nearly two years of sharing my home with lodgers, to help with the mortgage payments, I made the decision to sell up and rent somewhere else to live. Don had a male lodger liv-ing with him and, although I could have moved in too, I decid-ed against it.

"Hey Don, what do you think of this place I have found on a B.O.A.C notice board, advertising for females to share a river-side bungalow by the Thames, in Staines?"

"Why don't we go and check it out?" Don replied. So I made a phone call and fixed a date to meet up with one Lesley Reyn-olds, the lease holder.

The bungalow looked rather shabby as we approached it but it certainly was on a beautiful stretch of the Thames, which drew me in completely. After ringing the doorbell a few times the door was suddenly opened by an attractive young wom-an, who was struggling to keep a silk dressing gown wrapped around her quite obviously nude body.

"I am so sorry to keep you waiting. I was on a late shift last night and my alarm didn't wake me. Please, do come in and for-give the way I am dressed as, literally, I have just got out of bed. Oh! My name is Lesley, by the way," she said with a big smile,

We were ushered into a spacious sitting room that had large patio doors that opened out to the river garden,

"Please, have a seat on the sofa here" Lesley indicated, as she grabbed a pile of clothes from it, sweeping them to the floor.

"Would you like some coffee? I am dying of thirst." Lesley offered. Receiving a welcoming nod from Don and myself, she dashed off to the kitchen, nearly losing her flimsy dressing gown in the process. While she was gone I did a quick scan of the living quarters. The place was comfortably furnished but every item had seen better days. I noticed there were three rooms leading off the sitting room which, I assumed, must be the bedrooms.

"Oh! S.H.I.T." Lesley screamed, as she stuck her head through the kitchen hatch. "I'm out of coffee. Do you mind tea, instead?" We responded in the affirmative and two cups of tea, without milk, were duly delivered to us on a tray.

"You won't believe it but the milk has gone off. Do you mind having tinned?"

We did mind but nodded in agreement, mainly not to embarrass Lesley any further.

"I hope you don't take sugar. I have none. Do you mind treacle, it usually does the trick?"

"Don't worry. We can manage without sugar this time," I said, and quickly drank down the disgusting tea full of what turned out to be condensed milk.

"Let me show you round the place," Lesley offered, as she led me into a cosy bedroom, furnished with a single divan bed, dressing table and wardrobe. The room was fitted with a fading carpet and there was a small window with a river view. I could see myself, quite happily, sleeping in this room. Then she showed me her room and explained:

"As you see, this room is the biggest one, and I want to split it in half, so another person can have one end of it while I will have this end. There is plenty of room for another bed."

I looked, in shock, at Lesley's bedside table which was smothered in cigarette ash from an overfilled ashtray and, even worse, on the carpet around her bed were several carefully arranged cigarette buts, standing on end.

Surprisingly, I moved in with Lesley a couple of weeks later, by which time there were two other young ladies coming to join us: Bernadette, was a twenty-three year old red headed extrovert, who worked behind the bar in the fashionable 'Flower Pot' club by the river Thames. Yvonne, by contrast, was a twenty-year-old, extremely shy and laid-back girl from Malaysia. The first thing I did after sorting my room out was to clean the whole bungalow, much to Lesley's complete joy. We all bonded very quickly and Lesley wanted to join the Thorpe Players and turned out to be a talented actress.

She was cast in quite a saucy role and had to make her way onto the stage through a central door. It turned out to be quite an unrehearsed, dramatic entrance when, suddenly, the whole set shook as she wrenched at the door which was meant to open out wards. Lesley was pulling at the handle in the opposite way and muttering: "What's wrong with this bloody door?"

The eighteen months I resided at the bungalow were the happiest, craziest, and most frustrating ones I can remember. One weekend Lesley was in charge of the place on her own and when I returned from a short holiday break with Don, Lesley was out and the patio doors were wide open to the world. An ironing board was still assembled upon which, to my absolute astonishment, a travelling iron was still plugged in and the iron had, somehow, peeled itself in half!

During one of the frequent party nights that were organised, no less than fifty persons would descend upon the bungalow for dancing and drinking into the late hours. On one occasion I heard screaming coming from the river garden and dashed out into the moonlit night, to observe a group of people watching two men frantically rushing to catch an obviously drunken, young woman, who was 'roly-polying' herself down the lawn and headed straight for the flowing river Thames! She was rescued just in time.

When we gave up the bungalow, Lesley went off to South Africa for a sabbatical from the hectic BOAC ticket desk, where she worked. While there her car broke down in the Bush and she was rescued by a crocodile farmer, whom she later married. Bernadette finally wed the 'love of her life', who cheated on her with her best friend, after fifteen years of married bliss. A year later Bernadette died of stomach cancer, leaving behind a young daughter. Yvonne moved on to another rented place and we lost touch.

Act 2 Scene 10:

Divorce, Re-Marriage & Motherhood

'All spiritual growth comes through relationships'
- Lilla Bek

Eventually, in 1962 I moved in with Don, which caused quite a lot of scandal mongering and tongue-wagging comments from the neighbours on the estate, as we were not married and were living together.

Don was now in a position to seek a divorce from his estranged wife on the grounds of her desertion, because the requisite period of three years had passed, but first he had to track down his wife's whereabouts. This took time and was costly but eventually in 1963 the divorce Papers were served on his wife in California and a date was set for a Hearing in the High Court in London.

It should have been quite straight forward but for the fact that Don's QC had insisted that, as Neil's father, Don must ask for custody of his son, or the Judge might form a negative impression of Don. Care and control of Neil would remain with his wife. Quite how this could have been misconstrued by her wasn't clear. She was advised to cross-petition and it all ended up seriously unpleasant and expensive. The Judge ruled in Don's favour and awarded him costs but said as his wife lived abroad Don would have to settle on her behalf. In one fell swoop our joint savings were wiped out in the time it took to swat a fly. Happily, though, Don was now divorced.

He decided to sell his house and one day he telephoned me while I was at work:

"Audrey, you must come and see this place I've found by the river Thames. It's perfect for reconstruction and has a river garden and landing stage. It's empty now and the price is good."

"Okay. I'll be home soon and we can go straight round to look at it," I replied.

Nothing could have prepared me for the dilapidated, dark wooden hut-like dwelling, standing in the middle of a long and narrow plot of land leading down to the water's edge.

"It's ghastly," I uttered. "Admittedly it's a pleasant plot by the Thames," I agreed," but the bungalow is made of wood."

"Don't worry about that", Don replied enthusiastically. "The wood can be dismantled and replaced with new partitions and then rendered. I can do it."

Despite my being hesitant about living in a wooden dwelling, which would be a new experience for me, we jointly purchased the property and named it 'Water's Edge'. Don commenced what become an eight year project. I was amazed at his extremely talented building skills. He spent every weekend, with odd help here and there, creating a unique place for us to live in, converting the wooden bungalow into a beautiful Swiss style chalet, with all mod cons. Any resemblance to the original property was non-existent. Creative and colourful terracing swept around the unique home Don had created for us to live in and which all our friends admired and I loved. From the large sliding patio doors of our sitting room we could watch the constantly passing river traffic from the comfort of our own home.

Not forgetting the plethora of ducks and swans that I could feed from the newly constructed landing stage.

Aged thirty-two, Don and I married on February 22nd 1964 and we proudly held our reception at Water's Edge in the not quite finished lounge and the ghastly, untouched, other rooms still awaiting re-construction. Approximately forty family and friends joined us, some of whom must have thought we were crazy to take on such a building challenge in the first place.

Sadly, four of those years were extremely emotional and difficult ones for us. When I was twelve weeks pregnant with our first baby together, I was threatening to miscarry and spent four anxious weeks bed resting in hospital under mild sedation. My Consultant Obstetrician decided to carry out a surgical procedure under anaesthetic to insert a 'Shirodkar' stitch into the cervix. A few days later I returned to the operating theatre to have it removed, as I was bleeding heavily. I remember being very sleepy from the anaesthetic as I was wheeled back to the ward. I had an intravenous drip in my arm and became very anxious.

"Have I still got my baby? What is happening? Have I still got my baby? Please tell me."

Many painful and emotional hours later I delivered a premature baby girl - but not the afterbirth - which refused to yield. Another drip was put up to recommence labour pains and expel the afterbirth, but after a whole night of more pain and distress I was returned to the operating theatre for the afterbirth to be removed surgically. Both Don and I were really disappointed at the loss of our first baby together, while I was physically and emotionally drained after such an ordeal, but remained determined to try again.

A year later, when pregnant again and having retired from British Airways, everything seemed to be proceeding normally when, to my horror, my waters started to slowly leak. My doctor ordered me to bed, under sedation, and Don and I thought everything would settle down. I was already twenty-six weeks. Sadly, I started to experience niggling stomach and back pains which, over a week or so, began to build into strong labour contractions.

As I laid in bed I fought them off by visualising I was detached from them and enjoying a pleasant country walk in a scenically beautiful park. Although this helped it was obvious that things were building up and when the doctor arrived he said:

"I am most awfully sorry Mrs Copland, it would appear that you are in labour and will, unfortunately, lose your baby, as it is far too early for it to be born." It was just the worst news possible.

In the 1960s you were not sent to a maternity unit but to Accident & Emergency. It was late at night when the ambulance arrived at St Peter's hospital in Chertsey. I was in a lot of pain. The place was seething with out patients, some drunk and shouting obscenities. A medic informed us the duty Gynaecologist was not available as she was operating and would examine me as soon as possible. After a couple more hours in A&E in full labour, now, I still had not received any medical attention. Finally a couple of porters wheeled me on a trolley, out into the open, before arriving at a general ward. I was placed in bed and left there behind a screen with no one in attendance. Don had been sent home. My labour pains became more frequent and stronger and, suddenly, I had this overwhelming urge to push, which I hadn't experienced in other miscarriages.

Urgently, I called out: "Help me please. I need a nurse. My baby's coming."

There was no response and I was terrified, so I called out again, this time very loudly.

"Nurse... Nurse... please come at once. My baby's coming."

Unbelievably, there was still no response to my pleas and our baby son, Adam, was delivered stillborn while I was alone, in the middle of the night, in a general ward full of sleeping patients. Panicking, I didn't know what to do and kept calling out even more loudly.

"Nurse. Nurse. I need help."

Finally a junior nurse arrived and looked in horror as she drew back the curtains round my bed. I said to her:

"Help me please to sit up. I want to see my baby."

"No! No! Don't sit up. It's best not to look. It will distress you. Stay lying down while I fetch Sister."

With that she disappeared.

It has always been a terrible heartache for me not to have seen or held my little son Adam. He was just taken away from me. Later I was informed by a doctor that Adam was fully formed and appeared completely healthy but, unfortunately, too premature to survive. Again, I had not delivered the after birth so spent another two hours on a drip and in pain in order to do so. Nowadays, of course, some premature babies, with the right care, survive at twenty-six weeks or even less. If not, then the baby is dressed for you to hold; hand and foot prints are taken for posterity and there is a funeral. At least that gives one a measure of bereavement and completion. Feeling totally bereft, my heart ached with sorrow; my body empty of the longed-for baby I had lovingly been carrying, I remained even more determined though to try again. It didn't help either when I could hear patients bemoaning the fact they had spent a disturbed night. A nurse reprimanded them saying a young mother had just lost her baby son.

Relieved to be home once more but feeling quite desolate I pondered upon whether I should give up on motherhood completely. Then something powerfully maternal stirred deep inside me and I knew without any doubt whatsoever that I definitely would try again. I felt really positive about the outcome and cherished the feeling that I would become a mother next time round.

To ensure a safe outcome for what would be my fourth pregnancy, and acting on the advice of my Obstetrician, I spent three months bed-resting in hospital, until the baby became viable, when I underwent another operation for a 'Shirodkar stitch' device to be placed into the cervix. When finally allowed home it was on the understanding I would spend at least five hours a day in a horizontal position. Don bought me a Jack Russell puppy which provided me with endless joy and support. My Dad, who had just retired, offered to live with Don until I was out of hospital. He enjoyed the peace and quiet of the riverside and unmercifully teasing 'Digger', our puppy, so much so that he remained with us for the duration of my pregnancy, returning to my mum at weekends. For the first time in my life I felt able to 'bond' with my Dad which was a real blessing and I began to appreciate and understand him much better. Don needed company, too. He was feeling quite emotionally fragile with all the constant visits to me in hospital.

A week before my baby daughter was due to arrive I returned to the Maternity unit to have the 'Shirodkar stitch' removed and remained overnight in case I went into labour. I didn't. Baby Ruth arrived seven days later, on the due date, 6th October 1967 at 2.50PM following a thirty-six hour long and arduous labour which finally ended in a forceps and suction delivery. Ruth was born in a posterior position, face-up, which evidently accounted for the chronic back aches I suffered before she was born. Evidently. the 'Shirodkar' device acts as a clamp which results in very slow dilation of the muscles during labour. Although a good birth weight of seven pounds Ruth was cot nursed for three whole days before I got to see her. As I was being wheeled on a trolley from the labour ward, completely exhausted, my heart was full of joy; at last I had succeeded in becoming a mother. All the previous trials and tribulations were instantly swept away. In the end it had all been worth it.

Resting in a room on my own to recover from what was a totally exhausting and prolonged labour, I was overcome with joy and happiness when our sweet baby daughter was, finally, placed into my arms in front of her proud Daddy.

She was a miracle; and I really did give grateful thanks to God for her safe delivery. Don presented me with a beautiful gold bracelet in celebration, which I still wear to this day, and it truly does signify a golden moment in my life.

Many years later when Ruth was growing up I consulted Frank Coulsting, the first Osteopath in the UK to be trained in cranial/sacral treatments, as I was suffering from lower back pain.

Frank was a Theosophist Minister and we had many interesting discussions. While treating me for this persistent back problem he asked if I had ever been in a car accident and whether I had experienced difficulties in having a baby as my pelvic area was so misaligned it would have made it almost impossible for me to carry one to full term. I was flabbergasted.

The previous maternity team always maintained my problem was hormonal, not structural and, for the duration of my pregnancy while carrying Ruth, I also endured weekly hormon-al injections into my backside from a visiting Midwife. All that misery and pain and lost pregnancies may have been due to a misalignment in my pelvic area, not diagnosed and caused by that motorcycle accident many years previously.

Act 3 Scene 1:
Uncle Bert and Spiritualism

'This above all, to thine own self be true'
- William Shakespeare

During our many trips to the great City of Lincoln in the 1960s, during Don's mother's lifetime, it always intrigued me how much the family were in awe of elderly bachelor, Uncle Bert, brother of Don's deceased father.

Uncle Bert, born in August 1891 in Bradford, left school at the age of 14 but studied hard and eventually qualified as a Solicitor. Later in his career he became Clerk of Lindsey County Council in 1947 and after retiring in 1957 he was awarded an OBE. He then became President of the charity Age Concern for a number of years. He lived alone across the road from Don's now deceased mother and was highly intelligent, a little eccentric, and shy. I warmed to him immediately and instinctively sensed he needed some tender loving care. I invited him down to 'Water's Edge' to stay with us every year even taking him away with us to Majorca on one occasion. He was thrilled, too, to be part of young Ruth's life during her first four years, until he passed away from cancer on 27th September 1972.

During our last visit to Uncle Bert he particularly asked Don to secure a certain book he claimed to have been his 'bible for life' entitled 'How to Build Mental Power' by German author Grenville Kleiser. We retrieved it from Uncle Bert's bookcase and along with other stuff – including an attractive wall clock in a wooden frame with pendulum – were all packed into the car for delivery to our Thames-side home.

On reading the book I noted that there was a chapter on spiritual development and Uncle Bert had meticulously written notes in his neat handwriting in the margins and some sentences were underlined. One, in particular, caught my eye: '**The soul is eternal'.** *How interesting*, I thought, making a mental note to read more on this subject as soon as possible.

Act 3 Scene 2:

Odd Happenings

Having received a legacy in 1972 from Uncle Bert's estate and beginning to find the accommodation in our existing home too restrictive, it was with an extremely heavy heart we eventually moved from 'Waters Edge' in Staines, to 'Thames Creek' to a new build and much larger detached and elegant property, situated on a backwater of the Thames in Wraysbury. It lacked the unique charm and warmth of 'Water's Edge' which I sorely missed. (I actually have had recurring dreams for over twenty years that I still live there).

Following this move I began to feel decidedly downhearted for a number of reasons regularly chiding myself for being so when I knew I had so much in my life to be grateful for. Most marriages have their problems for one reason or another and I tried really hard to accept the personal incompatibility that existed between myself and Don but there was always this empty ache in my heart for the 'something else' that seemed to be missing from our relationship.

We had only lived in the new property 'Thames Creek' for a few weeks when I became disturbed by some strange happenings while alone in the house. Lights appeared to be switched on in rooms I had not previously entered. I thought it was weird and questioned if I might be losing my mind and became determined to pull myself together. I wondered if the electrics were faulty but sensibly reasoned the house was brand new. Then things got worse.

Returning from shopping, I approached the front door, put my key in the latch and was startled to discover the door was already open. There was no sign of forced entry and I suspected this was yet another fault for the builder to sort out. Entering the hallway, looking straight through to the large patio windows in the living room, I was astonished to observe my Jack Russell dog Digger, running around the lawn chasing ducks. I had left him on his blanket, asleep, in the laundry room with the outside door locked and bolted. Somewhat shocked I immediately thought of burglars and bravely checked the rooms downstairs. Nothing seemed amiss. When I walked into the utility room I was startled to observe that the door to the garden was unbolted and wide open. Digger came running in to greet me, grinning from ear to ear. Perhaps burglars had fled the house this way as I was entering through the front I rationalised. What other explanation could there be I pondered?

Shaken to the core, I grabbed Digger, bolted the garden door securely for the second time that day and turned off the lights. I then made sure the front door was safely locked before getting into my car to collect six-year-old Ruth from school. I was too early and decided to walk Digger down the road to a small park when an attractive, smartly dressed, tall, fair haired, lady, I presumed to be another mother, walked towards me, with a little black poodle dog by her side.

"Hello. We are rather early, aren't we? My name's Augusta. I believe my son Simon is in the same class as your little girl. Shall we kill some time and walk the dogs down to the park?"

"I'm Audrey and, yes, Simon is in the same class with Ruth. I don't usually arrive quite so early as this but I have just had a really odd experience at home which has quite unsettled me."

I then went on to describe the incident. Why I am not sure because I hardly knew her.

"What a perfectly intriguing story" she cheerfully remarked. "It's obvious to me that someone from the 'other side' is creating this kind of phenomena in order to get your attention and make contact with you."

I was completely taken aback at this suggestion.

"It just so happens that next week I'm attending the Spiritualist Association of Great Britain, in Belgrave Square, for my regular three monthly session with one of the Mediums there. Would you believe it, the SAGB is situated near to all the foreign embassies in the square? *(It has since moved).* Oh, I have a super idea, why don't you come with me and have a 'reading' with another Medium to find out what's going on? I can make an appointment for you and we can travel up to town together."

Augusta was so enthusiastically sincere and I was excited by her suggestion so I found myself accepting her offer. Both our dogs were tugging at their leads and once we reached the park we let them loose to have a playful time with one another, while we continued talking.

Act 3 Scene 3:

Revelations from the 'Other Side'

'When you expand your awareness seemingly random events will be seen to fit into a larger purpose'
- Deepak Chopra

Not having any idea of what to expect while seated in a small, pleasant sitting room at the Spiritualist Association of Great Britain (SAGB), having left Augusta at the reception desk, the door opened and in walked a friendly, smallish man, who announced himself as Roy Morgan. He smiled at me as he spoke very fast with a strong Welsh accent.

"Hello my dear. Please don't get up. I know this is your first visit to the SAGB and that you are quite nervous. Just relax as I have a lovely gentleman standing here, beside you, who is extremely happy to be able to communicate with you at last as he has been attempting to attract your attention."

Intrigued, I thought about the odd happenings that had been taking place in my home. Roy Morgan had my full attention as he continued:

"Well now, dear, this elderly gentleman informs me that he passed away a couple of years ago, with cancer of the brain. The undiagnosed primary growth was located in the chest area. He wants you to know how much he always appreciated your kindness to him and how much he enjoyed his visits to your home. Especially getting to know your small daughter. He informs me he never married as he had the responsibility of looking after his aged mother and he led quite a lonely life."

Surely, I thought to myself, this had to be Uncle Bert the Medium was channelling. Roy Morgan then remarked:

"He says he enjoyed his funeral and was quite touched by the flowers you laid upon his coffin. He was pleased, too, that a number of his old colleagues had come to pay their last respects and was very touched by this gesture."

(Uncle Bert had specifically requested no flowers only donations to Age Concern, of which he was local President, but we covered the top of the coffin in mixed white blooms).

It was difficult to take in this kind of information. Uncle Bert deceased since September 1972 was not only making contact with me but said he had attended his own funeral! How on earth could this be, I wondered?

Roy Morgan continued:

"Uncle Bert is aware that you have moved to another house, by water - which he never visited during his lifetime - but he often stands behind you now as you look out of a large window at some movement outside."

I thought to myself he must be referring to the sliding patio doors I opened each day to scatter lots of bird seed onto the lawn while watching the ducks, geese and swans leave the river and come up to feed.

Now sceptics believe that Mediums are 'mind reading'. To a certain extent this is true but I was told things about Uncle Bert's life that I knew nothing about as I only knew him for a few years. So Roy Morgan could not have been getting that information from my mind.

Through Roy Morgan's clairvoyance, Uncle Bert talked about his young life: he had owned a black dog when he was fourteen and bought a blue car when he was eighteen which he didn't drive much but enjoyed spending happy hours polishing every Sunday. Elderly relatives subsequently confirmed this.

The most startling piece of evidence that totally convinced me Uncle Bert really was communicating from beyond the grave, came when the Medium said Uncle Bert was upset that his clock in a lovely oak case hanging on our wall in the hall wasn't chiming. Transporting the clock by car from Lincoln had affected its chiming mechanism. A clock repairer informed us it could not be fixed. Oh dear! I knew what a meticulous person Uncle Bert was, while alive, and that the clock had been one of his prized possessions!

Roy Morgan then appeared quite serious when he commented:

"It would appear that Uncle Bert is concerned that his favourite nephew - (*my husband of course*) - is smoking too many cigarettes each day for his own good. Especially as he has the potential to use his hands for healing!"

Roy Morgan paused for a moment. Then he uttered these words.

"And remember, the soul is eternal."

(*Those very words Uncle Bert had underlined in the book he wanted Don to have.*)

At the end of this mind-blowing session I prepared to leave the room when Roy Morgan turned to me and said:

"You do realise that you are a very psychic lady yourself and you will be 'sitting in circle' here in about one year from now."

(This puzzled me no end as I had no idea then what a 'circle' was and felt too embarrassed to ask).

Roy Morgan also mentioned that I would personally develop both the gifts of mediumship and healing. (This certainly was precognitive –as much to my surprise, it did happen later.)

Following this clairvoyant session, in which deceased Uncle Bert was able to communicate staggering information from the 'other side', I was left with much to ponder upon: deceased Uncle Bert was not dead. He had communicated telepathically through Roy Morgan that he still cared for myself and Don and provided me with indisputable evidence that he was still very much 'alive' and that we do survive death! I knew for sure nothing in my life would ever be the same again after such a revelation. From 1974–1977 I took several classes at the SAGB and joined two development circles!

Act 3 Scene 4:

Church Matters

'The Soul is Eternal'
- Grenville Kleiser

As a result of receiving this remarkable proof/evidence of life after death I began to explore reincarnation and to read books on comparative religions and their roots. One Sunday, after morning Service at St John's Anglican church in Egham I discussed the 'Uncle Bert' experience with my vicar and we got into quite a deep conversation on 'soul survival'. The Catholic church does, apparently, believe in something called 'the perpetuation of the soul' and Don and I asked our Vicar his views on this, especially as we had shared with him the Uncle Bert experience. He did not dismiss the possibility of re-incarnation but preferred to consider it as a 'plane' in time and space. In retrospect, I realise now what a progressive thinker he was. The Reverend suggested there were 'planes' in time and space where people who have previously lived on earth, are collectively established, and with whom one might be able to contact.

Regretfully, I doubt his views were shared by members of the Parochial Church Council who called round, unexpectedly, to our home one evening, evidently concerned we had not attended church for some weeks. They seemed horrified and alarmed at what we shared of our contact with mediums and deceased Uncle Bert's messages and argued against such practices as being unchristian.

They were unaware that the Church of England had published a report on their investigation into spiritualism in which there was an admission that there was the possibility of the soul's survival and that communication could take place. The three visitors were not aware of the report, which we showed them, but they only skimmed through it and continued to express their deep concern for us.

Eventually, after several hours, they gave up and left saying they would pray for us.

(NB: The Original Church of England Report on Spiritualism completed in 1939 as published by the Psychic News in 1960s, approved by the Archbishop Lang and Archbishop Temple, can be read, in full, on line. The preface is by A.W. Austen then Editor of Psychic News.)

For nine years the report was kept secret then one morning it mysteriously appeared. The final paragraph of the report is of particular interest as it may be the reason why this report was suppressed for so long by the Church of England. It reads: 'It is in our opinion important that representatives of the Church of England should keep in touch with groups of intelligent persons who believe in spiritualism. We must leave practical guidance in this matter to the Church itself'. Signatory - The Archbishop Dr. Francis Underhill, Bishop of Bath and Wells.

In seeking to quench my own thirst for more knowledge I discovered that early Christian Bishops and other religious hierarchy viewed reincarnation (and healing) as a threat to their authority and that, subsequently, all mention of it was forbidden by order of the General Council of the Church in 553AD.

The order said: 'If anyone shall assert the fabulous pre-existence of souls, and shall submit to the monstrous doctrine that follows it, let him be anathema.'

I acquired the following information from the numerous researched articles available from the Internet:

'In 553AD the Fifth Ecumenical Council anathematized Origen. Until then Origen had been highly regarded as a Church Father; he was the pupil and spiritual successor to Clement of Alexandria; he worked for many years at the library in Caesarea that the evangelist Matthew established. He was no lightweight Christian. But for the dubious purposes of the Emperor Justinian, heavily influenced by his power greedy and former prostitute wife, he had Origen condemned, so that Origen's teachings were soon forgotten. The hidden reason for condemning Origen was almost certainly his understanding of reincarnation as deeply compatible with Christianity. Justinian as temporal ruler did not want his authority threatened like Herod the Great rebuilding the Jerusalem Temple. Justinian sought to appease his religious public in his time by building the most beautiful church he could conceive 'Haga Sophia' in Constantinople. But he played dirty with Origen'

I started to attend a Christian Spiritualist Church in Windsor (not far from the Queen's Castle) where I was warmly welcomed and was impressed by the loving and healing messages that came through to bereaved persons during the sessions of Clairvoyance.

One Medium directed her attention to a rather sad looking woman sitting across the aisle from me. In a very firm voice she asked this person to look up at her as she stood on the platform. The lady did so.

The Medium then said:

"I've been given a wedding ring by spirit and believe that I'm in touch with your late husband who passed over to the 'other side' about a year or so ago. He informs me that he is seriously concerned for you because you're still grieving and spending days looking at old photographs of when you were together."

The lady nodded vigorously inferring this to be correct.

The Medium then continued.

"Your husband says that all his clothes are still hanging in the wardrobe and it's about time you cleared them out. It is time to move on and to stop moping because he's fine and as you won't be joining him for quite a while you should get on with your life."

The transformation in this lady's appearance was a joy to behold. She had listened, intently, agreeing with everything the Medium was saying. She looked rejuvenated and one could only assume she was going straight home to clear out the wardrobe and put away the photo album. In one simple moment of proof, that her deceased husband was far from dead, this woman's grief was wiped away. I wondered if a visit from the church parochial council could have achieved such a remarkable result as this?

On my next visit to the Spiritualist church, I had convinced Don to come with me and after some persuasion he reluctantly agreed. Incredibly, for the next seven consecutive weeks, different visiting Mediums singled him out with similar messages from Uncle Bert which were:

'You have exceptional healing power in your hands which you must develop and use'.

Don was quite taken aback and became determined to follow up this directive from Uncle Bert.

Naturally, I was thrilled but also a bit miffed that Uncle Bert was completely ignoring me but, nevertheless, pleased, too, that he was still communicating from 'the other side'. Eventually, Don became a most remarkable spiritual healer. A path I followed myself in 1976 after previously participating in two psychic development circles at the SAGB while Don was busy attending healer development classes with renowned Healer/ Medium Ursula Roberts.

Act 3 Scene 5:

A Personal Healing

For more than a year or so I had been suffering acutely with a very painful neck condition for which I was receiving heat, traction and other treatments from an Osteopath to alleviate the condition. Driving was difficult as I could not turn my neck in either direction as it was so stiff and uncomfortable. One evening I was feeling particularly miserable as my neck was really hurting and I had wrapped a rolled up towel around it for support. Perceiving my discomfort, Don approached me saying:

"If I'm supposed to have healing power in my hands why don't I try and work on your neck? **I don't suppose it can do any harm!**" This was to become a famous saying of his during his time as a Healer.

Standing behind me Don placed his hands either side of my neck. Instantly, I felt a warm glow emanating from them that was soothing and comforting. He continued for about twenty minutes after which I retired to bed feeling very relaxed. The following morning all the pain and neck stiffness had disappeared and I had regained complete mobility. It was nothing short of a miracle considering the misery I'd been through which none of the other year-long treatments had managed to eliminate.

Act 3 Scene 6:

Sitting in Circle

Following Uncle Bert's revelations I enrolled in 1974 in my first development 'Circle' at the SAGB; these were held explicitly for the development of clairvoyance and consisted of a number of people sitting in a room in a circle, together with the leader of the group who was, herself, an experienced platform medium. After welcoming the participants, all of whom had introduced themselves, the group leader would recite a beautiful prayer then switch the main room lighting off leaving only a red light glowing above us in the centre of the room. We would then sit silently for approximately thirty minutes.

I was not quite sure what one was supposed to do during this 'silence'. With hindsight and much more experience now in understanding meditative practises, including the change of brain waves that occur in this state, I would not attempt to put myself into an alternative state of consciousness without first utilising the protective and necessary tools of good breath work, relaxation and grounding exercises which are important procedures. In such a situation one's consciousness is moving the kundalini - the creative life-force energy - up the spine from the reproductive area to the top of the head. In other words, the chakra system is transforming and opening the energy body to higher vibrations. To achieve this safely, and not overcharge the heart chakra, one has to be deeply relaxed, and very well-grounded. Sometimes, sitting in circle, I felt too much energy moving up the spine so fast I became dizzy or felt the need to stand up with my arms raised over my head due to the lack of energy underneath my feet, rendering me unable to 'earth' this powerful electrical charge moving through my body. I understand now that we have invisible roots of energy underneath our feet which we can push down, deeply, to ground our consciousness as it moves upwards into higher levels. I will be explaining more about this later in the second part of the book.

Nevertheless, as the silence in the room continued, I was definitely in an altered state of consciousness and it was as if I was looking at a video which had, somehow, switched itself on inside my forehead and I was viewing an array of beautiful coloured moving objects: a vividly coloured stained glass window appeared through which radiant shafts of light shone brightly followed by a gleaming silver sword which appeared to be hanging in space. What did all this mean? With every week's circle meeting I began to 'see' more and more with my inner eye.

In some sessions, I saw and felt the strength of a Native American Indian Chief; the gentleness of a sweet Oriental lady; the wisdom of a Tibetan Sage with a silver beard that fell down to the ground. On one particular occasion I saw Jesus Christ. He appeared to look the same as I would have imagined Him, or had seen Him in certain illustrations. The feeling of being overwhelmed by such love is hard to describe. Circle members were encouraged to share their own meditative experiences and it was absolutely fascinating how different they all were from my own. I continued to psychically 'develop' in this way for a couple of years and, as my personal sensitivity increased, I became quite alarmed, when sitting in the group in meditation, I began to have distinct and quite weird impressions of being overshadowed by another 'being: my facial skin seemed to be changing colour to dark brown; my nose and lips felt huge; then sensations that I was growing taller and my hands were becoming larger began to freak me out. I was being squeezed out of my own body which didn't feel mine anymore; especially when, in my mind's eye, I could 'see' I was wearing a magnificent feathered Indian head dress that swept to the floor.

I didn't fancy this at all! Whoever it was overshadowing me I didn't care. I just wanted it to stop. I considered leaving the circle but the Medium persuaded me to stay. She was excited that I was developing trance mediumship – about which I knew nothing – and that the Indian Chief was a part of me from a past life and was now acting as a Guide.

Eventually this discarnate 'entity' spoke to me by manipulating my voice box; my throat felt very dry and peculiar; he called himself 'White Feather'. Unable to control my throat area, suddenly a strange and deeply guttural voice, spoke. I wondered how it could be coming from me. This is what 'White Feather' said:

"Birds can teach humans so much. With their microscopic sight they always remain focused on what is important to them at any one moment. The Eagle remains the wisest and most focused of the bird kingdom."

Panicking, I forced myself to release this entity before he could speak anything else from my voice box. Especially as it didn't make sense to me anyway.

After this episode I was very emotional and burst into tears and told the group leader I was leaving as there was no way that I wanted a repeat of this performance. She was extremely disappointed with me as she was really excited to have a potential trance medium in her circle.

I have often wondered what would have occurred if I had overcome my fear and let White Feather use my energy.

Act 3 Scene 7:

Public Demonstration of Clairvoyance

In 1976 I joined a more advanced development circle after having been interviewed by a modern-thinking medium. She had been tasked by the Board of Trustees at the SAGB to train fledgling mediums for platform work. I felt very comfortable with her procedures – which did not include any trance work - and I confidently signed up for six months and confirmed I would give a public demonstration of Clairvoyance in the main demonstration hall at the end of it. (Where this confidence, or was it arrogance, came from I do not know).

The training was pretty intense but also exciting as my intuition developed sharply when asked to 'read' or 'sense' the thoughts and feelings of other fledglings in the group. The psychometry lessons were challenging at first. One had to hold and 'sense' a hidden object sealed in an envelope and then relate whatever vibrations (or information) this object was 'giving off'. (As we had all sealed our own item in an envelope and knew its identity we were able to judge if the information being picked up by another group member was acceptable or not. In nearly all instances we achieved good results!) We then had to learn how to respect and 'tune-in' to the 'spirit world' and act as a medium to make contact with a discarnate entity (with permission) on a group member's behalf. Contact was not always possible for whatever reason and one had to respect this. When someone did come through the results were astounding. How could someone, who had passed on some time ago, be able to transmit, telepathically, from another dimension, and identify who they were?

Too soon the 'big day' arrived when, much to our group leader's disappointment, only three of us out of the original six fledglings were present on the platform one evening in 1976 in the demonstration room facing an audience of one hundred members of the public. Where, oh where, was my confidence now? I was shaking like a leaf and could hardly breathe! I thought I was about to humiliate myself big time if I managed not to pass out!

After initial introductions my turn arrived. The audience was silent and full of expectation. I sent a silent prayer for help to 'upstairs' and then spoke to an elderly, sad-looking woman. Opening my heart to her I said:

"Good evening dear. I don't have a message for you from Spirit but I have to tell you that you do have a lot of love and support around you at this time".

The lady nodded at me and smiled.

"Just you take care now," I continued, "and all will be well".

Suddenly, there was considerable activity occurring in the aisle of the first row, in which a young man was seated.

Building up, etherically, beside him was a middle-aged, very small man, quite shabbily dressed, who was removing a cap from his head and stuffing it into a pocket. Then, he put his hand into an inside pocket of his suit and took out a 'baccy tin', which he opened and started to roll a cigarette from. Immediately, he shook his head, closed the tin and put it away, after which he started patting his chest and coughing frantically as he telepathically communicated with me:

"I believe I have your father here". I said to the young man. "He says he was a heavy smoker and died of lung cancer a few years ago".

The young man seemed transfixed.

"Your dad is bringing you a lot of love and encouragement. He says whatever you do please don't smoke as he would not like you to end up with a terrible cough like he suffered."

Later that evening the young man informed me that he had never stepped foot inside the building before that evening but passed the premises on his way home each night. As it was his dad's birthday that day he decided, on a whim, to enter and find out what went on there. He confirmed it was his dad whom I had contacted and yes he was a heavy smoker and had died of lung cancer three years ago.

Before I had a chance to wonder to whom I might go to in the audience next, I became aware of a very smartly dressed lady sitting in the back row. I pointed to her and she looked up.

"I have a tall, athletic, handsome young man standing behind you who is dressed in shorts and shirt like a footballer or rugby player wears. He says he was only eighteen years old when he was killed in a car crash. Wrapped round his forehead is some kind of white cloth. It could be a bandage. He says he was an enthusiastic sportsman and that he is related to you."

To my complete surprise I found out later that this lady was a Trustee of the association and she confirmed it was her nephew who had, indeed, been killed in a car crash when he was only a young man. She said the most convincing piece of evidence was the white cloth around her nephew's head. As a rugby player this skull cap was worn underneath a protective helmet during matches!

Happily I had passed the test of Clairvoyance and thanked 'upstairs' but I knew, instantly, I did not want to pursue a career as a platform medium. I was too stressed out. I decided to devote myself to becoming a spiritual healer instead.

Over the next decade I pursued and studied all manner of interesting subject matter, including understanding and exploring the human energy field, dowsing, life after death, sacred geometry, and any other subject allied to spiritual development. Subsequently, although I did not become a platform medium, I was eventually invited by the SAGB's general manager, in 1978, to lecture on healing and meditation and organise practical group workshops which, over a two year period, were most enjoyable and well supported once I was able to control my nerves. There was a beautiful chapel in the building there where I would always go and pray before the start of the talk or workshop asking for guidance and support.

Act 3 Scene 8:

California

'Certain things catch your eye, but pursue only those that capture your heart'
- Native American Proverb

Having waited so long to become a mother I wanted Ruth to have as many of the opportunities that were lacking in my own childhood as possible, especially a good education. It was obvious, very early on, that Ruth was not only academic but very artistic as well. From a very early age she composed the most beautiful poetry and shone in her studies of literature, music and drama. I couldn't have been more proud and counted my blessings that my dreams of motherhood had been fulfilled in such a wonderful way. Ruth was such a precious and long-awaited gift.

She was christened in St John's Church in Egham, where Don and I worshipped on an *ad hoc* basis for several years, and we thought very highly of the young, married vicar. We both felt we could discuss with him certain contentious religious subjects without falling foul of too much criticism.

When Ruth started her first pre-school in Virginia Water, Surrey, aged three, we were still living at our beloved bungalow 'Water's Edge' and I started working lunch times at a beautiful pub on Thorpe village green convenient for collecting Ruth from school. I have always been a 'people' person and thought this would be fun as well as a distraction from personal disappointments. Life was comfortable: I was still an avid acting member of Thorpe Players, organised a number of home-entertaining dinner parties and barbecues, and enjoyed sunshine holidays. So, why wasn't I happy and content? Something (or someone) was missing from my life. And I was constantly consumed with guilty emotions.

As much as I truly loved and admired Don as a person for his kindness, loyalty, generosity, security and friendship, I felt I wasn't 'in love' with him romantically; in some areas we were completely incompatible. There was also this distinct lack of passion (or chemistry) between us which I longed for. I would do anything for him and he would do anything for me but, somehow, we seemed to have more of a 'brother/sister' relationship. After what he had suffered in his first marriage and losing his little son, how could I even begin to contemplate separating him from Ruth if I left him - to do what? In any case I was too scared to think about what that would mean and how I would manage if I did. I was still very insecure in myself and the last thing I wanted was another failed marriage. It was a constant struggle for me. There were often depressing periods of nostalgia. I started to fantasise how romantic my life might have been if married to Kit instead of Don. Life is sometimes very confusing! So, I determined to pull myself together, count my blessings and be as good a wife as I could despite how I felt. I had married a good man; and I considered him to be my best friend. Thankfully, as things worked out later, there was to be a much greater and spiritually karmic purpose to our relationship; and a much bigger and more important spiritual mission to be fulfilled. When fate did finally intervene life was never quite the same again. In so many ways it became totally fulfilling.

It was during this personally unsettling and difficult period in 1976 that I was invited by my cousin Anne, who lived in California with her three children, to pay her a visit The invitation appealed to me and as I still had ongoing travel concessions with British Airways, Ruth and I flew out to California at the beginning of her school summer holidays with Don's blessing.

To be honest, I desperately needed the change of scenery and also some respite from the continuing pangs of guilt and misery I kept inflicting upon myself about my personal situation. Six weeks in California was just what I needed. Unfortunately my visit turned out to be extremely challenging due to a difficult family situation.

One beautiful, sunny day, while we were enjoying a family picnic in a scenically beautiful State park, I was leaping like a gazelle across sparkling streams of water tumbling over rugged rocks which provided stepping stones for me to cross to the other side of the bank. Suddenly, in the midst of this enjoyable, childlike behaviour, I had a mind-blowing experience that stopped me dead in my tracks.

In the distance, I perceived with some astonishment, a Native American Indian encampment full of wigwams, camp fires, horses and Braves moving around. Intriguingly, an older, wise looking Indian Chief adorned in a magnificent feathered head dress, was seated on the ground smoking a peace pipe which he then passed around to other members in the group. For a moment I was spellbound, hardly able to believe my eyes. Then, to my utter dismay and, suddenly, in the blink of an eye, the vision disappeared. Eventually, a long time later and with increased awareness and understanding, it dawned on me that what I had witnessed then in that magical moment, could have been some kind of cellular memory; was it possible that I had once lived within this Native American Indian community in a previous life time and I had experienced some kind of flashback? I already did have a deep rooted and natural connection to America from the first time I had stepped foot in the country.

A month on from this this incident, I cut short my stay with cousin Anne. Each of her children's behavioural patterns were totally bizarre and unacceptable. Sadly, they had not been taught to share anything: the two girls and boy competed with one another and each had their own TV, separate food stocks, toys and books which, if touched by another sibling, for any reason, resulted in a full scale screaming match. Ruth went to stroke the family cat, on one occasion, and was immediately instructed to leave the cat alone as it did not belong to her. Returning from a walk one day I was horrified to hear screaming coming from an upstairs window, followed by a shower of clothing being flung to the ground.

"How dare you come into my bedroom and move my things", screamed twelve year old Polly as she hurled toys and books to the ground. Neighbours appeared from their homes to witness this event and I heard one person mutter:

"Oh dear God not again!"

Ruth was totally unnerved and asked me if we could leave. Fortunately, we were rescued by a visiting English family next door, with two young very well behaved girls who invited us to accompany them on a trip to Lake Tahoe. It was with great relief we ended our stay with Sarah.

Another time Ruth and I joined a group of other friends on a houseboat trip in Arizona cruising on Lake Havasu in Colorado. This place was famous for having erected a replica of London's historical bridge, built from the original bricks after it was dismantled. It was rather bizarre to witness a little bit of 'old England' all along one stretch of the arid shoreline. A carpet of lush green grass spread across the banks of the river, kept alive in such heat, by dozens of water sprinklers. A real English telephone kiosk, post box and taxi cab added some authenticity to this 'little bit of England' in the middle of this hot, bleak, desert area.

Such heat was blistering and we lived in our bathing costumes leaping from the boat onto sand dunes, whenever we were able to and cool off in the water, washing our hair and splashing around. We hand-fed breadcrumbs to golden sun fish swimming all around us. Ruth and the other children were having such fun and it was truly a memorable and magical experience.

Early one evening after another intensely hot day cruising and relieved of any cooking chores I decided to watch the sun set by lying down on the flat roof of the house boat. The terrain we were passing either side of the lake was intensely bleak. Vast, jagged, black rocky peaks loomed high and unwelcoming against the silhouette of a blazing sunset sky streaked with colours of gold, apricot, deep pinks and rosy red and purple hues. Previously I had learnt that when the Native American Indians of this land had been banished from their lush green pastures by the USA government in order to appease white settlers, it was to hostile and infertile areas such as these where they were resettled without much hope of survival.

Pondering upon this cruel situation that the white man had forced upon these rightful owners of their long established territory, I experienced a powerfully intense inner pain in my heart and an acute awareness or 'knowing' that I, too, had lived and died in this place during a past life. Sighing deeply, a sudden shift in my consciousness inexplicably occurred: I became the sky above me, the setting sun, the flowing waters of the river, the heron skimming the surface, the bulrushes and reeds along the shoreline. I became 'one' with everything.

It was a unique, memorable, peak experience never, ever, to be forgotten. For one glorious moment – in or out of time – I had touched the hand of God and totally connected to 'His' creation!

What did all this mean? I wondered. I knew I would have to make an effort in order to find out.

Act 3 Scene 9:

Mind-Body-Spirit Festivals

I loved being involved with the NFSH office each day and the spiritual awakening taking place within my consciousness.

It was such a privilege and blessing to be a part of this spiritual healing process and exciting to be part of the team that was involved in setting up and fronting the **first ever** public NFSH Healing Stand at the first-ever-in-the-world Mind, Body, Spirit exhibition at Olympia in London in April 1977. The event was launched by Graham Wilson and was entirely devoted to the pursuit of healthier living and offered a home for spiritual seekers and pilgrims and attracted tens of thousands of visitors. It amused me that, finally, my flower arranging classes came in handy as I nervously dressed the large NFSH Stand, decking it out with hanging baskets of flowers and other floral arrangements.

Teams of registered and insured spiritual healer members were on hand each day during the exhibition to offer to the clamouring public a spiritual healing taster and also to provide them with a better understanding of the act of healing and our organisation. Many members of the public who were observing the healing sessions commented on the beautiful, relaxing, vibrations they, too, were soaking up, as loving healing energy flowed in every direction from our Stand, despite all the noisy jostling of the crowds around them.

Over the years at subsequent Mind-Body-Spirit Exhibitions we also provided demonstrations of spiritual healing in front of huge audiences who were invited to come on to the platform and experience the laying-on-of hands and offer feedback about their experience; it was encouragingly positive and resulted in a huge boost of members joining the organisation.

I didn't lose sight of the fact that here I was, on a very public stage, albeit not in an acting capacity, but in front of a very large audience, to whom I was explaining and demonstrating the act of healing.

Act 3 Scene 10:

Spiritual Teachers

*'Once the Soul awakens the search begins and you can never
   go back'*
- **John O'Donohue**

Both in and out of the office I continuously craved more spiritual knowledge and understanding, and sought it from every source available. The charismatic and lovingly described 'new age Guru' Sir George Trevelyan, launched the prestigious Wrekin Trust in 1971 as a spiritual educational charity which organised residential courses and weekend retreats at big country houses owned by the National Trust on subjects such as Buddhism, meditation, trans-personal psychology, healing and other subjects too numerous to mention, with renowned international Speakers of all persuasions. Sir George graced the NFSH conference platform on several occasions eloquently addressing mesmerised audiences on the importance of us being here on earth now, during what he described as one of the most important eras in the whole history of evolution, and of the major part humanity had to play.

The renowned French Mystic, Frederic Lionel, once a French engineer, World War II resistance fighter, writer, philosopher and spiritual teacher helped me to understand more about the ancient wisdom which he was so adept at teaching. At one of his small house group meetings he told us that during the war he spent four years working with the French underground movement in his native France. On a particular mission the Gestapo boarded a train on which he was travelling. Frederic was very likely to have been arrested. He related that unexpectedly and quite suddenly an intuitive message flashed into his consciousness and he received some inner guidance which he acted upon immediately, resulting in his being able to make himself 'virtually invisible' to the Gestapo officers. Frederic was then able to continue his journey unhindered. From that moment on Frederic said he was under a 'higher authority' which greatly assisted him in the special operations work in which he was involved until the end of World War II. During the war he became clearly aware that he was being led and taught by invisible guides working through his Higher Self. He saw that he had to jettison old beliefs and learn to obey his intuition implicitly in split-second reactions.

Both Frederic and Sir George held some inspiring spiritual retreats together down in Cornwall, close to St Michael's Mount. On one retreat I was present when Lord and Lady St Aubon – being great friends of Sir George – invited the group participants to take tea with them at their home, (or castle), on St Michael's Mount.

Preceding this we had permission to meditate as a group within the ancient and atmospheric chapel on the Mount. We were surprised to be joined by the resident Vicar and disappointed to be denied our expected 'silent time' in this beautiful setting when the Vicar proceeded to address us with quite a dreary sermon. More so, because I felt it was not delivered from his heart but from his head.

I loved the Alice Bailey Teachings which were channelled through her by the Tibetan Master, Djwal Khul and published by the Lucis Trust Publishing Company. It would take practically a life-time to absorb the amount of spiritual knowledge and intellectual wisdom these writings contain, some of which I studied by myself and in groups. My favourite publication is 'Ponder on This' which is a pot-pourri of all the other books.

My most profound personal teacher and subsequent life-long friend, was and still is Lilla Bek, yoga teacher, author and psychic energy researcher, who certainly enhanced my interest in the composition of consciousness, the mechanics of healing, and the meaning of colour and energy.

Back In 1978 an office colleague recommended that I contact Lilla for a remote reading on the state of my health following a partial hysterectomy. I posted off a letter to her, including my date of birth, signature and asked a couple of questions. After a two month wait I finally received in the post two one-hour cassette tapes; as I listened enthralled at what she had to say it all but 'blew my mind' away.

Lilla's reading read like a history book of my current life and previous ones. While 'tuning' into me more deeply, Lilla perceived certain colours in my auric field and within my individual energy centres (chakras) up the spine. She advised that I had black and ice blue colours in my reproductive area which, ordinarily, should not be present except following surgery which I had recently undergone. It seemed as if she was sitting inside my body consciousness from which she was able to ascertain information about my body, my past, present and future; and we hadn't even met. Not in this life time but most certainly, according to her, in previous lives.

Lilla related we had shared some past lives together: one in ancient Greece as sisters, and two as members of the Essene community situated on the shores of the Dead Sea in Israel. She was particularly intrigued by a life I had lived during the time of Christ's crucifixion and said that it was an important life as one would have been exposed to 'His Great Light'. I was Roman, not Jewish. She encouraged me to regress this life at some point.

Lilla explained to me why I had 'come down' to earth in this life time; that I had a specific role to play in developing and opening people's consciousness through meditation and healing. Evidently, I would undertake quite a challenging role which meant a lot of personal study, hard work, commitment and extensive travel.

My head was spinning as I listened to Lilla's revelations as she gifted me with her psychic insight and knowledge and certainly awakening within me the realisation and purpose of why I was born.

Lilla informed me that the colours she perceives in a person's aura, through tuning into her third eye, change according to how one thinks, feels, and acts, whereas the colours she 'sees' over someone's head are permanent and derived/earned from previous past life experiences or initiations. If she 'sees' the peach ray over someone's crown it indicates to her that the person has previously undergone a number of special lives of initiation to become what she describes as an 'old soul' who can then choose whether or not to re-incarnate here on earth. Lilla explained to me that the 'third eye' situated in the centre of the brow, is similar to a computer and contains past, present and future events. If you cut an orange in half you will find there are many segments to it. Such is the third eye in which each segment depicts a past or future experience. Through a very special awareness that Lilla has developed (at first almost reluctantly) Lilla has gained the capacity to see the energies around people which indicates their inner state of physical, mental and spiritual wellbeing.

During a chat on a later occasion Lilla laughingly shared with me a personal story - this is what she said:

"I was at the kitchen sink one morning washing dishes when I heard this male voice in my head announcing that he was the Count of St Germain. I immediately retorted somewhat cheekily by saying, 'Oh yes, and I am the Queen of Sheba.'" She continued:

"That afternoon I went to work at my local charity shop where I sorted out donated books. As I was reaching up to put them on the shelf, a book fell down on my head and then to the floor. As I stooped down to pick it up I noticed with interest that I was holding a copy of 'The Life of St Germain' who had in one life-time been a 16th century aristocrat alchemist who held the secret of life. Some time later the Count spoke to me again and this time I listened with more respect."

It appeared that the Ascended Master of Ancient Wisdom, St Germain, wished to train Lilla for the purpose of researching the evolution of consciousness, the human energy field and the mechanics of healing. Thus it seemed fortuitous that the deeper purpose for our connection was to bring Lilla into contact with healers.

During the reading Lilla did for me she stated:

"I could talk to you for hours whereas I have just completed a reading for a gentleman and found it difficult to fill an hour. With you I needed two hours and more. It would be wonderful if we could meet up some time."

Subsequently I invited Lilla to visit us; my ten year old daughter Ruth and I met her off the train at Wraysbury station. A small, slim, fair haired and very ordinary looking lady ran towards us with outstretched arms and one really big beaming smile. We embraced and it felt as if we had known one another forever. Lilla made a great fuss of my young daughter Ruth.

What a unique weekend it turned out to be. Most certainly one could describe it as "challenging boundaries" of time and space. All our spiritual questions were effortlessly answered by Lilla in great depth. Through her many hundreds of personal readings Lilla was making an extensive study of the human energy field and the composition of consciousness. She remarked:

"Every time I look, and look again at a person's aura and energy system, with its myriad of fluctuations, I can 'see' more and delve deeper."

I learnt that Lilla had developed her extraordinary abilities through teaching yoga classes for ten years, when she became aware that something was awakening inside her and that her psyche was beginning to 'open'. She was able to 'sense' the atmosphere around her changing and could feel vibrations through her body. There was certainly much more to Yoga than she had imagined.

It was later that Lilla began to 'feel' the quality of people's auras and the colours they transmit and that by tuning into them she could 'feel' a great deal about them. She received a lot of 'out of body training' while asleep at night and was able to sit at the feet of great Masters who provided her with vast amounts of wisdom and knowledge and instruction on how to use it.

The consequence of Lilla's reading was the realisation that I was not just a body but that my body was in my consciousness and my consciousness existed on many different levels, even into infinity.

Never again would I be able to think of myself in the ordinary sense that one tends to do. Lilla's insight taught me that, energetically speaking, I am composed of a multi-dimensional system that operates simultaneously, both physically, emotionally, mentally and spiritually.

As a result of Lilla's reference to the Essene past lives we had shared I became increasingly interested in leaning more about them and I became a member of The Essene Healing Network whose introductory pamphlet states:

'Essene communities lived over two thousand or more years ago on the banks of the Dead Sea. At the highest level they were seers, mystics, prophets and healers, who had come down to prepare the earth's energies for the birth of 'The Christ'. Others were called neophytes and the community all shared their work in the fields. They were custodians of an ancient wisdom and were responsible for writing the Dead Sea Scrolls, which they wrapped in cloths and hid in caves at Qumran, to be found for posterity, by the Bedouin shepherd boy in 1947.

Seven days a week, morning, noon and night they downed tools to commune with the Angels. Thanks to inspired and beautiful translations, capturing the very essence of their message, of the Aramaic scripts held at the Vatican, we know that they had something unique to offer us in this troubled century.

These ancient communions or invocations are ways of linking to natural and cosmic forces. Through the angelic realms, we are able to draw energy for healing, rejuvenation and spiritual growth. From their early writings we learn that we are meant to commune with God as both female and male and that Jesus taught 'Our Mother' as well as 'Our Father'. The original commandments told us to - Honour our Heavenly Father and our Earthly Mother, not to take life from any living being and to commune with the Angels of the Earthly Mother and Heavenly Father, so that we may bathe in the Fountain of Light, and enter into the Sea of Eternity.'

Edmund Szekely's writings on the mysticism of the Essenes captured my interest which had prompted my decision to join the Essene Network and attend their retreats.

Max and Isobel Cade played an extraordinary part in my development as a spiritual healer. A Zen Buddhist for forty years and British biophysicist Max, together with Geoffrey Blundell, in 1976 invented the first and one and only 'Mind Mirror EEG led Awakened Mind Training' which monitored and demonstrated the level of brain activity during meditative practises which measured alternative states of consciousness. Max and Isobel Cade organised a series of training workshops exclusively for NFSH healers. Initially we were seated at tables with skin resistant meters attached to one wrist while we listened to a series of relaxation techniques, after which we were able to ascertain from the skin resistant meter reading to what degree of relaxation we had achieved. Another time Max linked up one healer and one client to two separate Mind Mirrors during the healing act. The healer commenced by attuning to their own Higher Self and then the Higher Self of their client, in preparation for becoming a channel for healing. Uniquely the healer's brain waves were being monitored by the Mind Mirror to ascertain whether they were able to reach and maintain the fifth state of meditation or the healing state or a theta brain wave, during the laying-on-hands. In most cases we were able to reach the healing state of meditation, but were unable to sustain the theta brain wave for more than ten minutes which meant the healer would then be generating their own energy and more likely to absorb, rather than transmute, any negativity the client might be releasing. An exciting and important development of this exercise was to prove that the healer and client could achieve total brain wave synchronicity during the act of healing. It was a complete revelation and would focus any future training and development of our healers to better understand how important and instrumental the process of deep relaxation, breath work, and meditation, was in reaching a state of spiritual attunement. Max wrote the book 'The Awakened Mind'.

The renowned successful painter and author, Vera Stanley Alder who died in 1984, wrote the book 'The Finding Of the Third Eye' the cover of which states: 'She had a rare gift of condensing and synthesising the essentials of esoteric teaching'. I found her books both fascinating and illuminating and especially loved the 'Fifth Dimension'.

In 1988 on two separate occasions I travelled to California to attend conferences organised and hosted by Dr. Brugh Joy, a Fellow of the American College of Physicians and a Phi Beta Kappa graduate of the University of Southern California and the USC School of Medicine and author of Joy's Way. 'It is a book that shows the process of individual and group transformation that rattles and reforms the reader's concepts of the nature of reality.' Similar to Lilla Bek Dr. Joy could 'see' into the physical body. Attending a lecture of his in London he made this fascinating statement:

"The reason we become interested in spiritual healing is because all healers are wounded and trying to heal themselves. Once we can achieve this there will be no need for anymore healers."

Act 3 Scene 11:

Health Concerns for Healers

Sitting at my desk in Central Office I was beginning to have some serious doubts as to whether or not it was actually healthy for a person to be giving spiritual healing to sick people when, it seemed, so many of our own healer members appeared to be quite unhealthy themselves. Sifting through the annual membership renewals I was shocked and concerned by the number of members who were not renewing their subscriptions for the current year and the reasons why:

'I am recovering from a stroke'.

'I have developed angina'.

'I have had a heart attack'.

'My blood pressure is sky high'.

What on earth was going on? I wondered. I took my concerns to Lilla with about a hundred questions, all of which she was able to competently answer.

Healers had to understand the nature of healing and the part their nervous system played in the process. It wasn't good enough to just feel you had a 'gift' for healing and could express that gift, however lovingly, through the laying-on-of-hands without first having any understanding of the mechanics of healing and the importance of self preparation through understanding and practising good breath work, relaxation, meditation, attunement and a healthy lifestyle. Lilla's research revealed that there was an invisible energy system involved in healing and that, when fully understood, healers would be protected from damaging their own health and well-being through personal lack of knowledge of the wondrous process they personally were involved in. The second part of my book explains this in detail.

That is why Don and I encouraged Lilla to consider lecturing for the NFSH and to teach us about the evolution of energy, how consciousness was composed, and the mechanics of Spiritual Healing. Lilla was totally inexperienced in facing the public and shy in doing so but she put her faith and trust in us and permitted Don to make all the necessary arrangements for her fledgling debut as a public lecturer. Lilla always said Don and I took very good care of her while she, subsequently, proved to be an outstanding asset to the healing organisation and to healers at large.

Thus for the next fifteen years, throughout the 1980s and 1990s, Lilla Bek shared with us 'Source/Wisdom' material while teaching her advanced courses which enabled us to establish a much needed ground-breaking two part basic foundation course to educate potential healer members and ensure that the act of healing was a healthy and risk-free vocation.

In 1982 the NFSH launched the first-ever professional healer development training weekend which attracted over seventy intensely interested personnel from other organisations and was held at the Berkeley Arms Hotel near to London's Heathrow Airport.

Made thoroughly nervous by the challenge of being a founder member of the lecture team and having to face such a large and prestigious gathering without an acting script to follow, or another character to portray, I suddenly became full of self-doubt and prayed several times for help and support to quell my fear.

'Meditation – A Channel for Healing' was my chosen subject. When I finally made my presentation my nerves were not quite under control and I was shaking inside so much I decided to rely heavily upon my previous stage experience of making contact with one's audience by sensing and gaining eye contact with them and smiling! Thankfully it worked. Little did I realise then this was to be the beginning of the next twenty-five years of my life and that I would be travelling to many different countries and far away places and that there would be such an international interest in our organisation and spiritual healing.

We had much to thank Lilla and the Ascended Master Count St Germain for in providing a plethora of uniquely essential and knowledgeable information into the mechanics of healing.

After further study and practice, a team of four tutors, of which I was one, together with my husband Don, and John and Jean Dreghorn (all now deceased), was able in 1983 to start teaching a residential basic healer development programme on behalf of the NFSH for the next 10 years. Lilla continued to teach much more advanced material. Much later, in preparation for her withdrawal from presenting so many courses, she passed on some of her lecture notes to me and provided me with personal tuition on certain subjects which, later, were incorporated into more advanced workshops which I helped to teach.

Countless hundreds of people from all walks of life flocked to attend this healer development training programme and, eventually, dozens more tutors were trained to teach the courses in every part of the country. The prestige and the membership of the NFSH continued to grow and it was quite exhilarating, though somewhat challenging too, being in charge of the busy office on a daily basis and teaching healer development courses most weekends.

I wouldn't have changed anything for the world. My life was so full of all the wonderful things that were taking place that I felt extremely spiritually blessed and more able to stop dwelling upon other unsuccessful areas of my life. I likened it to being at the 'hub of the wheel' because everybody and anybody from all walks of life who had an interest in spiritual healing seemed to be contacting the office for information. One could say that I had been 'thrown in at the deep end' and I was so grateful to Don that he had persisted in persuading me to agree to 'help out' in the office– albeit on a supposedly temporary basis – in the first place.

I realised, of course, that all of this must have been pre-determined and that from the moment I was born – or before I was born - I had been on a journey towards such an outcome and, fortunately, had been willing to accept the challenge and the part I was destined to play in this major production of what it meant to be a healer. All my former heartache and disappointments with my personal life, though not completely diminished, seemed more bearable as I embraced the privilege and opportunities Spirit had blessed me with.

Perhaps there was, after all, an unselfish, valid or karmic reason for marrying Don. His major input into the organisation for twenty years wearing the numerous hats as an executive officer trustee, regional chairman, President for seven years and eventually Administrator and media consultant, is incalculable. In this respect we were a great team although we subsequently amicably divorced but we remained in a solid and loving friendship, living next door to one another, despite his other romantic involvements.

Act 3 Scene 12:

Healing in the Community

'When you bring cleansing, healing, soul-light into your body you heal the neglected, tormented places'
- John O'Donohue

During the 1990s Don and I were part of a team of spiritual healers offering healing sessions at the newly built and spacious Ashford Community Centre, where each week approximately fifty members of the public came along for healing. They were greeted by a friendly Receptionist and made to feel very welcome with a free cup of tea and biscuits. Ten fully insured registered healers were in attendance and the healing was freely given and any donations to the charity were optional.

The plethora of ailments the clients brought with them varied considerably from a headache to something much more serious. The spiritual healer knew it was important to remain empathetic rather than sympathetic and refrain from becoming emotionally attached. This was sometimes difficult. I recall when an elderly lady whose face was eaten away with cancer became my next client. The smell of her cancer was putrid and made me feel quite nauseous as I stood behind her ready to commence the act of healing through the laying-on-of hands. Once in the 'healing state' such physical concerns disappear as you enter a state of non-attachment and unconditional love.

Prior to the commencement of the healing session healers and helpers would gather into a circle holding hands for the purpose of attuning to universal love, light, peace, healing and protection, such as my example below of leading this procedure:

'Centre yourself into a beautiful circle of protective golden light. Sense this golden light above and below you, in front of you and behind you, sweeping underneath your feet. Gently breathe in this protective, healing light, as you expand into its golden essence. Breathe in 'Divine love' and breathe out 'peace' and feel your heart filling with this love and peace. Silently ask your Higher Self for permission to be used as a healing channel of love, light and peace. Then 'earth' this energy through your feet making them strong and grounded.'

These evenings were a huge success and many of the clients claimed it was the highlight of their week, particularly if they lived alone. Some stayed on after their healing session to chat with one another, drink some more tea and ask questions. A few of them even signed up for membership as probationer healers and others were interested in attending the day workshops I began offering on self-healing, relaxation and meditation so they could become involved in their own healing process and spiritual development.

In addition Don and I set aside time each week to offer spiritual healing from our own home. We had organised a special healing room and sometimes worked together on clients but mostly separately. Don had a particular healing gift for such ailments as arthritis, spinal problems, injuries, etc. while I seemed better able to help people suffering from cancer or emotional problems. As spiritual healers we completely accepted that when channelling healing to a person, the resultant outcome is not always on the physical level, much as we would hope for it to be.

Healing works in many different ways and on many different levels and is used by the person as their body and soul wishes. Healing is holistic and happens on mental, emotional and physical levels with sometimes healing promoting resolution of seemingly unrelated issues. Here are a few examples:

Baby Susan:

This youngster of twenty months had been starved of oxygen at birth when her parents were told she would never talk or walk due to the damage sustained. After attending for healing, given mainly by Don, we were thrilled when baby Susan took her first steps at two years old and was making strides in being able to speak. Her parents were so overjoyed they invited the press to Susan's third birthday party, which we held for her in our home.

Celia and Marjorie:

There was a particular occasion when we were visited, separately, by two ladies both of whom were suffering with multiple sclerosis. Celia, the younger of the two, was newly married and worked as a hairdresser. Celia planned, eventually, to have children, and was positively determined from the outset that she would overcome this illness and attended regularly for healing sessions. She had researched nutrition, diet, supplements to find out more about how she could be involved with her recovery.

Her MS was diagnosed shortly after she had collapsed at a bus stop and tests were carried out to determine why. Celia was so positive about the whole situation that after six months her MS had gone into remission and she had returned to work at the hairdressing salon.

Marjorie, the older lady, had not long been diagnosed with MS when we started treating her and she arrived in a wheel chair for her appointment. Marjorie was a very strong character and seemed to dominate her husband Ron, whose task it was to push the wheel chair in which she regally sat. Marjorie told me:

"I don't really need to use the wheelchair too often and, usually, I walk with a stick when Ron is at work but I like it when he pushes me in the wheelchair."

In preparation for healing, I would guide Marjorie through a relaxing visualisation after which Don would place his healing hands on different areas of her body. Each week Marjorie appeared to be much the same while Ron had become very depleted and anxious. Don and I decided to give Ron some healing as well as Marjorie. Every week he seemed more relaxed, he had also lost some of the excess weight he was carrying which had relieved the painful arthritis in his knee. Ron was overjoyed.

To sum up the situation, after a year of healing one has to conclude that if we really don't want to get well, for whatever reason, conscious or unconscious, then healing won't supersede this. It is possible in Marjorie's case that she was very aware of the benefits of being ill so she was blocking the healing process.

"I rather like being the centre of attention: my daughters are taking care of the housework and Ron, bless him, does most of the shopping and cooking. Before my MS diagnosis I had to do it all."

One has to ask whether Marjorie had, unconsciously, created an invisible shield or barrier around herself which made the spiritual healing ineffective.

Alistair:

When he came to see me Alistair had just returned from his honeymoon. Sitting down he began to talk about his problem:

"I got married two weeks ago and my honeymoon was a complete disaster. I had hay fever pretty badly, which completely ruined any kind of romance because my eyes were streaming and red and I was sneezing and blowing my nose constantly. I could hardly breathe, let alone make love!"

I explained to him how spiritual healing takes place and guided him through a relaxation and a creative visualisation to ease his stress.

As my healing hands moved over his heart centre Alistair seemed to be absorbing more energy there than in any other places where my hands had been. While this was occurring I silently asked my Higher Self:

"Is there anything I need to know? Is there any way I can be of help to this young man?"

Instantly a voice in my head told me:

"It is to do with his mother when he was three."

I held on to this information and the young man came for several more healing treatments but reported that he was still suffering miserable symptoms of hay fever even though he felt less stressed.

During one of his appointments I asked Alistair about his wedding.

"I expect your mother likes having a daughter-in-law and was pleased to see you happily married." He paled, visibly, in front of me.

"My mother did not attend our wedding. I left home when I was fourteen years old and went to live with friends, since when I have avoided all contact with her. Sometimes she might be walking down the road towards me and I deliberately cross over to the other side so I do not have to speak to her."

During the third healing session Alistair opened up to me and told me:

"When I was three years old my mother suddenly left home and my Dad explained that she would not be coming back as she had gone to live with another man. I missed my mother dreadfully and felt very hurt that she had not taken me with her. I thought it was my fault that she had gone away. When I was five she came back and pleaded with my Dad to let her stay. He did. I then lived in fear that she might suddenly leave again. The only way I could protect myself from such an event was not to trust or love her."

We looked at how his mother might have made a huge sacrifice in leaving him behind and was probably heartbroken in having to do so. She may have felt he would be safer with his Dad and in his own home. Then I asked:

"Alistair, when did your hay fever symptoms first commence?"

Astonished, he replied: "When I was three!"

Alistair didn't keep his next appointment and didn't telephone to make another one. I did wonder why? Three months later he made a date to have another healing session with me.

He seemed happy and quickly said:

"I am so sorry for not being in touch with you and sincerely apologise for my tardiness. My boss sent me on a training course and I have been really busy."

I accepted his apology and explanation and asked him:

"How is your hay fever?"

"I feel absolutely marvellous! You are not going to believe this but for the past week or so I have not suffered any hay fever, even though the pollen count has been at its highest level this year."

In reacting to what Alistair had just shared with me I asked:

"That is wonderful. How do you account for this?"

"I have been to see my Mum. After some long chats I have forgiven her and we are now the best of friends."

Alistair looked and sounded very content and I sent up a silent prayer for such a blessed outcome. It also made me realise that when a person asks for healing it is not just the current problem you have to deal with but their whole life experience. Alistair had released his longstanding resentment and anger towards his mother and, with the help and support of spiritual healing, had released such negative energy and had found it in his heart to forgive his Mother.

Spiritual healing had opened Alistair's heart for him. Twenty-three years on he was, finally, in the real process of healing himself. He had started to release all the pain, anger, and torment he had locked away there since childhood.

Helen:

Helen was three months pregnant when she came to see me accompanied by her husband. This is what she said:

"My husband and I have always longed for a baby but I am anorexic and it has been difficult for me to conceive. Now that I have I am anxious about my weight and I am not sure how I am going to cope. I keep looking in the mirror all the time and I really hate how fat I am. My husband is worried sick about me and the baby as I can't eat without feeling fat all the time." Helen still appeared chronically thin.

I responded by commenting:

"I would like to suggest that you come for regular healing treatments and, in addition, I will add your name to my distant healing list, so that you can feel really supported at all times. "

Attuning to my Higher Self before giving Helen healing, I asked for spiritual guidance and support. On completion of the healing act I said to Helen:

"Place your hands on your tummy and speak to your baby about how much you are looking forward to the birth. Imagine holding this precious gift in your arms. Let your baby hear your voice and know how much love there is waiting for him/her."

At each healing session Helen was encouraged to stroke her swelling stomach as if she was stroking her baby and reassuring it of how happy she was to be pregnant. Instead of focusing on how fat she was getting Helen tried to look forward to her baby's birth. Eventually, Helen and her supportive husband, were absolutely delighted by the arrival of their baby daughter whom they both brought round for me to meet.

Act 3 Scene 13:

Awakening my Inner Child

Alice Miller, a pioneer in the recovery field said: 'Only when I make room for the voice of the child within me do I feel myself to be genuine and creative.'

- Alice Miller, a pioneer in the recovery field

In my quest for deeper knowledge and understanding of myself throughout the 1980s and 1990s I signed up for a weekend workshop on trans-personal psychology to study and discover the sub-personalities from which we are composed. It all sounded very mysterious and not knowing quite what to expect I was more than happy to be accompanied on the course by two close married friends. The course leaders explained to us that, buried deep within the psyche, a number of sub-personalities make up the different aspects of who we really are: feminine/masculine, negative/positive, prince or princess and so on. The most important and strongest archetype being the 'child' who might possibly be vulnerable, angry, loving, kind, resentful, optimistic, pessimistic, creative, magical or spiritual. Evidently our inner child has the power to influence the whole of our life depending upon how they were treated by and reacted to their parents, siblings, friends, and school teachers in their most formative years. As the saying goes:

"Give me a child for the first seven years and it's mine for life."

I really wished that one day I would get to know my inner child and love and support her in every way possible.

After a really challenging day participating in lectures and practical sessions, I joined my class mates for the evening meal and discussion. We were all intrigued by one visualisation exercise in which we were able to call forth three of our sub-personalities from a house we had been guided to enter and explore only by listening outside the different rooms. My house was pleasant and there were a few rooms on the ground and upper floors; much as I wanted to enter the rooms and explore them I followed instructions from the group leader and just listened outside of each door. I remember there was a landing upstairs with a beautiful oval window through which the sun was shining brightly, creating a kaleidoscope of rainbow colours. Upon leaving the imaginary house by the front door, I then followed the path to the gate and crossed the road into the meadow from whence I started and waited, anxiously, while my three sub-personalities came out of the house:

First, came a small fair haired little girl aged about four, dressed in a night gown, head down and looking sad. She hugged a doll.

Next was an old crone in widow's weeds, walking behind a magnificent glass hearse, which contained an ornate coffin smothered in beautiful flowers, being drawn by two large black horses whose heads sported an exotic array of black feathers, which tossed and turned as the horses trotted by.

Third, and last, a joker came forth, jauntily skipping and dancing, clothed in a costume of Lincoln green wearing a tall, floppy, pointed hat from which dangled silver jingling bells.

Left to my own devices I had to discover who these sub-personalities were: I surmised that the little girl must be my 'inner child' who could certainly do with some cheering up; the old crone being the 'wise woman' seemed to be intent upon making me bury all the negative thoughts and feelings lying deep inside me. The joker I recognised as that part of me that longed to perform in front of an audience and entertain and delight them.

Later on that evening while reading in bed I began to sense a presence in my room; looking across to the door I couldn't believe my eyes. There stood a child; a lifelike replica of the little girl who had exited the house earlier in my visualisation still wearing a nightgown, head bent down and holding on to her doll. Sad to say I was absolutely freaked out. Where had she come from? This was no hallucination but a completely physical, life-like child. I began to panic and, breathing heavily, acted totally irrationally and dived under the bed covers.

After a while, as I slowly emerged and came up for air there she stood by the side of my bed staring at me – my inner child.

"Oh! Dear God!" I exclaimed. Then, to my great shame and huge regret, I confess that fear drove me to shout at her:

"Go away. Go away. I don't want you here!" And she vanished.

This experience became a 'watershed moment' in my life and I became continuously disappointed in myself for having missed such a wonderful, heaven-sent opportunity to engage with that part of me that was so intensely meaningful. Especially when I came to accept that we are composed of archetypal sub-personalities, of which the 'child' is the strongest and has the most influence over our adult life.

"I must find a way to contact her," I vowed.

And, as if by magic, I discovered the book, 'Recovery of Your Inner Child' by Lucia Capacchione, Ph.D. which explains how one is able to have a first-hand experience of their inner child, actually feeling its emotions and recapturing its sense of wonder by writing and drawing with your non-dominant hand. This technique led to some intensely revealing and magical communications with 'little Audrey' at various stages of her life, and resulted in being able to understand the kind of reassurance and validation she was desperately seeking from me.

Louise Hay, author of 'You Can Heal Your Life' wrote on the back cover of Capacchione's book: *'Healing is making ourselves whole. Healing our inner child is a major part of our recovery.'*

On the following pages are some examples of direct written communication with little Audrey.

THIS IS LITTLE AUDREY
AT LAST YOU HAVE SAID HELLO
TO ME!

Has it seemed a long time?

FOREVER.

WILL YOU FORGIVE ME?

OK. YES BUT YOU HAVE
TO PROMISE NOT TO IGNORE
ME ANYMORE.

I Promise.

What Would you like to do now.

I WANT TO DRAW A PICTURE
FOR YOU.

That is very kind of you.

OK. BUT YOU HAVE TO
PROMISE NOT TO LAUGH AT ME.

I Promise.

OK.

This is little Audrey. At last you have said hello to me.

Has it seemed a long time?

Forever.

Will you give me hug?

OK. Yes. But you have to promise not to ignore me anymore.

I promise. What would you like to do now?

I want to draw a picture for you

That is very kind of you.

OK. But you have to promise not to laugh at me.

I promise.

OK.

These FLOWERS ARE FOR YOU.

Thank you — they are really beautiful.

Do you, LIKE THE SMELL?

Yes — very much indeed. I will put the flowers in water.

OK — HERE THEY ARE.

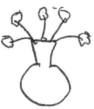

I WILL PICK SOME MORE.

Do You LIKE THEM.

THEY ARE BEAUTIFUL THANK YOU.

I LOVE YOU. I LOVE YOU.

These flowers are for you.

Thank you. They are really beautiful.

Do you like the smell?

Yes - very much indeed.

I will put the flowers in water. OK - here they are. I will pick some more. Do you like them?

They are beautiful. Thank you.

I love you.

I love you.

Hello — How Are You Feeling To-day?

I feel very good.

How old are you?

I am ten. No. Nine!

What are you doing?

I am playing with my friends.

What are you playing.

We are playing actors!

Do you like to act?

Yes very much. I want to be a film star
when I grow up!

How old are you now?

I am ten.

What are you doing?

I am sitting on the door step of
my Aunt's house in Hadon!

Are You Happy!

No — I am not!

Hello. How Are you feeling today?

I feel very good.

How old are you?

I am ten. No nine.

What are you doing?

I am playing with my friends.

What are you playing?

We are playing actors.

Do you like to act?

Yes. Very much. I want to be a film star when I grow up,

How old are you now?

I am ten. I am sitting on the doorstep of my Aunt's house in Hendon.

Are you happy?

No! I am not!

Why are'nt you happy.

Because I hate it here and I miss
my mum. She's in Feltham!

What don't you like.

Not going to school. Not having any
friends. Not being with my Mum.

What would you like to do now?

I would like to go home.

Will you draw me a picture please.
A picture of what you would like to do.

Why aren't you happy?

Because I hate it here and I miss my Mum. She's in Feltham.

What don't you like?

Not going to school. Not having any friends. Not being with my Mum.

What would you like to do now?

I would like to go home.

Well draw me a picture please. A picture of what you would like to do.

Do you have any other brothers or sisters.

YES. I HAVE A BIG Brother

Do you play with him?

No, He is mean to me.

WHAT DOES HE DO?

He wont share — and he pinches me.

How old are you now?

I am five. I have started school.

Do you like school?

Yes — I feel safe at school.

Don't you feel safe at home?

Yes but not when MUMMY Screams. It scares me.

Why does Mummy scream.

She screams at my daddely when he is funny. I dont like him when he acts funny.

Do you have any brothers or sisters?

Yes I have a big brother.

Do you play with him?

No he is mean to me.

What does he do?

He won't share and he pinches me.

How old are you now?

I am five and I have started school.

Do you like school?

Yes. I feel safe at school.

Don't you feel safe at home?

Yes. But not when Mummy screams. It scares me.

She screams at my daddy when he is funny.

I don't like him when he is funny.

WHO ARE YOU?

I AM YOU AND YOU ARE ME — WE ARE ONE.

HOW OLD ARE YOU?

I AM 3.

CAN YOU REMEMBER WHAT HAPPENED WHEN YOU WERE 3?

NO.

Were you happy?

I DONT KNOW.

What did you like to do.

PLAY.

What did you play?

BABIES.

Do you like babies?

Yes I have a baby brother.

Is he good?

He cries a lot. But I kiss him.

Who are you?

I am you. And you are me - we are one. How old are you?

I am three.

Can you remember what happened when you were three?

No!

Were you happy?

I don't know.

What do you like t do?

Play.

What did you play?

Babies.

Do you like babies.

Yes, I have a baby brother.

Is he good?

He cries a lot but I kiss him.

Are you afraid?

· Yes - I am very afraid.

What do you do when you are afraid.

I cry.

What else.

I try to hide.

Are you frightened now?

I am when I remember.

Were you often afraid?

YES   YES   YES

Did your big brother protect you?

No — he ran away
and was very naughty.

Did you love your mummy + daddy?

Yes but not all the time.

How old are you?

SIX
What happened when you were six?
The war,

Are you afraid?

Yes, I am very afraid.

What do you do when you are afraid?

I cry.

What else?

I try to hide.

Are you frightened now?

I am when I remember.

Were you often afraid?

Yes! Yes! Yes!

Did your big brother protect you?

No - he ran away and was very naughty.

Did you love your Mummy and Daddy?

Yes but not all the time.

How old are you?

Six.

What happened to you when you were six?

The war.

Were you afraid in the War.

Sometimes.
Tell me about this.

When my Mummy didn't love me.
When was this?

When she left me in Wales and
Sunderland.

Tell me about it.
I tried to run away from the Williams
house. She was Omhed to me. I hated
it there. I am very angry — it. makes
to me feel very bad. I am angry
with my mother for leaving me.
Draw me a picture of your Anger,

I AM
TRAPPED!

I AM TRAPPED.
I AM A PRISONER.
I AM VERY UPSET.

Were you afraid in the war?

Sometimes.

Tell me about this.

When my Mummy didn't love me.

When was this?

When she left me in Wales and Sunderland.

Tell me about it.

I tried to run away from the Williams' house. She (Mummy)
was mad at me. I hated it there. I am very angry - it makes
me feel very bad. I am angry with my Mother for leaving me.

Draw me a picture of your anger.

I AM TRAPPED. I AM TRAPPED. I AM A PRISONER.
I AM VERY UPSET.

Hello Little One.
I am your
nurturing parent who
loves you very much.
What is your name?

I am Audrey
but I think
it should be
Elizabeth!
How are you feeling?
Very unhappy!
Frustrated!
Angry!
How old are you?
I am 11!
Why are you angry.
Look what my mum
is doing to my
hair! she is
ruining it.

Don't worry - it will grow strong & beautiful!
I love you and won't let this happen anymore.

Hello little one. I am your nurturing parent who loves you very much.

What is your name?

I am Audrey but I think it should be Elizabeth.

How are you feeling?

Very unhappy. Frustrated. Angry.

How old are you?

I am eleven.

Why are you angry?

Look what my Mum is doing with my hair - she is ruining it.

Don't worry. It will grow strong and beautiful.

I love you and won't let this happen anymore.

Hello Audrey — little Audrey —
I love you so much. Do you love me?
YES VERY MUCH! I AM
HAVING SO MUCH FUN!

WHAT ARE YOU DOING?

I. HAVE ALL THESE OTHER
CHILDREN TO LOOK AFTER.

IS THAT FUN? WOULDN'T YOU LIKE
TO PLAY WITH THEM?

NOT REALLY BECAUSE SOME
OF THEM ARE REALLY
SAD!

HOW OLD ARE YOU?
I AM ONLY LITTLE — FIVE.

YOU ARE VERY YOUNG TO HAVE
SO MUCH RESPONSIBILITY. LET
ME LOOK AFTER THE CHILDREN SO
YOU CAN DO WHAT YOU WANT.

Hello little Audrey. I love you so much. Do you love me?

Yes. Very much. I am having so much fun.

What are you doing?

I have all these other children to look after.

Wouldn't you like to play with them?

Not really because some of them are really sad.

How old are you?

I am only little. I am five.

You are very young to have so much responsibility.

Let me look after the children so you can do what you want.

OK — I AM GOING TO RIDE
MY BIKE THEN TAKE MY
DOLLS FOR A WALK.

WHAT A LOVELY IDEA. CAN YOU DRAW
A PICTURE FOR ME OF WHAT YOU LOOK
LIKE?

OK !

YOU ARE REALLY
LOVELY —
BEAUTIFUL —
I LOVE YOU
VERY MUCH
AND WANT
TO TAKE CARE
OF YOU.

THANK
YOU.

I LOVE
YOU
TOO !

THAT'S ME !

OK. I am going to ride my bike then take my dolls for a walk.

What a lovely idea. Can you draw me a picture of
what you look like?

OK. That's me.

You are really lovely - beautiful. I love you very much
and want to take care of you.

Thank you. I love you too.

Would you like to tell me anything else?

OK.

How old are you.

Eleven. And I am very sad.

What is making you sad?

I haven't passed the 11+. My friend
Kathleen didn't pass either so her
mother took her to Carlisle & she
got another chance & passed.

Don't you like the school where you attend?

It's ok but I haven't got a uniform.
My friend Kathleen has. She looks posh.

Is there anything else you would like to tell me.

Yes. I am fed up with everyone
making fun of my hair, they all
call me dyed hair - its horrible.

Is your hair dyed?

Yes - my stepid mother bleaches it
when she dyes her own hair.
She is ruining my hair. She is a
stupid cow - I hate her.
She never listens to me. She
doesn't care about me. My dad is
not always drunk - they are always

202

Would you like to tell me anything else?

OK.

How old are you?

Eleven. And I am very sad. I haven't passed the 11 plus.

My friend Kathleen didn't pass either so her mother took her

to Carlisle and she got another chance and she passed.

Do you like the school where you attend?

It's OK but I haven't got a uniform. My friend Kathleen has.

She looks posh.

Is there anything that you would like to tell me?

Yes. I am fed up with everyone making fun of my hair.

They call me dyed hair - it's horrible.

Is your hair dyed?

Yes. My stupid mother bleaches it when she dyes her own hair.

She is ruining my hair. She is a stupid cow. I hate her. She won't

listen to me. She doesn't care about me. My Dad is always

drunk - they are always

forgetting — I am fed up.

OK. let's do some Healing. You are Safe now. You are surrounded by love — you are all right. I will look after you & take care of you. Just sleep now and let the Healing Angels soothe & comfort you.

That sounds nice — OK!

When we talk again I want you to list some of the happy things you liked doing.

OK — but now I am resting.

Hello Audrey darling. I am just letting you know I love you and want to be with you. How are you?

I am fine!

How old are you?

I am ten!

Are you happy?

Sometimes — but I do get very angry.

fighting. I am fed up.

OK. Let's do some healing. You are safe now. You are surrounded by love. You are all right. I will look after you and take care of you. Just sleep now and let the Healing Angels soothe and comfort you.

That sounds nice. OK.

When we talk again I want you to list some of the things you like doing?

OK. But now I am resting.

Hello Audrey darling I am just letting you know I love you and want to be with you. How are you?

I am fine!

How old are you?

I am ten!

Are you happy?

Sometimes - but I do get very angry

Act 4 Scene 1:

Healing into Death and Dying

'Love is the optimum strategy for healing'
- **Stephen and Ondrea Levine**

Spiritual healing is not only about recovery but plays an important part in the dying process. A spiritual healer is really only a catalyst for the healing process to take place at whatever level it is required. Essentially the act of healing is a release mechanism for the client to let go of what they no longer need to hold on to – even if it is their physical body. Unknowingly clients bring their whole life with them (including past lives) when attending for a healing session.

Spiritual healing is channelling the power of unconditional love thus enabling a person to feel safe and supported as the healing transmutes any stored or blocked energy which will either take several treatments to bring to the surface or after only one healing session. It is a remarkable transformational procedure which can be extremely empowering for the client to heal themselves or, if suffering a terminal illness, prepare them for their transition to the 'other side' – a place I call 'home'.

Dealing with death had never been an every day occurrence for me. My only real confrontation with it was the 'passing away' of some elderly relatives. In my wildest imagination I could never have considered it possible until practising as a spiritual healer that death would take on a whole new meaning and that it would become so up close and personal.

In John O'Donohue's book Anam Cara which in Gaelic means 'Soul Friend' he states: 'Death is an invitation to freedom.'

Thus it was heartening to receive the following comments from some of the terminally ill after a healing session:

"I feel so relaxed and peaceful during and after the healing. Your voice is so soothing and comforting. It makes me feel safe."

"Thank you so much for the healing; I feel so much lighter, free from all my fear."

"I love the healing meditations you speak to me during the healing because your voice takes me to another part of myself where I experience so much love and peace."

When carrying out spiritual healing on someone it has always felt completely natural to use my voice simultaneously for the purpose of relaxation and guided visualisation. My voice seemed to reach a higher level of consciousness and produce certain healing colours/vibrations and became an integral part in the healing process. So much so that I became inspired to create a set of healing meditation CDs after many requests to do so which enabled the listener to experience an uplifting and supremely creative life-force energy of unconditional love and healing.

Act 4 Scene 2:

My Best Friend - June

During the many years we were friends June, being a natural healer and clairvoyant, often used to say:

"I won't make old bones Audrey, I am fairly certain."

In 1990 While I was teaching courses in California June wrote in a letter to me:

'I have ovarian cancer and have to undergo a full hysterectomy before you return home. Please send me distant healing and come and see me as soon as you are back.'

I visited June, who was sixty years old, for many months and channelled healing to her. One day she started talking to me about her situation:

"I am not afraid to die, Audrey, because in a way I am really looking forward to leaving this world behind. And, of course, I have already visited the spirit world and talked to my mother. In our world there's so much cruelty to animals, particularly the overworked and neglected donkeys whose charity I support. My husband and daughter will miss me, but they are both so self-possessed I feel certain they will be okay."

As time passed and she became weaker June's aura began to shrink around her and she became very emaciated. One afternoon her daughter telephoned me:

"My Mum has gone into a hospice this morning as she collapsed in pain and my Dad phoned for the doctor."

"Oh dear, I'm so sorry to hear this and I will visit your Mum first thing tomorrow morning. Give me the details of how to get to the hospice and try not to worry too much."

After putting down the phone, I started to prepare my evening meal but suddenly a voice in my head shouted:

"Go now. Do not leave it until tomorrow."

Upon arrival at the hospice June's bed was empty when a nurse directed me to her ward and my heart sank believing I was too late. Then another nurse said:

"Mrs Marcham is sitting in a wheelchair outside by the little pond and waterfall." I sighed with relief. I was not too late.

"Hello dear." I said in a cheery voice. "It is lovely out here, isn't it? So peaceful."

June didn't respond at first so I knelt down in front of her for a moment looking up into her face. She seemed miles away, even though her eyes were open, and didn't acknowledge me. Then she smiled, looked down at me and said:

"You've just missed Ken. He'll be back shortly but went home to get something for me. How are you, Audrey? Tell me all about your travels. I love to hear about them."

I began to relate to her some interesting little anecdotes but she wasn't listening, she seemed to have disappeared again. An orderly was serving refreshments and asked June if she wanted anything:

"No thank you, just my Bach flower remedies, please, and my lighter and cigarettes."

"I will bring them immediately and a smoking blanket to put across your lap," he replied as he walked away. When he returned June sat with the lighter in one hand and the packet of cigarettes in the other. She did not attempt to have a smoke but sat very still.

It became obvious to me that she was in the process of 'coming out' of and 'coming in' to her body. Then she spoke to me:

"This dying process is very difficult Audrey. It's so complicated." Then silence.

Where was she now I wondered, if only she could tell me?

For over an hour I talked to June while channelling healing to help her on her way, telling her how much I loved her and how much our friendship had meant to me. June nodded. Her husband had returned and I decided it was time for me to leave. I put my hands on June's shoulders and leaned down towards her face.

"I love you June, I love you with all my heart dear friend. I love you. Safe journey." Sadly, I knew I would not see her again in my life time.

June passed away around 3AM the following morning and left a note pad open on her bed, which read:

'Dear God. I'm ready now. Please take me!"

It made me feel that June was very well prepared to make her transition from this world and I was in awe of the mystery surrounding the dying process and the part we play in it.

Act 4 Scene 3:

Deidre

Deidre was in her forties and had been diagnosed with stomach cancer. Her husband accompanied her to the healing session and appeared to be very kind and loving towards his wife. He waited in another room of our home while his wife was receiving spiritual healing from me. While chatting together Deidre became very agitated and told me:

"My husband is having an affair with my seventeen year old niece Sandra. He doesn't think I know about it. We have two daughters aged ten and twelve and I don't want a divorce. It is driving me mad and I am so angry."

It can be quite difficult, sometimes, when people share such intimate details about their situation. In the role of being the healer one also has to become the empathetic listener, not making any comment, but just allowing the client to offload what they feel they need to.

Regular healing sessions followed until Deidre became bedridden when I then undertook home visits. She lived in a luxurious mobile home on a winter fairground site. I noticed a big deterioration in Deidre's condition and asked her if she was in pain.

"Not really. The medication deals with it. I am in emotional pain though about this affair between my husband and Sandra, although I think it might have ended now".

"Does your niece come to visit?" I queried.

"Yes, frequently. Sandra is a lovely girl and very loving towards me, but I can tell there is something going on with her".

Just then Deidre's twelve year old daughter arrived home from school, unexpectedly, and snuggled beside her mother on the bed. She was not feeling well having just started her period. It was a poignant moment for me witnessing mother and daughter comforting one another.

During my next home visit I sensed the deterioration in Deidre's appearance and felt that her life force seemed to be ebbing away from her. She looked peaceful when she spoke to me:

"I have talked to my niece and asked her what was going on between her and my husband, her uncle. To my utter astonishment Sandra informed me that, as she had not seen her father since she was five, she was asking my husband (her father's brother), if he knew where he was, why he had left, and had not been interested in contacting his little girl."

As it was a delicate subject, Sandra had wanted to keep it as confidential as possible, and had thought it necessary to meet with her uncle clandestinely to do so. I thought to myself if only Deidre had not been so suspicious about whether her niece and her husband were having an affair. If only she had spoken to one of them sooner, would she not then have stomached so much anger, fear and disappointment and, possibly, not have manifested stomach cancer? I don't know but it certainly reinforced what I had been taught about the strong mind/body connection.

Ten days after this disclosure Deidre passed away quite peacefully. Her husband informed me that the fairground community had given his wife a glorious send-off and were supporting him and his two daughters in a quite remarkable and caring way. It was reassuring to hear this.

Act 4 Scene 4:

Martin

I took a telephone call at the office one day from a desperate Mother.

"Please can you provide spiritual healing to my fourteen year old son, Martin. He's suffering from terminal leukaemia and has been discharged from the Royal Marsden cancer hospital in London; there is nothing further they can do for him. They've given him only three weeks to live. We are a Christian family and pray constantly for his recovery but our church doesn't perform healing treatments so we've been advised to contact this organisation".

It was arranged that she could bring Martin to our home as they lived quite close. Martin was a good-looking, tall, thin, teenager, with a cheeky grin and, as it turned out, an acute sense of humour. He was wearing a woolly hat which sadly when he removed it, revealed his totally bald head. He didn't seem a bit bothered or self-conscious about it. Martin was keen to find out all about spiritual healing and inquisitively asked:

"What is it? Where does it come from? How does it work? What do I have to do?"

I explained:

"The spiritual healer, through attunement and meditative processes, opens up a channel through their Higher Self to connect with a divine energy, that is loving, peaceful and healing, which flows into their consciousness from a divine level. The healer then transmits this balancing and harmonising vibration into the consciousness of the recipient through their Higher Self. The healer is just an instrument and understands and accepts that although they are involved in the process, ultimately it is 'Thy Will be done; not my Will be done'."

Martin then asked a profound question:

"Does everyone have a Higher Self? If so, can I heal myself?"

I answered 'yes' to both questions.

With a medical prognosis of three weeks to live, my husband Don and I decided to team up together for Martin's treatments. This way we knew the healing energy would be amplified. In preparation for this joint laying-on-of-hands, I sat Martin down on a dining room chair in order for Don to be able to scan down Martin's spine, with his hands, while I relaxed Martin with a creative visualisation, similar to the following:

"Make yourself comfortable Martin. Take one or two deep breaths in and out. Feel yourself letting go on each out breath. Your breath is relaxing and releasing all that you no longer need to hold on to. As you breathe in, imagine that you are drawing into your whole being a loving, peaceful, healing vibration which is full of light. Sense this light filtering into every part of you, flowing into your cells, muscles and organs. As you begin to feel this universal love and peace embracing the whole of your body consciousness, imagine that you are sitting in a small, beautiful, garden beside a modest pool, in the centre of which is a sparkling fountain. It is a pleasant, sunny day, and you are soaking in the gentle warmth of the sun. The tumbling water of the fountain cascades downwards into the shimmering pool, creating colourful rainbow swirls on the surface of the water, which is bathed in sunlight.

In the garden there is a path leading to a gate at the far end. You walk towards the gate and open it. You now find yourself in a lovely leafy lane, full of overhanging trees, from which birds are chirping happily. You can feel the crunch of the earth beneath your feet.

At the end of the lane you open another gate which takes you up a gently rising grassy hill leading towards a large oak tree. When you reach the tree you sit down with your back resting against the trunk of the tree. The spine of the tree is full of powerful and supportive energy which is flowing into your spine. As you sit on the ground, you can feel the strong roots of the tree spreading out all around you.

While you rest here you gaze up at the leaf laden branches of the tree, through which the sun is filtering shafts of golden light. You become aware of the calming blueness of the sky above and the peaceful scene all around you.

You feel totally rested and at peace. Remain here as long as you need. This is your healing tree and it is a great and loving support system for you to embrace. So enjoy your time here.

When you are ready to leave you reverse your journey, walking back down the hillside, closing the gates you came through, until you are once more in the leafy lane that leads you back to your familiar garden."

At the end of the healing session Martin declared:

"That was just the best experience. And I love that healing tree on the hill and intend to visit it often."

During the three months Martin received healing, he was always accompanied by his mother and, on occasion, by his father as well. Martin was such a cheerful boy; he would joke with his serious and strain-ridden parents.

"Look at their long, serious faces. It's a good job I am the one with leukaemia. I don't think they would be able to cope."

On the occasions Lilla came to stay with us she would join in the healing sessions and recommended Martin should drink plenty of beetroot juice and wear something red; she also suggested he should have a red bed cover which would help to boost his red blood count.

Despite the original medical prognosis of three weeks, Martin was still very much alive after three months. His Consultant wanted him to have more chemo. Martin refused at first, but was encouraged by his parents to reluctantly return to the hospital. In preparation he had composed his very own visualisation exercise; he asked me to record it for him so that while he was being treated intravenously he could listen to the meditation and in his mind be somewhere else much more interesting. It is worth while reporting that Martin suffered none of the nasty side effects of sickness on this occasion.

Before Martin was discharged from hospital and because he was so popular with the medical team, who knew he loved golf, they had arranged a surprise for him. There was a celebrity golf tournament taking place at nearby Sandown Park golf course. The veteran Hollywood star, Bob Hope, was among those teeing off. Early in the morning, Martin was taken by golf buggy on a tour of the golf course where he met many of the celebrity players. He was ecstatic.

A day later, I received a telephone call from Martin's mother.

"I'm so sorry to bother you but Martin is laid low with a nasty cold and a high temperature. The doctor came at once and will call again later. We are so worried because his immune system is non-existent. He must have caught a chill at the golf course with it being so early in the morning and quite cold. Please send healing to Martin as soon as possible."

After lighting a candle and sitting quietly in meditation I interceded on Martin's behalf using distant healing. Late afternoon I received an update on his condition from his mother:

"The doctor has called again; Martin's fever is worse and he looks terribly weak".

I decided to pass all this information on to Lilla who said she would 'take on' Martin's fever when she went to bed to give his body a better chance to recover. Lying in bed, sweating, with a high temperature, Lilla 'tuned in' psychically to Martin who was struggling with life or death. Martin spoke to Lilla's higher consciousness saying:

"I have to make up my mind whether to remain in this wasted shell of a body or leave it and get a new one." The choice was his.

At that moment Lilla's fever abated; psychically, she watched Martin leave his body, hand in hand with his Spiritual Guide and Teacher. There was a wonderful light all around him as he turned towards her, smiling, and spoke to her:

"I decided not to fight anymore. This body is no good to me. It is burnt out. I might go back briefly to Royal Marsden though, and haunt my doctors, just for the fun of it. Please give this message to my Mum and Dad............"

When Martin's message was duly conveyed to his parents they were overjoyed, even though distressed at losing their son. Whatever the message was (and it has to remain confidential) his parents were totally convinced that it could only have come from their beloved son.

Don and I were invited to Martin's funeral and Don was asked to speak the committal at the graveside. Martin's parents thanked us for providing spiritual healing support to their son which, they confessed, had served a beneficial purpose for them as well because they now meditated and felt stronger in themselves. A family healing had taken place.

Act 4 Scene 5:

Nancy

In her middle forties, mother of two girls aged seven and nine, and a boy of eleven, Nancy had been diagnosed with breast cancer. When she came to me for healing it was just after a mastectomy. Nancy had been brought up as a Spiritualist and her mother, when alive, had been a Medium. During the nine months Nancy came for healing at our home, she tried hard to be optimistic about her condition and appeared to be making good progress. Sadly, the cancer spread into her liver and the Oncologist informed her husband that Nancy's condition was terminal.

To back up the weekly healing sessions, Nancy began using one of my healing meditation CDs, 'Healing Light' which she told me helped her to deeply relax and feel peaceful. As Nancy's condition deteriorated home visits for healing became more practical. During one of these I found Nancy resting and lying down on a sofa in her sitting room, while her husband was in the kitchen. As Nancy greeted me she said:

"See that disgusting glass of bright green vegetable juice my husband expects me to drink, well I am not going to. Please can you throw it out of the window before he comes in here?"

"Oh dear. I don't think I dare do that Nancy. Your husband has gone to a lot of trouble to make that for you," I replied.

Just at that moment her husband John walked into the room. He looked straight at his wife and then at the glass of green, unappetising liquid on the table. For one moment I could feel the tension between them. Picking up the glass, John addressed his wife in a kindly voice:

"Come on, now, Nancy. You know you have to drink this as it will do you good and is helping to make you stronger.

"You drink it. I can't. It tastes disgusting."

John pleaded:

"Nancy, darling, you have to drink this. Please. There's nothing more I can do for you. Don't you realise you're dying."

"Don't be so ridiculous, of course I am not dying. Whatever gave you that stupid idea?" she replied.

Frustrated and angry, John stormed out of the room without speaking another word. I felt so sorry for him.

After guiding Nancy through a twenty minute creative visualisation, followed by a longer healing session, Nancy was sleeping peacefully. I quietly went towards the kitchen to speak with her husband. He looked quite fraught.

"John, I am unable to call next week as I am on holiday but I have arranged for another healer to come in my place. Her name is Shirley and she is very experienced. I have explained the situation to her. I hope this is okay?"

Wiping his wet hands on a towel he pointed to the kitchen table, "All these organic vegetables are delivered every day. The Oncologist told me Nancy's condition has worsened as the cancer has continued to spread even more. He suggested juicing might help Nancy and he put me in touch with an organisation that has provided me with a juicer and arranged for a free delivery of these organic vegetables. I have had to give up work to look after Nancy and the children. The juice I gave her to-day was raw lettuce. I followed the recipe book and it took me ages to juice enough lettuce to make a glassful which she has now refused to drink. I am at my wits end. I do not know what more I can do?"

We had a little chat and I allowed John to give vent to his emotions and suggested that, perhaps, he would like to have some healing himself and to think about it.

Two weeks later, upon my return from holiday, I telephoned Shirley prior to making another visit to Nancy.

"Hi, Shirley. Audrey here. I am just enquiring about your visits to Nancy. Was everything okay?"

"No, Audrey. Her husband cancelled them. He said his wife was too ill and that the Macmillan nurses were in attendance."

I then telephoned John and asked if I could visit Nancy? He was adamant that I could not and explained:

"Nancy is very ill and I feel she should now be left alone, in peace, as there have been too many comings and goings by this person and that person."

Sensing his frustration and anguish I said:

"All right John. I understand. I am disappointed not to be able to see Nancy and I will send her distant healing. Perhaps you will let me know how things are progressing please."

At seven AM the following morning my telephone rang and my heart sank. I knew it must be John calling me.

"Hello". I said.

"It's Nancy's husband, John, here. I wish to inform you that my wife passed away at three AM this morning."

"Oh John, I am so sorry to hear that. Did Nancy die peaceful-ly?" I asked.

"No. It was awful. She started screaming and shouting and woke up the children. They were banging on the bedroom door asking me what was happening? I told them to go back to bed and not to worry as their mother had woken up from a bad nightmare. I tried my best to comfort Nancy and held her in my arms and cuddled her close to me but she was in a hysterical state. The Macmillan nurse had gone home and I didn't know what to do. Then I noticed your 'Healing Light' cassette on the bed side table. Nancy must have been playing it so I put it into the tape recorder and your soothing voice filled the room. Instantly, Nancy went quiet, snuggled into me and we both listened to the healing meditation. Nancy died later, in my arms."

With fresh tears pouring down my face I couldn't think of anything to say except.

"God bless you John. You have my sincere condolences."

As I pondered on what I had just heard I wished so much I had been able to visit Nancy and give her some healing one more time. I had to respect John's wishes. How ironic, though, that in a blessed way I had managed to bring Nancy healing via my healing cassette, and that Nancy had found some comfort in listening to my voice. God does, surely, work in mysterious ways, I thought.

Act 4 Scene 6:

The Death of my Father

In 1984 my dad was eighty-two and he was suffering dreadfully from arteriosclerosis which was causing him intense pain in his legs. The situation was so dire it was more than likely that one of his feet might have to be amputated, due to gangrene. He was adamant that he would not lose his foot, under any circumstances.

During a visit I observed that my father was still making the effort to neatly dress, shave, and look refreshed - due, no doubt, to his military training - but was constantly rubbing his leg to ease the cramping pain. He never requested healing from me but I was praying for the pain and discomfort to ease. With the advent of gangrene in his foot I became deeply concerned and decided to speak to him:

"Dad, I'm sorry you are suffering so much and this problem with gangrene in your foot surely means you should consider surgery. They can do wonders these days."

"I am not prepared to lose my foot, Audrey. It will be all right," was his stubborn response.

"You don't want the gangrene to spread up your leg, do you? This is a possibility?" I queried.

My mum, who had been sitting and listening to the conversation, then intervened:

"He is screaming in the night with the pain, something has to be done about it."

She then went into the kitchen to make us some refreshments.

"Dad, can I talk to you please?" He nodded affirmatively.

"What is it you feel you still want to achieve or complete now that you are 82?"

"Nothing much at all." He replied.

"In which case, why are you hanging on and suffering all this pain if you have nothing more to achieve? Why don't you make peace with yourself, your situation, and just let go and let God take care of everything?"

There was a glimmer of understanding in his eyes as he looked at me.

Two weeks after this chat my Dad contracted pneumonia and after his lung collapsed the doctor informed us that my father was dying. He was lying, propped up in bed in his room, a ghost of the father I last saw; I sat holding his hand listening to his laboured breathing. He started to speak to me but his voice was rasping and I had to lean in closer to hear what he was saying:

"I have reached the end of my life, Audrey… and I want you to know that I am very sorry I have been such a poor husband to your mother… She deserved much better as she is a good person. Please take care of her and make sure she is all right."

Utterly exhausted he could say no more but I nodded and reassured him.

"Don't you worry. Mum will be fine, we will all take good care of her. I love you dad."

Five hours later my father passed away, free at last, from all his agony.

Act 4 Scene 7:

My Mother's Death

The next ten years of my mother's life up to 1994 were extremely fulfilling for her. She really enjoyed her new-found freedom and joined several social clubs for seniors and took herself off on long train journeys which she relished. As a diligent grandmother to 10 grandchildren she spent much of her time visiting them or keeping in touch by letters, which she loved to write. By the time she was 82 her health seemed impressive.

I had not long arrived home after flying in from Portugal when the telephone rang. It was my brother:

"Hi Audrey. I am at mum's flat and she is not at all well and I have called the doctor. Can you come round as, unfortunately, I have an urgent appointment?"

I immediately drove over to see my mum and, fortunately, arrived before the doctor, who was not long behind me. After examining my mother the doctor referred her to a Consultant for further tests; these were carried out within a week as my daughter's partner paid for a private consultation. Meanwhile, my mother stayed with my daughter, Ruth, as she had a spacious home whereas I didn't even have a spare room. Mum was experiencing considerable pain in her back and was on four hourly pain killers but otherwise seemed comfortable.

The medical test diagnosed a small growth in mum's lower bowel and an operation to remove it was advised, in case it caused an obstruction. She took one look at the Consultant from the wheelchair in which she was seated and addressed him:

"I came into this world in one piece and I am leaving it in the same condition. The only time I have been in hospital was to have my five children. I will leave things as they are and take my chances, thank you very much. Audrey, take me home."

The Consultant looked startled and then dismayed.

Two weeks later my mother collapsed in pain and was taken into hospital. She settled well and seemed almost recovered when I saw her. The next morning I visited early, accompanied by my sister, and the Registrar greeted us and said he wanted to speak to us in his office.

"I am very sorry to inform you that your mother is in renal failure and does not have long to live. She only has one fifth of a kidney. We are going to remove her to a side ward and then insert a morphine shunt into her arm to control the pain which, without it, could be severe."

I looked at the Registrar in shock and dismay and queried what he was saying:

"The tests my mother underwent only revealed a small lump in her lower bowel. Renal failure was never mentioned before. How was this missed?"

He looked at me uncomfortably and attempted to offer a feeble but totally unacceptable explanation:

"The Consultant obviously was not looking in that area."

"Surely blood tests would have revealed renal failure?" I remarked. "This is most unsatisfactory."

My sister and I left his office in a daze to make urgent telephone calls to our siblings to break the awful news to them. By that afternoon, my mum was settled in a side ward and the morphine shunt had been inserted into her arm.

"Off you go all of you. I know you are very busy all of you and have lots to do. I am fine. I have my new copy of 'Majesty' which I haven't read yet and intend to do so now."

We were summarily dismissed and decided to visit the hospital cafe but not leave the premises. My mother never spoke again.

The following day the entire family of my three brothers and one sister, together with their partners and all the adult grandchildren, were hovering outside my mum's private room, waiting to greet her, unable to comprehend that she was actually dying. We took turns around her bed and she looked very peaceful but had her eyes closed. Eight days passed and I was becoming anxious. I contacted Lilla and asked her:

"Why is it taking so long? Where is she in this dying process?"

"Your mum is doing well, Audrey, it won't be long now because the head is out. Think of it as labour when you are about to deliver a baby. There is a specific process taking place, etherically now, before your mum is delivered to the other side, where a cosmic midwife is waiting to assist." Lilla then described this process to me which involved a reversal of the human energy system.

After that conversation I sat with the other members of the family in my mum's room and, gradually, one by one we left to return home, leaving my younger brother to spend the night with her, on a camp bed by her bedside. At 3AM he telephoned me:

"Mum has died. I must have fallen asleep for a while and woke up aware that she wasn't making that snorting breath anymore. The night Sister confirmed mum had stopped breathing."

"I will come to the hospital immediately", I replied with some relief that mum was in safe hands.

When I saw her she looked at peace; not dead. I had so much I wanted to say to her but more family had arrived and in the end I requested some time alone with my mum. I cuddled her close and told her how much I loved her and then clipped one of her silver curls from her head for a keepsake.

When I returned to my flat I sat down and wrote this message to my mother:

'To-day is 1 August 1994 and it is hard to believe that it was only hours ago that my mother's life ended - it already seems like an eternity to me. So much has happened in the last five or six weeks it is really difficult to come to terms with. Of course, I realise that my mum was 83 years old, but she seemed always to be so strong, in body, mind and spirit, that it came as a complete shock to see her so frail and fragile, becoming weaker in body but certainly not in her mind, at least not until that morphine pump was connected to her. Even then, there were moments, when visitors from the family arrived, when she tried so hard to let us know she was aware of them even though she was unable to speak to them.

I am lucky really. I have had a mother for sixty-one years and that's not bad going, is it? I think the problem is that when we have them around, we take so much for granted - but then that's life, isn't it? Our relationship has always been marred by all the various difficulties my mother had to deal with throughout her married life - and they were continuous - but she dealt with them the best and only way she knew how and this sometimes meant that, unintentionally, she could not always be there, in the way that I would have liked, to support me when I needed her.

Her marriage was very distressful at times and she came through several "wars", including the world war of 1939 - 1945. She never had much money, gave birth to five children, struggled to take care of them and be a loving wife when, it seemed, all the odds were against her. Nevertheless, all five children admired and loved her even though they were affected in various ways by the family situation being stressful and disturbing.

There have been times in my life when I seemed not to have deep feelings for my mother. I felt cheated, rejected, unloved. Now I know that this was silly. My mother was doing her very best to love us and love herself, too, by trying to honour her ability to succeed as an independent woman, capable of working and having some kind of career. This was important for her; she needed to know she had gifts: intelligence, capabilities. Looking after five children takes a hell of a lot of energy and, having to supplement the family income too, and be a wife, housewife, mother and whatever else, meant she needed some space of her very own, where she could just be herself. Why, has it taken me so long to understand this? God only knows we all have limits and she was only human.

Now I just want to thank her from the bottom of my heart for all her courage and fortitude. It now seems a great privilege to have been able to take care of her in the last month or so of her life. It was as if she knew. I wish she could have shared her feelings with me about how she really felt. I think she was frightened and didn't really want to know.

So here, at last, was an opportunity to get close to her as she was dependent upon being nursed, cared for, loved and comforted. It was demanding both physically and emotionally for my sister and I. Staying in Ruth's home and in my sister's home helped; the surroundings were so peaceful and restful, My mum really appreciated the lovely bedroom, the view from the window and our attention.

I shall never forget how hard she tried not to be too much trouble or in the way. She coped valiantly with an inner strength to retain her dignity and she succeeded, virtually to the end, even though at times *it was so painful and drained her of what little energy she had left. She even told the doctor: "I am getting better every day."*

Finally, admitted to hospital, the doctor informed me my mother was dying from renal failure, as cancer was destroying her kidneys, and it was spreading. She only had days, she was at the end of her life, and all we could think was thank God she had been spared an operation. When it began to sink in that this really was the end I was overwhelmed by sadness. This was my mother, who always seemed so fearless, endless, indomitable, and was now going to die, just when I had begun to establish a close and more intimate relationship with her. Tragically it seemed so unfair. Now I wouldn't have time to share my thoughts and feelings with her. All too soon she became weaker; her spirit never faltered. Slowly, so slowly, she had to succumb to her weakened body. Unconsciousness crept over her like a thin veil until it became a tangled web and she let go... she broke free... left the old body, the old pattern, for a new beginning, free, at last to be herself.

May God bless you mum, for all that you were in this life. I love and honour you. I know now that I always loved you, even when I was angry, upset, or didn't want to see you. I wanted so much more of you and didn't understand that, with all the demands life had placed upon you, it could not be. You had a limit to how many pieces you could cut yourself into if you were going to be able to save a piece for yourself. You gave and gave - all of your life.

So mum, thank you for what you saved for me.

I love you, I love you. Until we meet again, God bless you and Peace be with you always.

Your loving daughter Audrey'

Act 4 Scene 8:

Jane

Our home healing sessions were becoming quite busy so Don and I made use of another room to see clients separately. On one occasion I remember having three ladies coming to see me on alternative weeks. The first was a young, attractive, and very distressed mother close to death. Supported by her husband and brother, Jane could hardly stand. Jane's cancer had spread all over her body and her husband confided she might only have a week or so to live. Under such circumstances the Healer always has to be mindful of the fact that it is 'Thy Will be Done' and not my will be done! You want so much to help in any way possible. After settling Jane comfortably I guided her through an appropriate and spontaneous intuitive healing visualisation. Jane relaxed very deeply and as I opened up a channel for the laying-on-of-hands there was no doubt she could feel the flow of unconditional love reaching deep into the recesses of her mind and body.

I never saw Jane again. A few days later her husband informed me of her passing. Then, to my utter amazement, about a month after Jane's death, the post delivered a hand written card in which Jane thanked me sincerely for the healing; she wrote that it had released all her fear of death and that she was at peace within herself. It taught me that Spiritual Healing is not always about recovery but preparation for 'going home'!

A Spiritual Healer is really only a catalyst for the healing process. We have to heal ourselves. Essentially, Spiritual Healing is a release mechanism for the client to let go of what they no longer need to hold on to. A Spiritual Healer is not only dealing with someone's symptoms when they come for an appointment. Realistically, they bring with them their whole life. And even past lives. During the healing act the recipient is able to relax very deeply

Spiritual Healing is channelling the power of unconditional love, enabling a person to feel safe and supported. It breaks down any stored or blocked negative energy bringing it to the surface. It is a wonderful and transformational procedure which is extremely empowering for the person to heal themselves.

Act 4 Scene 9:

Thelma

When Thelma came for healing she was in her sixties and was a high-powered business woman. Thelma told me she had been diagnosed with liver cancer. She lived alone and had no contact with family. I sensed she was very unhappy with her life.

Following the healing visualisation session I guided Thelma through she began informing me that she was full of regret and anger over an unresolved situation that she herself was responsible for but could not forgive. Thelma kept her fortnightly healing appointments with me for around six months. While I felt she had softened considerably within herself and eagerly accepted the healing visualisations and the laying on of hands, there still remained this shield of self-protection which needed breaking down.

Then for some reason or other she ceased to keep her appointments and I was unable to make contact with her. It was very frustrating as I had thought we were really making progress.

Three months later I received a telephone call from Thelma's estranged daughter, Mary, who informed me of her mother's passing several weeks prior. While going through her mother's belongings she found my telephone number in her mother's diary, in which all her appointments with me were listed. It appears that Thelma had contacted her daughter Beverley, after twenty years of estrangement when Beverley, aged sixteen, had a baby by a married man, whom she later married, but whom her mother despised and said she wanted nothing more to do with them.

Realising she had not long to live, Thelma had contacted Beverly to ask if they could meet up. They had spent the last two months of Thelma's life healing old wounds. Beverley said it was a miracle she had always prayed for and wanted to thank me for all the healing support her mum had received, which she felt had been instrumental in bringing about this special reunion at the end of her mother's life.

These ladies taught me an important lesson about healing into death and dying. It confirmed for me that spiritual healing takes place on many levels and none, more especially, when a person is going through the dying process. What a privilege.

Act 4 Scene 10:

Emily

Emily was eight years old and the adopted only child of rather mature parents. When they arrived for their appointment with me for Emily's healing session, they all alighted from a beautiful chauffeur driven Bentley. Emily was tiny for her age, totally bald, and I was shocked by the size of her stomach. She looked about nine months pregnant. Her doting and quite elderly parents explained to me, privately, that they had taken Emily to see many different medical consultants but none of them could offer a cure and they were desperate. Hence they wanted to try spiritual healing.

I had prepared for Emily's visit and, once in the healing room, gave her a set of coloured pencils and paper and asked her if she would like to draw me a picture. The purpose behind this request was to find out more about her and whether she would choose dark, dreary, sludgy colours as a result of her illness and her state of mind. She didn't. Emily's picture was delightful and full of bright, cheerful, uplifting shades of rose pink, purples, light and deep blues, bright orange and yellow, red and lots of green, which very much suited her lovely personality. There was not a dark colour anywhere. She externalised positive healing colours which was extremely encouraging. Emily then signed her picture and addressed me, saying:

"Thank you for the healing, I really enjoyed it and I would like you to keep the picture I drew for you and I have signed it with my name."

"Oh how kind of you. I am going to put it on my fridge when I get home."

There was no doubt Emily had loving parents: they had sent her to ballet classes, provided her with her own pony, and clothes that were obviously very expensive and exclusive. I loved the multicoloured, soft cotton, ankle-length, dresses she wore but felt very sad, too, because they couldn't hide the huge bump protruding from her stomach.

Lilla came to stay with us a few days later and happened to see Emily's drawing on the fridge. Studying the drawing Lilla said to me:

"Please don't raise your hopes up about being able to heal this child. Her picture is lovely and is giving me a lot of information as I tune into it and the signature."

With some dismay I stared at Lilla, with a questioning gaze and commented:

"Oh dear! What are you seeing?" I queried.

"This little girl is on a mission. She is a special soul and her life, this time round, will be short. Emily has 'come down' this time to experience cancer for herself. In her next life she will be an important researcher of this disease."

Emily did not keep her next appointment. Sadly, her distraught parents telephoned the news to me that she had passed away peacefully in her sleep and they asked me if I would mind returning the picture Emily had drawn when she came for healing. Of course I did not mind and posted it off to them with my love and condolences. Perhaps. I mused, Emily's lovely colourful picture would act as a healing balm for her parents in their sad loss.

Act 4 Scene 11:

Shock & Grief

In 1998 Don's health had been deteriorating daily. Ten years prior he had survived major surgery for a leaking aorta aneurysm when he had been taken in an ambulance with a police escort to Bristol hospital where crash teams rushed him into surgery. Afterwards the operating surgeon told me:

"He only has a one in four chance of surviving the night, I am afraid, as his heart stopped four times during the surgery, which took seven hours in all, as he had to be resuscitated so many times."

Don's miracle survival was due I am certain to him being linked to a prayer chain of distant healing groups and colleagues throughout the country.

Some fifteen years later on 24th April 1998 his death came suddenly and was a huge shock to my daughter and I. We had all eaten dinner together two nights previously at Ruth's home when I realised Don seemed depressed and unwell. Before leaving Ruth's together in Don's car, he reminded Ruth and me (for about the umpteenth time) where his Will was kept. Nothing, though, could have prepared me for the early morning phone call I received from Ruth, two days later.

"Mum, I have just phoned Tekels Park, where Dad is staying, and they went to his room so he could take my call, but they found him dead in bed. Mum, Dad is dead! Phone for the doctor to meet us at Tekels Park. I am going there immediately and will meet you there."

My lower back suddenly went into an agonising spasm as I spluttered out these words:

"Dead! What do you mean he is dead? He can't be dead"!

In that moment a great emptiness overwhelmed me. I gasped! I put the phone down and automatically picked it up again and dialled the doctor's surgery. The receptionist answered: I was in such shock that I was rendered speechless.

"Hello. I know there is someone there as I can hear you breathing." The receptionist stated in a very calm voice.

"Take a moment to breathe in and out deeply and try to relax and you will feel better."

Following her instructions I was then able to blurt out:

"A doctor is needed at once at Tekels Park Guest House as my former husband, a patient of Dr... has been found dead in bed this morning."

There, I had said it, but the agonising words meant nothing. I still kept repeating to myself:

"Dead! He can't be dead. That means I will never see him again in this life time. We have known each other for over thirty years."

At that shattering moment I fully realised what a great support system we had been to one another and how much true love remained for one another, despite having been divorced for ten years.

When I arrived at Tekels Park Guest House my daughter and the doctor were just going into the room where Don lay in bed in his pyjamas.

After examining Don the lady doctor proclaimed:

"Well, he is very dead indeed!"

I queried what she was inferring.

"I don't understand what you mean when you say he is very dead."

The doctor stated:

"He must have been dead some thirty hours or more. It looks as if he came to bed, two nights ago, and died in his sleep, probably from a heart attack, since when he has lain here. His bedding is undisturbed, his hands are not clutching the bed clothes, so he must have died peacefully in his sleep."

This information comforted me no end. Don had always remarked that he wasn't afraid to die but he wanted to go quickly and peacefully.

The next three days felt like a whirlwind making arrangements for the funeral, informing family and friends, of Don's passing. The shock waves were considerable. Ruth went onto auto pilot. She dealt efficiently with everything, including writing her father's obituary for the newspaper 'The Independent':

DON COPLAND was one of the most important figures to emerge in the field of spiritual healing in the last 20 years. (1987 - 1997).

Having been brought up a Christian, over the years he expanded his interest into comparative religion and early Christian history, including the Dead Sea Scrolls and the Essenes. He investigated healing through the ages and this led him to his first healing encounter in 1968, when he healed his second wife, Audrey, of a chronic neck condition.

With the preamble "Well, it can't do any harm!", he held his hands over his wife's neck and in one session cured her of a year-old problem that had failed to respond to medical treatment. This success led him to train as a healer with the National Federation of Spiritual Healers; and the words "It can't do any harm!" became a catch phrase.

Spiritual healing is the channelling of healing energies from a "divine source" through the healer to the patient, with the intention of boosting the body's own recuperative abilities to combat a wide range of physical and psychological conditions. A variety of research has been undertaken to demonstrate the scientific validity of healing, including studies on animals, plants and micro- organisms, as well as humans. Results have indicated the existence of a real healing effect.

The National Federation of Spiritual Healers (NFSH) was founded in 1955 as the first non-denominational professional body for spiritual healing. Copland became a Healer Member of the NFSH in 1977 and in 1982, after two years as Vice-President, was elected President. He held this position for seven years, only relinquishing it to take on the full-time job of Administrator for seven years, after retiring from his job as a company director. His final role in the NSFH was as Media Consultant and Spokesperson.

Copland's experience in business, running his own engineering company, Winvic Engineering, with two partners for more than 20 years, meant that he brought practical administrative skills to the NFSH as well as a deep spiritual commitment. These combined qualities enabled him, with other colleagues, to transform the NFSH from a sleepy cash-strapped "club" into the professional organisation that it is today - the largest spiritual healing charity in the world. He worked tirelessly to bring spiritual healing into mainstream acceptance, gaining the British Medical Association's approval of the NFSH Code of Conduct and helping to form the Confederation of Healing Organisations (CHO).

He frequently appeared on television and radio to explain the value of spiritual healing and was the subject of many newspaper and magazine articles citing his healing successes. In attempts to produce measured evidence of the healing process, Copland's healing was monitored by Biofeedback Mind Mirrors (which measured brain wave changes in both Copland and his patient) and infra-red cameras (which showed white light building up in his hands and passing into his patient), but the real proof of its efficacy was in his results.

He was a founder member of the NFSH Healer Training programme and was a gifted tutor, well-known for his relaxed yet informed approach and notorious for his jokes. His luck was also legendary: no healing fund-raiser or tombola was immune to his winning streak; he was constantly donating prizes back.

He wrote a definitive book on spiritual healing, So You Want to Be a Healer? (1981), while his "Spiritual Reflections" column in the NFSH magazine Healing Review (now Spiritus) was one of its most popular features. He edited the magazine for many years and loved to write. He published several books of spiritual verse including Verses and Prayers for Children (1977). The Healer's Prayer which he wrote is used by healers throughout the country.

Don Copland was born in Lincoln in 1930. He was called up for National Service when he was 18 and spent a large proportion of it in Malaya during the bandit war. In his bureau he kept a scrunched-up bullet which had flown in through the window of a troop train, hitting the seat behind his head. His love of Oriental food dated from this period and led to a general interest in cooking.

He was also a keen gardener and his healing hands meant that everything he grew was bigger and better; he used to say that he channelled healing through the water in the hosepipe. He was very practical and as well as building sets for years for Frank Muir's amateur dramatic company, the Thorpe Players, he also as a young man built a home from scratch on the banks of the River Thames near Chertsey, in Surrey. He was a talented sportsman, playing hockey and tennis, and also loved driving, especially in car rallies.

He had an affinity with animals and birds and found that they responded particularly well to healing. Several of his most recent *"patients" were dogs, who sat as still and contented as could be while Copland's hands were laid over them.*

By Ruth Copland

Donald Frank Copland, spiritual healer and businessman: born Lincoln 25 November 1930; Vice-President, National Federation of Spiritual Healers 1980-82, President 1982-89, Administrator 1989-96; married 1954 Anne Taylor (one son; marriage dissolved 1964), 1964 Audrey Murr (one daughter; marriage dissolved 1986); died Camberley, Surrey 24 April 1998.

So many wanted to pay their respects we reckoned on about two hundred people attending the Service. My daughter recorded her own song 'Outside Time' for the funeral service and Ruth and I agreed to have a reception afterwards at Tekels Park, where Don and I had taught so many healing courses together and where he had been temporarily lodging when he passed away.

At the funeral I read an extract from 'The Mystical Union' Don's last book manuscript.

"Our meeting with the Angel of Death is never far away. It cannot be avoided. As the raindrop falling on the ground finds its way into the sea, so our specks of living consciousness will return to that great cosmic ocean from whence it came. Realising all of this:

Let us therefore now accept that each moment is precious and should never be wasted. Let us be loving and compassionate to everyone we meet. Let us appreciate the gift of life God has given to us. Let us not waste a moment of life in anger, jealousy, envy, or greed.

Let us radiate God's love. Let us remember we are not alone We are an atom of God and therefore the sacred life energy of our Soul is eternal."

Relaxing quietly at home the evening after the funeral I was suddenly disturbed by a very strange incident. My large white teddy bear which sat on the top of the sofa near to where I was sitting suddenly, with tremendous force, crashed face downwards beside me. Completely startled I attempted, unsuccessfully, to repeat the pressure in which the teddy bear had fallen. No matter how many times I pushed it down, with all my strength, I was unable to repeat the initial impact. I knew for certain it was a signal of some kind.

Tentatively, I asked out loud:

"Don, is that you? Are you here?"

Mysteriously, a shimmering but jagged, circle of fiery light then appeared in a corner of the room. In the midst of this bright golden light, Don then emerged, looking years younger, and dressed in his favourite tennis clothes.

I sat very still and wondered if I was hallucinating.

The golden circle of light expanded and I could see Don more clearly. He then spoke to me:

"I just want to thank you for all you have done for me and for all the love you have given to me!"

Then he was gone; the circle of light disappearing with him.

For an hour or so I sat silently pondering what had just occurred, thankful for such a blessed but nevertheless totally unreal experience.

What a wonderful gift. Thank you Don.

Act 4 Scene 12:

A Special Dream

My 'baby' brother aged seventy-two, had been terminally ill in hospital for six weeks throughout January/March 2018 and had asked to be able to 'come home to die'. His loving family fulfilled his request and a hospital room was set up for him from which he could look out onto his beautiful garden through the large patio doors. With his loving family all around him and two hospice nurses checking on him each day, he finally experienced the peace he had sought but lacked while hospitalised in a busy acute respiratory ward.

Due to the distance and extreme weather conditions I was unable to visit him in hospital but prayed for him on a regular basis asking that he be surrounded with God's healing light for his highest good and highest purpose.

After so much frustration at my inability to visit I was, at last, sitting at his bedside the day after he was stretchered home from hospital. Taking it in turns with his precious family I spent the next five days with my lovely younger brother totally in awe at his dignity, heroism and complete awareness of everything that was happening around him. Even when he seemed fast asleep he spoke to me thanking me for coming such a long way to see him. When it was time for me to say my final goodbye I felt extremely emotional. Speaking very softly and touching his face very gently I said:

" I have to leave you now. I love you dearest brother with all my heart. You have been so loving and kind to me in so many wonderful ways. Thank you. I will miss you until we meet again."

He spoke very softly:

"I love you too Audrey. Drive home carefully."

Two night's later I went to bed, praying as usual for his peaceful transition and upon awakening was astonished by the dream I had experienced.

'Keeping watch at my brother's bedside I was shocked and concerned to watch him sit up. I asked him what he was doing and to lie back down. Ignoring me he then left his sick bed and stood up. Horrified I told him he must return to his bed and lie down because he was very, very ill. He ignored me and started to smile broadly as I witnessed him looking fit and well but most astonishingly much more youthful. He seemed to be glowing with good health. It was a complete transformation. Then he spoke to me:

"Where are my car keys Audrey? I need my car keys."

"Don't be silly. You mustn't drive anywhere."

He insisted he must have his keys which I found for him while still protesting he shouldn't drive."

He left the sick room saying:

"There's somewhere I have to be. Something I have to do."

With that he left and drove off. I then had a vague glimpse of him reprimanding someone about some previous behaviour. Then he spoke to this person.

"I have nothing more to say. It's your problem now. I have to leave as I have somewhere I need to be."

At 8AM the morning after this dream the telephone rang and it was my sister informing me that our brother had passed away the previous night at 11.15PM but she had waited until the morning to let me know so my night's sleep wouldn't be disturbed!

A huge sadness overwhelmed me but also an extreme feeling of joy. I knew in my heart I had 'seen' my brother leave his sick bed fit and well again, completely transformed. I lit a candle and prayed silently with grateful thanks for all that he had shared with me.'

Late that day I was handed a book to read by a friend who was enthusing about its contents. She was unaware that my brother had died. The book was 'Journey of Souls' by Michael Newton.

"How odd," I remarked, and shed tears as I mentioned the passing of my brother.

Michael Newton's book was a great comfort and confirmed in detail so much of what I had already been taught, experienced and accepted. I remembered what Uncle Bert had said during a channelled session years ago.

"The Soul is Eternal."

Act 5 Scene 1:

The Magical Process

'I do not fear death. I had been dead for billions and billions
of years before I was born and had not suffered the slightest
inconvenience from it'
- **Mark Twain**

With so much emphasis on death and dying in the world today I have sometimes wondered whether I am alive and dead at the same time? As a spiritual healer and a spiritual being, I sometimes have to ask myself: "Am I really here? And which part of us belongs to the 'other side?" When I meditate or channel spiritual healing a distinct alteration in consciousness occurs; a part of me is no longer here; I am somewhere else as I enter a calm, uplifting, peaceful state of attunement (at-one-ment) and begin to sense the changes that are occurring on different levels. It is a truly magical, transformational process as the creative life-force energy, condensed in the lower part of the body, begins a journey up the spine, opening all the invisible energy transforming centres, so they gather more light. At the top of the head this light energy then takes me beyond the physical realm or, from the 'Lower 'Self' towards the Higher Self and it will be the same for the person who is receiving spiritual healing. Their feedback has been invaluable to me as it is rewarding to know that the healing process moves the consciousness of the recipient to such a deep level that they felt they wanted to stay where their mind had taken them, rather than have to return to all the hustle and bustle and daily challenge of physical living.

A magical process occurred when I was 'sitting' in meditation with a friend. During the silence I opened my eyes only to behold in front of me, to the left and to the right, two columns of brilliant spiralling, light, rising upwards to a great height from the ground. At the top of each column sat a spinning silver crown. All I could do was stare in astonishment until I was completely and emotionally overcome by the purity and magnificence of what it was I beheld. Tears were falling from my eyes and the pure love filling my heart overwhelmed me. There was no doubt in my mind that I had just been blessed by an Angelic Presence.

Near Death Experience (NDE) Versus Meditation:

Many recipients of spiritual healing start to practise meditation and it is not uncommon for some to feel that they may have experienced a near death experience, as related by some people in television programmes on NDE, who say they have 'died' and come back.

I can personally vouch to having had such experiences myself and know of many others with whom I have worked who have also had similar ones. Very early on in my own spiritual development my meditations would take me through the misty tunnels of consciousness where I could perceive the light at the end of the tunnel which became brighter and brighter and the radiating force of pure love and peace became overwhelming. Suddenly my body seemed to be breaking up into geometric shapes, sizes and colours. My arms became detached and were floating either side of my spinning form, as did my legs. Instead of a solid, physical body of bone and tissue it had energetically broken down into this other form, but even though I felt shapeless I knew I was still totally connected.

Scientists have tried to dismiss the NDE by saying our brain creates this phenomena. So, if we can experience similar phenomena in meditation, you might ask are we really dying when we meditate? The only difference between the NDE experience and my own in meditation is that there is no one at the end of the tunnel saying: "Go back. It isn't your time yet" - which seems to be the case of people who have passed through this tunnel of consciousness, prematurely, after having been involved in a traumatic situation during which they have 'died'.

Language of Death

Dr. Elizabeth Kubler-Ross, Swiss-American psychiatrist and Founder of the Kubler-Ross Foundation, gained international fame for her landmark work on death and dying. She claimed even blind people who have experienced NDE 'see' everything at death before coming back into the physical and again being blind. Whether it is rebirth or death - you are using another set of senses. Why is it then that dying people see wonderful images: halls of light, shimmering buildings, tunnels of light, things that they have never experienced while alive and the scientists say it is to do with brain phenomena? Why, for instance, don't they see things they are familiar with: children's faces, familiar pictures, cream buns or cups of tea? Why do those people having a NDE see balls of light, angelic forms and other beautiful images?

Perhaps the language of death is totally different from what we are used to. Balls of light are Angels, shapes are higher levels of consciousness, crystalline buildings made out of light. All talking another language. After someone has died, a relative or friend of that person may smell their perfume or might even see part of the deceased. At the age of three my daughter, Ruth, asked me one night when I was putting her to bed:

"Mummy, did you know that Nana Copland comes to visit me at night, before I fall asleep, but I wish she would bring more than just her face."

And when my friend June clairvoyantly brought through a message from Mrs Copland Snr. we knew it must be her because June was overwhelmed by the smell of my mother-in-law's favourite perfume, Apple Blossom. Why is this?

I have also witnessed how a dead person can help the alive person feel all the pain of bereavement being lifted away from them.

Death and Rebirth

What we need to recognise is that we can die and be reborn while we are living in this life. Lives fall apart. Something dies. Something is reborn. Relationships break up; falling in love means you will never be the same again. Bits of you have to die and a new energy has to be reborn. If, every night, when we go to sleep we 'die' then every morning when we wake up we are reborn. It is up to us what that rebirth is all about.

With every new inhalation of breath we have a new beginning; with every exhalation of breath we have an ending. Constantly, we are only one breath away from physical death. Death is discarding what no longer matters and resurrecting what matters the most. When we become interested in death we begin to realise that there is no end.

Student to Guru: "I want to be very happy and experience Paradise now. How can I do this please?"

Guru to Student: "That is very simple. All you have to do is enjoy all of your problems."

Last Thoughts Before Death:

Supposedly, the last thoughts before death are very important. They classify you. They have a strong influence on your next life. In the end the quality of your life is much better than the quantity. Quite a thought to ponder upon.

Act 6 Scene 1:

Unexpected Developments

'Remember that no one is where he is by accident and chance
plays no part in God's plan'
- from 'A Course in Miracles'

With so much publicity about spiritual healing not surprisingly the Christian churches seemed at last to be waking up to the fact that they had not established any significant healing services within their ministry for years and decided to do something about this neglect. Conversely, the Spiritualist Churches had always offered healing – through the laying on of hands – and kept the practice alive. The NFSH was inter-denominational and their Healer members were of all persuasions but understood that the source of spiritual healing was divine.

At the office one day in the Autumn of 1983 I was surprised to receive a telephone request from the Vicar of St Mary's Church in Marylebone (opposite Madame Tussauds in London) asking if it would be possible for 12 of our healer members to attend a talk on Saint Francis of Assisi, to be given by Mrs Lilian Carpenter, wife of the Very Revd. Edward Carpenter, Dean of Westminster Abbey, which would then be followed by offering individual healing sessions to anyone in the congregation. St Marylebone Church was unique in that it had become a Christian Healing Centre. The crypt of the church had been cleared of some 850 dead bodies in order to (in the words of the Rector Christopher Hamel Cooke) "make way for the living."

In opening the St Marylebone Healing and Counselling Centre in the crypt of the church in the summer of 1983, Prince Charles had stated 'that complementary medicine could often be efficacious. Medicine has thrown out the baby with the bath water and what we're doing is bringing the baby back. The church has a healing mission together with the rest of the healing agencies for the benefit of the people'.

Although a range of alternative/complementary therapists practised from the crypt, the Vicar mentioned he was anxious to include the laying-on-of-hands but, as yet, the church did not have any healers. Mrs Carpenter's talk was riveting and, after introducing myself to her, I invited her to be a keynote Speaker at our next NFSH national conference. Meanwhile the spiritual healers, much to the delight of the Vicar, were kept very busy for a couple of hours while the members of the congregation patiently awaited their turn for the laying-on-of-hands.

Subsequently, and to my great joy, I became a life-long friend of Lilian and her husband the Very Revd. Edward Carpenter. Lilian, I learnt, was quite a remarkable lady who opened up her home in the Deanery of Westminster Abbey each Friday morning to feed the needy and to offer them healing and counselling.

Lilian was such a huge success at our Annual Healing Conference that she was invited back the following year, accompanied by her husband Edward who also addressed our conference.

A couple of weeks after Lilian had spoken at our healing conference she invited my teenage daughter Ruth to an audition at Westminster Abbey. Lilian said she had been impressed by Ruth's clear speaking voice while reciting a poem she had written herself for the conference audience. (Unbeknown to me at the time Lilian was a trained drama and elocution teacher).

Lilian advised that there was to be a '40th Anniversary of Peace in Europe Service' celebration at Westminster Abbey in May 1985, to mark the end of the war in Europe.

The Service would be attended by HM Queen Elizabeth II and members of the Royal family, as well as European Royals and Heads of State. Ruth was selected as a 'School Girl' to read a lesson from the pulpit following HRH the Duke of Edinburgh's address. Ruth and I slept overnight at the Deanery, to avoid the considerable travel chaos there would be the next day. It all seemed rather surreal. Lilian, bless her, had arranged for me to observe the momentous event from the 'Abbot's Pew' - which led directly from the Deanery into the Abbey and overlooked the 'Tomb of the Unknown Warrior' - near the Abbey's great entrance door, and across from the pulpit from which Ruth would give her Reading. Hence, I had a grandstand view of the arrival of our own Royal family, European Royal families, government Heads of State. and every single VIP known and unknown to me, from all the Commonwealth countries, who were attending this great and historic occasion. I had to pinch myself; it was unbelievable and absolutely thrilling! No mother could have been more proud when my teenage daughter, Ruth, delivered a heartfelt and impeccable Reading from the bible to the great and the mighty present that day in Westminster Abbey which included this text:

"The Wolf also shall dwell with the lamb, and the leopard shall lie down with the kid, and the calf and the young lion, and the fatling together, and a little child shall lead them."
(Isaiah 11.6)

Driving home that night we switched on the radio for the news which opened with Ruth's voice booming out and reciting her pulpit address. Together with a national newspaper there was a comment to the effect that a 'school girl's' delivery had brought a tear to the Queen's eyes – captured for the first time publicly – as she dabbed them with her handkerchief.

Earlier that year, prior to this important Abbey event, I had accompanied Bill Sykes, Editor of the 'Healing Review' (I was Assistant Editor) to the launch of the now famous book series 'A Course in Miracles' which took place in the Jerusalem Chamber within Westminster Abbey. The Very Revd. Edward Carpenter spoke a little about the publication before introducing everyone to Judith Skutch Whitson and her husband who had recently published the series 'A Course in Miracles' through their 'Foundation for Inner Peace' situated in Tiburon, California. Dr. Helen Schucman, an American Clinical and Research Psychologist from New York, Professor of Psychology at Columbia University from 1958 - 1976 said the book was dictated to her by an 'inner voice' she identified as Jesus. (This was quite surprising as I later learnt that Dr. Helen Schucman, was brought up in a Jewish family but was an atheist). She was helped in scribing the book by her colleague Dr. William Thetford.

Co-incidentally, I met Judith Skutch Whitson and her husband again, at Westminster Abbey, during the 1985 40th Anniversary Celebration of Peace in Europe as they, like me, were personal guests of Lilian and the Very Revd. Edward Carpenter and we were standing next to each other in 'The Abbot's Pew'. After Ruth had finished reading her Lesson from the pulpit Judith Skutch Whitson turned to me and asked who the enchanting teenager with the beautiful voice was? It was with intense motherly pride that I admitted she was my own beautiful daughter! At the end of the Service Judith and I had an interesting chat about healing, a subject dear to her own heart, and she invited me to visit her in Tiburon, California, that summer which I did. Judith Skutch Whitson was a great host and shared with me many of the handwritten notebooks that Dr. Helen Schucman used while receiving dictation on 'The Course in Miracles'.

Following the Abbey Service, Ruth and I were invited to attend the private luncheon in the Deanery, hosted by Lilian. The spacious reception room was extremely crowded with important church dignitaries from all across Europe all of whom were dressed in their colourful and assorted religious ceremonial garb, except one it seemed. A gentleman seated next to me was wearing a rather creased beige suit lamenting the fact as to how hungry and exhausted he was having just flown in from Australia and then travelling straight from the airport to the Celebration. He was ravenously tucking in to a plateful of food, while chatting away to me, when I did a double take and suddenly realised I was talking to Robert Alexander Kennedy Runcie, 102nd Archbishop of Canterbury!! You could have knocked me down with a feather.

As my friendship with Lilian became more established she invited me to join her weekly evening group gatherings in the Deanery for the purpose of studying 'A Course in Miracles' and presented me with the whole set of books on the course in beautifully bound black and gold hardback covering. It was quite a long drive from my home in Camberley to Westminster Abbey but I wouldn't have missed for anything the year long study, or what I gained from attending. Eventually I introduced the course to my own spiritual development group and they all purchased the paper back version and we set about exploring the contents, full of teachings and life-enhancing lessons. To all intents and purposes it seemed at the time that I was undergoing my own 'course in miracles' and could only feel truly blessed by the way my life seemed to be proceeding.

Every year His Holiness, The Dalai Llama, came to London on a visit and always stayed, for a week or more, in the Deanery of Westminster Abbey, and fondly called Lilian "His English Mother". His Holiness was due to preach to many of his followers and invited guests within the historic confines of the Abbey. Lilian personally handed me twelve invitations to share with other Healer colleagues and it was with great excitement and privilege that we all entered Westminster Abbey to hear His Holiness' address. To our utter amazement and disbelief 12 front row seats had been reserved for us. We were so close to His Holiness who, after his sermon, came across to speak with us.

A couple of years later I was visiting Lilian and helping her to prepare delicious food for a luncheon she was hosting on the day after His Holiness, The Dalai Llama, had just completed another one of his visits to their home. His Holiness always used the large guest bed room which his staff turned into a kind of sanctuary, placing cushions on the floor for praying etc. Lilian had arranged for me to stay overnight at the Deanery and so it was that unbelievably I found myself lying in the big double bed that only the previous night had been occupied by His Holiness, the Dalai Llama. As I stretched out my arms and legs on the bed I soaked up all the wonderful vibrations left behind by His Holiness and silently prayed to give thanks for all my many blessings. When I turned over in the bed and looked out of the window I could see towering Big Ben close by and listened as it chimed the midnight hour. I then fell into the most wonderfully sound and profoundly relaxing and deeply peaceful sleep within my living memory.

Act 7 Scene 1:

Challenging Events

'Strong reasons make strong decisions'
- William Shakespeare

1987 was a watershed year because Don and I were amicably divorced. We were still jointly teaching healer development courses and lived together, but separately, converting our Edwardian three-storey home into three separate apartments for the three of us. I added my maiden name to my married name in order to signify to all those concerned that there had been a change in our relationship. Thus I became known as Audrey Murr Copland in place of Audrey Copland. Somehow by doing this the vibration of my name became much stronger and more supportive.

Although I still loved and admired Don as a loving friend - we had known each other for thirty years - personal challenges still existed and it felt right to set ourselves free from marriage in order to pursue separate paths. Living on different floor spaces but still under the same roof proved to be unsatisfactory and, consequently, I became ill.

Practising What You Preach:

Office life seemed to become busier and busier. Combining all these office admin duties during the week with travelling and teaching residential healer development workshops nearly every weekend, meant moments of leisure and relaxation seemed fewer and far between, important though I knew them to be. I was taking on too much; and being a natural 'sensitive' and not entirely stupid, I heard my body talking to me and I listened to my tired mind.

"What should I do?" I asked myself. "Who will I be letting down if I retreat from this ridiculous situation?" I wondered. Common sense told me I wasn't indispensable, but I was certainly acting like it.

Following a winter holiday break in Scotland, with Ruth, at one of my staff's time shares, the matter was finally resolved for me. My tired mind and depleted body succumbed to a virus. Invisible to the naked eye, bacteria and viruses exist in our environment. Occasionally, they make their presence felt usually when we are in a weakened state or are out of balance. They remind us that we are not in harmony. Viruses could have wiped out humanity a long time ago, but I do not believe that is their intention. Viruses teach us lessons. This particular one laid me out flat with the worst headache, neck and body pains, I could ever remember.

"It must be flu," I thought to myself.

I felt absolutely wretched and needed to do something about it.

"All right," I thought. "Now is the time to practise what you preach."

I talked to the virus.

"I need to remind you that my body is not your home and I would like you to leave as soon as possible."

Then I visualised the virus leaving happily. Every day, for a week, during meditation, I 'bathed' my body in healing light and breathed love and peace into it. Each night I tuned in to the Angels of healing. Colleagues called round to give me spiritual healing. I endeavoured to draw in energy from the trees outside my window as I listened to chirping birdsong. Everything around me seemed normal yet I felt so abnormal. My body felt stiff and painful, the sickness was humiliating, my eyes felt sore and full of grit; it was time for a medical opinion, My doctor referred me to a Medical Consultant at the local hospital who, after examination and several tests, declared:

"I think you have got yourself through the worst of an attack of viral meningitis. The virus went into the brain and set up inflammation and also attacked the kidneys. However, the worst seems to be over. I don't know what you have been doing but you have done well to get through this."

"I have been doing self-healing as well as having other healers working on me," I replied.

"Is that so? We could do with them here," he retorted. "I would like to keep you under observation, in hospital, for a few days though, just to be sure of your recovery."

I declined his advice as gracefully as I could. Truthfully, I could not face being hospitalised and promised to return two days later for another examination. On the second visit I informed the Consultant I felt generally much better except for my eyes which were really hurting and that my vision seemed to be deteriorating. Within fifteen minutes I was being examined by an Eye Consultant who urgently called for his Registrar to take a look.

"This lady's eyes are haemorrhaging. She has acute iritis - bilaterally, in both eyes. We will have to commence intensive eye therapy immediately. She must be admitted at once."

The meningitis virus had set up some kind of allergic reaction in my eyes.

"I'm not going blind am I?" I asked as fear and panic gripped me.

"No, no!" He reassuringly replied. "But we do need to start administering drops every hour, immediately. I will admit you to a ward and as your daughter is here with you she can fetch whatever you need."

"No!" I exclaimed. "I will go back with her and collect my stuff."

"That is not a good idea," he retorted. "You must go to the ward now."

Panicking I said: "I am very sorry, but I do need to go home first." I insisted and headed out of his consulting room like a frightened rabbit caught in the glare of headlights, leaving the Consultant with a perplexed look on his face.

I realised I was out of control. My daughter lovingly attempted to allay my fear. When we reached home I went straight upstairs to my flat while Ruth apprised her father of my situation.

Later, as I lay in my hospital bed I felt shaken to the core. For years I had never been sick, not even a cold. This virus had set up some kind of allergic reaction in my eyes; these eyes of mine that I had always taken for granted which were now inflamed and full of drops that nurses administered around the clock. With vision blurred and time to think I knew there was a message here for me to grasp, an experience from which I would learn. Next day the Specialist told me my eyes had taken such a bashing he wanted to give me cortisone steroid injections into the eyes.

"I'm not going blind am I?" I asked as the fear returned.

"No, no, no," he answered. "This should clear things up much sooner."

I quickly telephoned my nineteen year old daughter Ruth, and put through a call to colleagues at the office to organise some distant healing for me. I felt terrified. Ruth arrived with a banana cake she had baked especially for my birthday - which I had forgotten about.

While waiting for the injections in the operating theatre I thought of all the loving support that now surrounded me as I knew many kind, dear people were all thinking of me and sending healing light. A beautiful peace descended and I became very calm, no longer afraid. Afterwards, with both eyes bandaged Ruth and a young nurse guided me back to the ward and into bed. I was in shock and very shaky.

It was the strangest sensation; I could hear, smell, touch and taste but was unable to see all my family and friends who had gathered around my bedside. Grateful to them all for their love and support my eyes were really stinging and I needed to be alone with my feelings but hadn't the heart to ask the visitors to leave me in peace.

Finally, when everyone had gone I started to think about blind people, the problems they faced, the beauty they missed. I listened to other patients talking in the ward and it was not the same as being able to study their faces and to observe their gestures.

Two days later the injections were repeated and the darkness descended once more. Lying in bed I considered why this was happening; whether I needed to look at my life, see things more clearly or differently? I slept for a while and took an inner journey where I seemed to be talking to my Higher Self.

"Look at your attitude to life and the way you look at everything and then make changes where you should," I was told.

I awoke to find my American healer friend, Joanne, by the bed. She had brought me a cassette player, with headphones, so I could listen to a reading she had recorded from Ernest Holmes' book, 'Science of Mind'. It was uplifting and inspiring:

'There is one vision and one perfect scene. My eyes are open and I behold perfect life. No suggestion of imperfect vision can enter my thought. I perceive that all people can see and that the one looking is not limited in vision. I AM one with the TRUTH. I do open my eyes and I can see. This world operates even through me and manifests through my eyes now. Open my eyes that I may see. The eye of the Spirit cannot be dimmed. Neither can it be limited in its ability to see. My eyes are the vision of my indwelling world. They are the windows of my inner Spirit and are always open to the vision of the Truth.

I see with the vision of the Spirit and this sight cannot be weakened or lost. It is forever a factor. My world which I now speak is the law of perfect sight. Spirit sees through me. My peace is found at the heart of God. The heart of God for me is found at the centre of my being. It does not matter how closely the confusion of the outer world presses against me, I am not even disturbed by the confusion in my immediate environment. I know that the only way to counteract confusion is to bring peace into play. Peace I leave with you. My peace I give unto you. These words of assurance stay with me and I hear them re-echoing in the depths of my being. I surrender all my fears. Those nameless fears which have beset me for a long time. Dulling my pleasures and clouding with misery and apprehension all of my days. I am now through with fear. I do not fear sickness or death, because the eternal and perfect life animates my body and goes always about its perfect work healing and renewing my body.'

After listening to this reading I said to Joanne "I will never take my eyes for granted again. I will try and look at life and see it through different eyes, using the perfect vision that exists and is there for us to see."

Once my recovery was complete we sold the house and purchased separate places in the same town. Some time later Don moved into an apartment in the same building as me and the unbreakable bond of loving friendship between us continued on a slightly different and less stressful level.

Act 8 Scene 1:

A New Phase In My Life - Overseas Experiences

'Whatever you can do, or dream you can, begin it. Boldness has genius, power and magic in it'
- Goethe

Early in 1989 I had begun to sense my life was about to change direction and that it was time for me to leave the administrative day job at head office that I had undertaken for 12 years. I planned a six month sabbatical in California and to accept an invitation from my healer friend Joanne and her husband to base myself at their home in Half Moon Bay where they would soon be returning as her husband's contract with his company in the UK had ended.

Fate then intervened in a most extraordinary way. I had previously given three months verbal notice to the NFSH Board of Trustees of my intention to resign and all that remained was for me to hand in my written notice to the Chairman. Entering his office, I handed it to Guy Batham just as his telephone rang. Guy looked at me beckoning me to sit down as he answered the call; he then passed the telephone over indicating it was for me.

"Hello. I believe you wish to speak to me. Who is this please?"

"Hi there. My name is Brett Dunne. I am over in the UK with my wife and we are down here in magnificent Glastonbury, calling from the home of a mutual friend."

"I see. In what way can I be of assistance?" I enquired.

"I am informed you are some kind of a healer and trainer, and that you intend visiting California soon; I wonder if you would consider coming to Mount Shasta?" said he.

"Manchester in England," I replied.

"Not Manchester," he exclaimed. "Mount Shasta. Have you never heard of this special place? It is on the Oregon border, in northern California, and is the most magical and powerfully energetic and spiritual place on earth, on a major ley line."

"Oh", I said: "No. I have not heard of such a place. It sounds interesting. Do you live there?" I asked.

"Yes, we do at the moment. And we would love to host some healing workshops for you there, if you would consider such a plan? I can arrange venues, publicity, radio interviews etc., if you will only take up my offer."

My head was whirling with excitement at such an opportunity and the synchronicity of the moment did not escape my mind. Spirit works in mysterious ways.

"Thank you for the invitation. Yes. I would like to accept your kind offer and wonder whether you and I can meet up to discuss everything in more detail?"

"Great. My wife and I will be in London next week." He announced: "Mount Shasta awaits you and I know you will love it there," he said.

"Can I enquire how you know this mutual friend of ours down in Glastonbury?"

"Sure! I hadn't seen him in 20 years and while staying in this wondrous town and visiting the sacred sites of Glastonbury, I was directed to a chiropractor for treatment for a painful back. Incredibly, the guy turned out to be someone I met in India when we both worked for the Maharishi and were invited to teach transcendental meditation (TM) by the United Nations."

"Well, isn't life just full of surprises"? I commented. "I look forward very much to meeting you and your wife very shortly," and put the phone down. Guy was smiling at me and said:

"I suspect this is going to be the beginning of a new phase in your life, Audrey, well done."

Act 8 Scene 2:

Mount Shasta

'Anxiety must go, It must be replaced by faith and solemn confidence in the outworking of the plan'
- **Comte de St Germain**

Nothing could have prepared me for the beauty, majesty and powerful energy of the volcanic Mount Shasta, rising 14,179 ft into the sky. The surrounding area is 3,600 ft above sea level and naturally landscaped with lush forests, pristine glacial waters, natural mineral springs and mountain air. Apart from the thousands of tourists who visit the area, intent on some skiing, mountain trekking, canoeing, etc., it also attracts countless numbers of people searching for spiritual growth and rejuvenation through all kinds of spiritual pursuits for mind, body and spirit available there. The City of Mount Shasta hosts the St Germain Foundation and the Ascended Master's 'I Am' Teachings and has a population of 3,292 residents and is a sacred place to the Native American Indians of Northern California.

Thankfully, my hosts had booked me into a homely and comfortable boarding house for the duration of my stay in this magical place. When I arrived in Mount Shasta in October 1989, I fell completely under its spell and, at the same time, became completely disorientated during my first week of settling in. I wasn't prepared for the purity and intense spiritual energy of Shasta and was, literally, 'knocked out' by it. My head ached for days and I felt exhausted; gradually, as I adjusted to the climate, it felt as if I had shed a life time of stress and that I was being given an opportunity to find my true self. A deep and inner part of me had, unconsciously, bonded to Mount Shasta. It was a really intense and wonderful feeling. It seemed a place like no other I had ever experienced, being much closer to God and heaven.

Co-incidentally, my daughter Ruth had been living in Mount Shasta for some months prior to my visit, arranged for her by Brett and his wife when they were in the UK. Consequently, Ruth was able to take me on some spectacular sight-seeing trips, including a thrilling drive up the great mountain to a place named Bunny Flat, where we parked the jeep and then hiked to higher parts of the mountainside, treading carefully between the loose rocks that were scattered everywhere. The hot sun shone relentlessly down upon us and the dry dust we created as we climbed and clambered over rocky terrain filled our nostrils making it hard to breathe. I wanted to turn back but Ruth was determined to share with me a special place she had previously stumbled upon - South Gate, previously called Squaw Meadow. Amidst all the rocks, stones and dust there suddenly appeared what to me looked like a mirage as I perceived an acre or so of soft green moss and crisp shaved grass in a meadow adorned with tiny, multi-coloured, mountain flowers and minuscule tumbling rivulets of water flowing through it all. In total awe, I sat down with Ruth and scooped up handfuls of the cool, refreshing water, gleefully drinking some and splashing it over my face. It was as if I was in a totally different dimension akin to paradise.

Ruth and I silently blessed Mother Nature's pristine beauty and creativity spread out all around us. We experienced the breathtaking views of the twin-peaked, snow-capped Mount Shasta rising high above the surrounding terrain into a clear blue and cloudless sky. The spiritual consciousness of the mountain dominated the community below and, like so many before, I was soon convinced that all the stories and legends of the mountain being the meeting point on earth of such Ascended Masters as St Germain were completely believable.

On this, my first of several subsequent visits, I remained in Mount Shasta City for some three months, such was the spiritual magnetism of the environment. As promised, Brett set up and advertised my healer development workshops at a couple of venues and arranged for me to be interviewed on local radio. Some of the participants were already therapists practising in their own right and their presence added another dimension to the classes, which included aura and chakra scanning and balancing, meditation, attunement and spiritual healing. Some of the therapists inferred they were 'burnt out' by their own energy work on clients and wondered why? They hadn't realised that working one-to-one in close proximity with a client could put them at risk of absorbing, instead of transmuting, any negative energy the client might be releasing if they had not first acquired attunement with a divine source. They were taught the 'cleansing breath' or 'egg breath' exercise which is outlined in section two of this book. It is easy to do and expands the auric field, strengthening and releasing, so that it remains strong. In sick people the aura begins to contract and might, therefore, contain such thought forms as fear, apprehension, anger, resentment and so on. The therapist's aim is to cleanse, clear, harmonise and re-balance the energy field thus enabling the client to feel safe and able to release and let go of what they no longer wish to hold on to. The cleansing egg breath is recommended for the use of clients as well as therapists. A strong aura is a strong protection.

Eventually, winter arrived in all is glory with prolific snow falls which transformed everywhere into a shimmering, white, wonderland. Downtown Mount Shasta had to be snow ploughed, resulting in high banks of snow being laid either side of the road. Temperatures dropped dramatically and the silence of the winter became awesome. The magical and majestic snow clad mountain reigned supreme over all its territory.

One afternoon I was cabin-sitting for Brett and his wife while they were away when a mutual friend Colin, a chiropractor, called round on a pre-arranged visit to do some promised regression therapy with me in which he was very experienced. The cabin was very cozy with a wood burning stove blazing away and Colin talked me through a deep relaxation followed by another hypnotic procedure that resulted in me feeling I was floating upwards above the room and beyond. Following Colin's guidance I began to descend very slowly and he instructed me to look straight down at my feet and at the ground upon which I landed. This is what happened:

'My feet were bare and the earth was very dry and dusty. I perceived my sandals where I had left them under a tree. It was a very warm day and my two teenage girl friends were calling out for me to hurry as it was late and time for them to go home. Gathering up my sandals I walked with them towards a small white windowless flat roofed stone building from which a delicious aroma of fresh baking filled my senses. Their mother greeted me and I was offered a piece of piping hot flat bread which tasted delicious. Realising how late it was I took my leave and walked quickly to a completely different part of town, which housed attractive villas with pretty colourful gardens. This is where I lived with my father, a Roman Centurion. I was Roman and my friends were Jewish and I loved them dearly and met up with them against his wishes.

When he walked into our villa my father informed me that I was to be interviewed for a special position in the household of an esteemed family the following day and that I must look my very best. A servant would come to collect me and it was important that I made a good impression.

Waiting nervously, a kindly looking plumpish lady led me by the hand away from my home towards an area which I knew to be one where important officials resided in opulent properties such as the one the servant was now hastening towards. The gardens were filled with exotic and colourful plants. Once inside I was told to wait in the spacious entrance hall until I was announced. I perceived a lovely young woman in flowing robes coming towards me and she beckoned me to follow her into another part of the house, whereupon she smiled at me very kindly and asked me to hold out my hands for inspection. She turned them over and over, palms up and then palms down and then rubbed my fingers one by one. Finally she announced that I would be hired as her personal hand maid and taught the art of massage with essential oils for which I would receive instruction. I would live in a separate part of the house from the other servants and be situated closer to the lady's bathing area. She then dismissed me and the original servant came and showed me the room in which I would live. I was disappointed as it was very small and the window was high up on the wall and would prevent me from seeing out into the beautiful garden below.

On hearing about the successful outcome of my interview my father was really pleased and excited that I would be serving the wife of a very important dignitary. He was adamant that I could no longer associate with my Jewish friends or ever visit that quarter again and that it was off limits. I was extremely saddened by this.

I loved my work and found I was a natural in hand massage techniques and also in understanding how essential oils were used for therapeutic purposes. Being in such intimate contact with 'my lady' who was the wife of the important official, whom I was yet to meet, she asked me if I had ever joined in any of the groups who gathered in the Jewish section to listen to the 'Teacher'? She mentioned that she liked to slip away incognito, with a servant in attendance, to hear the 'Teacher' speak which was a wonderful experience but warned me never to utter a word to her husband as he would be furious.

One day while I was carrying out her daily massage, 'my lady' informed me she was going away but could not take me with her and that I was not to mingle with servants in the other parts of the house. Naturally I was disappointed she was leaving without me. She told me that her husband, who was the Governor, Pontius Pilate, had said there was a great deal of unrest brewing following the savage breaking up of the Teacher's groups.

A while after 'my lady' had left her home I was sitting on the bed in my room when I could hear a lot of commotion outside. There was shouting and screaming which disturbed me and I was very afraid. Suddenly everything went black and the silence was terrible. I was absolutely terrified. That ended the regression which had lasted for over two hours and left me with much to think about as it all seemed so real.

I did not miss any opportunity to 'open' to and exchange energy with the spiritual wisdom that people shared with me about the St Germain Foundation and the 'I AM' teachings. It didn't escape my notice that Lilla Bek, my Teacher and friend, had originally been contacted by the Ascended Master St Germain, and placed under his direction in order to research the mechanics of healing and the evolution of consciousness and that what I was sharing in my workshops with attendees was the result of what she had been teaching us in her courses for the NFSH over a long period of time.

During a second visit to Mount Shasta Brett loaned me his jeep so that I could drive myself around. With great care I journeyed up to the Bunny Flat level and parked alongside a large camper van. Two very buxom and smiling ladies were giving their two Jack Russell dogs some water and food.

"Good morning," I cheerfully shouted, "your dogs remind me of my Jack Russell, Digger, who was such a character and dug holes all over the place. I really miss him."

"Gee, get that lovely British accent," one lady replied. "I just love to hear you talk so! Where are you from and what brings you here to this glorious mountain?"

We engaged in a chatty conversation when one of the ladies announced:

"I channel the Arch Angel Gabriel and my friend here channels the Arch Angel Michael. We visit the mountain every year and have travelled a long way. We are off now to find a place to sit and meditate. You are very welcome to come and join us."

Completely staggered at their invitation and their announcement, I mused on how I could not possibly miss an opportunity to sit on this sacred mountain with two Arch Angels and I gleefully confirmed I would like that very much indeed. My meditation was surprising. I was taken inside the mountain which seemed to be home to some extremely tall and silver beings. They seemed to be busily involved with certain tasks and completely ignored me. I was fascinated by their agility of movement and did not have any sense of them being robotic in any way. Quite the opposite. It was all rather strange. Was this another civilisation from another dimension I asked myself? The whole atmosphere inside the mountain was one of peaceful tranquility.

One of the areas in Shasta I grew to love was Castle Lake which rose 6000 ft above sea level. On a beautifully fresh perfectly sunny morning I drove up there, in Brett's jeep, parked it and then began a gentle hike around the glistening, sunlit lake, surrounded by pine forests, craggy boulders, and twisted woody shrub land underfoot. Gazing across to the far side of Castle Lake as I took care not to stumble, my attention was immediately drawn to a Native American Indian settlement close to the water side. Bustling women and children were busy with tasks outside their Teepees and smoke was rising over camp fires, horses were being handled by various braves. Startled, I attempted to achieve a closer look at all this activity but the vision suddenly disappeared leaving me disappointed and wondering, once again, whether I had, in fact, imagined it.

History relates that the Wintu Indian Nation first resided around Mount Shasta several hundred years ago, when they witnessed volcanic activity and believed that the smoke they saw came from the camp fire of the Great Spirit within the mountain.

Continuing my walk along the water's edge I pondered upon what I had just witnessed, realising it was quite similar to the previous vision that occurred a few years before when I was picnicking in a State Park in southern California. I became completely convinced I was experiencing flash backs of a previous life or lives as a Native American Indian and felt strangely excited and comforted by this thought.

During another of my visits to Shasta Brett presented me with a special book entitled 'The Magic Presence' by Godfrey Raye King, published by the St Germain Press: I was particularly taken by this extract from the Foreword:

'This book contains the second group of experiences which I was privileged to have through the Love and Assistance of the Beloved Ascended Master St Germain. He revealed many, many things which have been held in secret and sacredly guarded for many centuries.'

Further on the foreword explains:

'The purpose of This Book is to reveal to the Individual the whereabouts of his own Divine Self - God'. "The Mighty I AM Presence," that all who desire may return to their Source, receive their Eternal Inheritance and feel once again their Divine Self Respect.'

Godfrey Raye King reveals astonishing encounters with the Ascended Master St Germain, when the author and certain other chosen and mentioned individuals, were able to experience his wondrous wisdom under incredibly intimate and magical circumstances.

One of the spiritually enlightened groups I was invited to attend while residing in Mount Shasta, was held in the home of an elderly lady in her eighties, named Pearl Dorris, who was never present at the meetings, as she was unwell, suffering from a heart condition. Pearl remained close by in her bedroom and, apparently, had made a request for me to give her spiritual healing on my next visit.

When I kept our appointment and was shown into Pearl's bedroom, which was stunningly decorated in all shades of rose pinks and purples, I was surprised by her appearance, as she looked some twenty-five years younger than her age: her skin glowed and her eyes sparkled; as we chatted I became overwhelmed by the flow of glorious and radiant light that emanated around and from her.

"Why does this gracious lady want me to give her spiritual healing?" I silently asked myself, "when I am being bathed in pure, unconditional love radiating from her whole being?"

Pearl sat up and moved from the bed to a nearby chair and said: "Please commence your healing, now, dear, if you will."

Silently, I stood behind her and placed my hands over the crown of Pearl's head, attuning to my Higher Self, and asking for permission from Pearl's Higher Self, to carry out the laying-on-of-hands. Then, standing sideways on, with one hand near to her brow centre and the other hand at the top of the spine the intention was to scan downwards over each of the seven chakras, or energy centres, to harmonise and balance Pearl's main circuit of energy.

My hands were flowing with spiritual energy into Pearl's consciousness which, simultaneously, was being resisted by Pearl's enormously powerful energy field and swiftly diverting the healing energy back into me. There seemed no way I was able to penetrate Pearl's auric field as it overflowed with unconditional love into my whole being.

I began to feel completely euphoric; my head appeared to be 'in the clouds' while, at the same time, I was experiencing that 'perfect peace that passes all understanding.' Intuitively, I sensed that Pearl was being overshadowed by the 'Presence' of the Ascended Master St Germain.

"How could this be?" I asked myself.

"Pearl dear, I don't know who was giving who healing just now. I am so sorry but I seemed unable to penetrate your energy field," I said apologetically.

"Oh don't worry dear. I received what I needed," Pearl calmly stated.

I hadn't failed to notice the beautiful ring on Pearl's finger and commented.

"What a beautiful amethyst crystal you have set in your ring. I have never seen a stone so large and so clear. It is quite dazzling and draws you in to its purity," I remarked.

"Yes," Pearl said softly, "it is very special. The Master Saint Germain apported it to me on an especially significant occasion."

Following this visit, I started to read 'The Magic Presence' and, to my utter astonishment, it contained the name of a certain lady named Pearl Dorris as being one of the members of the small privileged group of people that entered a specific cave entrance, by invitation and, subsequently, found themselves under the Direction of the Ascended Master St Germain's authority and ability to create unique circumstances and experiences that only an Ascended Master could manifest.

A member of Pearl's house group presented me with a copy of her book 'Step by Step We Climb' - as given by the Arisen Masters.

Months later and to my utter joy, when I was about to leave England for another visit to Mount Shasta, Lilla said she wanted to join me there. We met up in San Francisco and I hired a car to drive the five hundred miles to Mount Shasta where we were to stay in Brett's cabin while he and his wife were away. As we approached the outskirts of Mount Shasta City Lilla started to experience great shudders of emotional concern.

"What is it Lilla? You seem to be in shock. Are you okay?" I queried.

"Oh dear God" she cried "something pretty dreadful has happened here at one time. I am picking up such intense pain and horror from the ethers."

While on a visit later to the Native American Indian museum in the town, we learnt that in the re-settlement of around 5,000 tribal people of the Wintu nation, they had attended a government feast in celebration of the new reservation they were being allocated, only to have all been intentionally poisoned by the meal laid before them, from which they died. Mass murder was what Lilla had been tuning into as we approached Mount Shasta, even though the shocking event had, supposedly, occurred some centuries ago.

Once we had settled into the spacious and comfortable cabin situated in a pretty secluded woodland area, where bears sometimes roamed, Lilla and I had a pretty wonderful and magical time together. Each night we would light a candle and sit quietly to meditate. In one meditation I saw a 16th century, immaculately dressed, silver-wigged aristocratic gentleman holding a young woman in his arms; she was stunningly dressed in a billowing ball gown as they waltzed together in the warm glow of a candlelit ballroom. When I related this vision to Lilla she giggled and replied:

"Yes. This often happens ahead of a more serious meeting with St Germain. It is his way of relaxing me and also reminds him of the period when, historically, there was a dashing Comte de Saint Germain on earth, who worked at the Court of France before and during, the French Revolution." The Comte became famous for being able to appear simultaneously, anywhere at any time, and perform wondrous acts of compassion and illumination. Our meditations together were always joyful, sincere and graced by the Ascended Master's presence.

During one of my extended visits to Mount Shasta I was invited to join a Homeopathic and Chiropractic Centre, taking on client referrals for spiritual healing and counselling, on a voluntary basis. It was a most rewarding period and I began to look very seriously at the possibility of moving permanently to America but regretfully it did not work out for many complex reasons. Though quite disappointed I accepted that 'what will be - will be'.

I have vacationed in Mount Shasta with my daughter and her family a few times, many years on from those first visits to give workshops, and it still feels as if I am coming home.

Act 8 Scene 3:

Los Angeles

'We work we believe in the power of Spiritual Healing and entrust the results of this to the One who knows everything and governs all things with Love'

- Harry Edwards, the Great British Healer

Dr. Kolah, tall and upright aged 90 plus, and looking years younger, was of Indian origin and was the second oldest healer member of NFSH. He lived near Hollywood, with his charming family, and in 1990 had invited me to his home to join a gathering of some 40 friends, to teach a workshop on self-healing and distant-healing.

Dr. Kolah had once known Harry Edwards some years previously and had visited Burrows Lea, in Shere, where Harry lived and operated the renowned healing sanctuary and famous world- wide distant healing service.

Starting out as a young medical doctor, in Bombay, Dr. Kolah explained that he could not accept the side-effects some drugs caused his patients so he had studied further in homeopathy. He combined this work with spiritual healing, an art he was still practising in the form of distant healing.

At this workshop I was introduced to Sarah, a British born healer, who very kindly invited me to stay in her luxurious mobile home in Pacific Palisades overlooking the ocean - an up-market area where the rich and the famous resided, some of whom were her clients. It was Thanksgiving when I arrived there and during my stay I witnessed some spectacular sunsets and sunrises as well as Sarah's amazing healing work. Bright as a lark and chatting non-stop Sarah worked her way through a dozen or so ailing folk, all gathered together in her living room for one of her regular morning healing sessions. In no time at all (assisted by what she calls her 'invisible helpers') I witnessed Sarah soothing and straightening arthritic joints and dealing with lumps and bumps and goodness knows what else, to very grateful clients.

Sir Andrew Lloyd Webber's famous and highly acclaimed musical, 'Phantom of the Opera', was celebrating its 1000th performance at the major performing arts Ahmanson Theatre in Los Angeles, and the British actor, Michael Crawford, was playing the leading role of the Phantom. A client of Sarah's, Michael had given her two complimentary tickets to the show which Sarah was generously sharing with me. On the day we were to attend the performance Sarah received a phone call from Michael. Putting the phone down she said:

"Oh dear. Michael has a horrid cold and a nasty sore throat and has asked if we can come back stage before the curtain goes up as he needs some spiritual healing. He says there is no way he can miss this important 1000th performance."

Thus I found myself in Michael Crawford's dressing room which was filled to overflowing with congratulatory cards, balloons, garlands of flowers and bottles of bubbly. Sarah introduced me to the star of the show and we chatted as if he had known me forever. He was just so normal! I told him:

"I remember you from your hit TV show 'Some Mothers do 'Ave 'Em'. It was one of my favourite programmes." He laughed and replied: "That was some time ago, wasn't it?"

Michael sounded very hoarse and was coughing when he asked to be excused so he and Sarah could slip away for a while, where they would not be disturbed, while he received some much needed healing. Waiting in his dressing room I cast my eye around it and peered intensely at all his stage costumes hanging neatly from big hooks; I gasped when I noticed the famous Phantom mask placed on his dressing table ready for him to don. All my own stage-struck memories were triggered as I waited, in awe, for Sarah and Michael to return.

Later, seated in the second row of the stalls, I was so excited and noted that the theatre was packed to overflowing for this celebratory 1000th performance. I said a little prayer for Michael whose voice, fortunately, never faltered once throughout the show; you would never have believed how hoarse and full of cold he had been earlier. Spiritual healing had, apparently, worked wonders.

After the show we joined the whole cast back stage for the celebratory party where a huge iced cake was cut and passed around to everyone, together with glasses of champagne. Michael gave Sarah a big hug informing her that the healing had completely sorted out his sore throat and cough about which he had been so anxious.

Lesley Flint Seance:

A few days later I accompanied Sarah to an elderly, former film director's spacious apartment, situated in the older and more prestigious area of LA, to attend a direct voice seance, being held there. This would be a completely new experience for me. Lesley Flint, the famous British direct voice and most tested medium in the world, made an annual visit to Los Angeles for the purpose of visiting his film director friend, during which he always gave a seance during his stay. Direct voice mediumship is considered the strangest, rarest, and most controversial form of mediumship. Through the medium's ability to create an ectoplasmic voice box within the room, it became possible for communicants to speak directly to deceased members of their family or friends, who would respond by using their once normal physical voice and language. In his time investigators had placed gags in Lesley's mouth, putting him into wooden and even steel boxes, to ensure he was not cheating.

Sarah had received an invitation from Lesley and had asked him if there was room for me. Lesley Flint had commented:

"Well Sarah, actually there is one more space available and Shirley Maclaine has begged to be allowed to attend, but as I don't want to be mentioned in the new book she is writing, perhaps I will let your friend come in her place."

On the night of the seance Sarah and I were seated comfortably together on a plush sofa, and I observed there were six other people, male and female, animatedly chatting noisily in this spacious sitting room. The walls were adorned with huge framed posters of past epic films, such as 'Gone With The Wind' which had been directed by our host, who was yet to appear, together with photographs of famous stars. It certainly portrayed a little piece of old Hollywood. I was rather surprised to observe how many of the invited guests, including Sarah, were all smoking and there was quite an unpleasant haze and smell of tobacco smoke in the room which was beginning to make me feel slightly sick.

"Surely," I thought to myself, "the seance isn't going to take place here?" And nervously I looked around the room. Everyone, including Sarah, had brought tape recorders with them.

A gentleman who had just arrived, sat down and beckoned to Sarah for us to come over to him. I was completely taken by surprise when Sarah introduced me to Lesley Flint.

"How nice to meet you my dear. I understand you are a healer friend of Sarah's and it is you who has taken the last space available this evening, instead of dear Shirley. She will be furious, if she ever finds out. Never mind."

We continued in pleasant conversation for about ten minutes and I grew more and more excited about the forthcoming seance.

Finally, an announcement was made for us to make our way to the seance room. There was more giggling and chatting by the group as we proceeded down a long corridor, each side of which the polished wood panelled walls displayed film posters.

As we walked Sarah whispered to me:

"Audrey hold on to my hand as the room will be pitch dark and you, literally, won't be able to see where to go."

It was like the blind leading the blind; the room was utterly blacked out. Childlike, I followed Sarah closely, holding on tightly to her hand as instructed when suddenly she pulled me down on to a sofa. To my surprise everyone was still laughing and talking as they entered the room. Inexplicably, I began to feel rather nervous as I had absolutely no idea what to expect. Then someone mentioned that Lesley Flint had arrived and was now seated in the blacked out room. Without any warning the seance began and I heard everyone's tape recorders being clicked on.

"Allo, allo, allo," spoke a deep cockney male voice as it resonated around the room. "Welcome dear friends once again. You all know who I am, don't you? I am Mickey your 'Door Keeper' and this evening I 'ave quite a few visitors from our side of the veil, all clamouring to speak to their loved one's on your side. In just a minute we'll begin but first of all I know we 'ave someone new 'ere tonight." There was absolute silence. Squirming with embarrassment I suspected he must mean me. The room was so intensely dark it was impossible to observe any one's reaction, even Sarah's, who was sitting next to me.

"Come on now, don't be shy, you know you're new to all of this caper, so let's be 'aving you and 'ere you speak your name dear, so we can welcome you." Mickey requested.

"If you mean me, Mickey, my name is Audrey and I am here with my friend Sarah." I quietly responded.

"There yer go! That wasn't too bad, was it? Little Audrey, eh, who laughed and laughed and laughed?"

(Ever since I was a child adults had quoted this very same phrase to me upon hearing my name and I have never known what it was 'little Audrey' laughed at. After the seance I decided to investigate: Evidently 'Little Audrey' is a famous folklore cartoon character used in a series of jokes popular to the 1930s, when a genre of cruel jokes became popular. The short jokes were pretty macabre but they also featured the catch phrase in that 'Little Audrey' just laughed and laughed and laughed. The name 'Little Audrey' was so well known - from either joke books or vinegar labels - that a British tank that first took part in the D-Day landings - well before another tank 'Santa's Surprise' was even conceived - was dubbed "Little Audrey II". A "Little Audrey I" commemorates the vehicle to-day in England. A nice thing about 'Little Audrey' is her integrity. She is no hypocrite. 'She does what she wants to do, says what she wants to say, and makes no bones about it.' I like to think that this last statement describes me, 'down to a tee', as they say.)

"Well, Audrey, it's luvely to 'ave you 'ere, darlin' so good luck me love."

Suddenly the voice changed to a woman's who was speaking in fluent French and a conversation began to take place between this discarnate entity and a man attending the seance. Spellbound, I listened as two formerly married lovers, one alive and one on 'the other side', lovingly talked to each other in French. It was astonishing and so touching.

Several more of these dual conversations took place between the other people in the room, excepting for Sarah and myself. Gertrude Lawrence, a one time iconic film star from the 1930s also communicated. Then Mickey's voice boomed out:

"Cor, blimey! Wot a busy night, eh? Well there is just one person left and I aint gonna introduce 'im cos he wants to do that imself."

There was an expectant silence in the room for about a minute. Then a very cultured English male voice spoke:

"Good evening to you all. I am delighted to have this opportunity to communicate. I believe there is one person here tonight that I wish to communicate with. She has worked ceaselessly within the healing organisation in which I was privileged to hold office as the first President. I speak of the National Federation of Spiritual Healers."

Until he spoke those last few words I had no idea who this communicant might be. Immediately I answered:

"Oh! My goodness, then you must be Harry Edwards. Sadly we never met when you were here on the earth plane but I have heard and read all about your wonderful healing activities. And I have visited Burrows Lea, your home and healing sanctuary at Shere, where I have also had the privilege of speaking. This is just incredible as you passed away quite some time ago."

Sarah then interrupted and asked:

"I know you help me when I am giving healing to my clients. I try to emulate your style of healing, Harry, and feel that you are supporting me. Are you?"

"The beauty of being this side of the veil means that I can help lots of people as there is no restriction here to my activities. It's very strange, really. People feel that because you are dead you don't exist anymore when, in fact, you are much more alive than ever you were before when you were living. It is all really rather sad. I carry on with my healing work now in so many more wonderful ways. And thanks to the organisation I was involved with at the start - The National Federation Spiritual Healers - and the dedicated input from people like yourself, Audrey, it remains healthy and of great service to many people who seek the support of spirit healing."

I responded by saying:

"Thank you Harry for all your kind words. I wonder, may I ask your permission, please, to be able to report this communication in the NFSH's magazine, 'Healing To-day' and also, perhaps, send it to the Psychic News as well?" I requested.

"By all means, my dear, please do so. Spread the word that I am not dead and continue my healing work much more now than ever before, as there is such a need for it on the earth plane. Thank you. I am leaving now. Good night to you all."

"Thank you very much. I am really touched by and very grateful for your presence here this evening. It is an experience I will always cherish."

Then Mickey took over, loud and clear:

"Well folks. That's it then. We don't 'ave time for anymore so off you all goes until next time."

The buzz of conversation began again and a chink of light from an open door helped us to adjust our eyes and to make our way out of the seance room and back into the sitting room, where tea and coffee was offered to us. When Lesley Flint walked into the room everyone applauded and thanked him profusely for being the direct voice instrument for those persons who were communicating from spirit.

Before leaving Sarah's home I spent time transcribing from her taped recording what Harry Edwards had said to me at the Seance so that I could send a transcript to the 'Psychic News' and write a report to be included in the next edition of the 'Healing Review'. The 'Psychic News' report took up all of their publication's front page which was heartening to see. I was just grateful that, once again, I had been witness to the proof of life after death and how we can still be useful and serve humanity.

Act 8 Scene 4:

Newfoundland

*'The ultimate lesson all of us have to learn is unconditional
love, which includes not only others, but ourselves as well'*
- Dr. Elisabeth Kubler Ross

In the spring of 1988, Francine Fleming, an NFSH probationer healer and film-writer travelled from her home in St
John's, Newfoundland, to attend an NFSH healer development
course in England. Francine told me:

"I have been given a grant by a Canadian TV company to
make a film about spiritual healing and I am thrilled by the way
in which the NFSH is teaching beginners to develop their healing abilities. In St John's we are devoid of any such training and
if you would be willing to come over I know, for sure, I could
guarantee a great welcome and a good attendance. We are, literally, starved of any courses such as I have just experienced."

Knowing I was taking a six month sabbatical in California, in
the Autumn of 1989, I replied:

"I could make a stop over in Newfoundland, on my way to
San Francisco, if you can set up all the arrangements."

"What about expenses, Audrey, air fare, fees, etc.?" Francine
queried.

"The air fare isn't a problem. I worked for BOAC for 12 years
and now qualify for concessional travel at 90 per cent discount

on all fares. You are providing accommodation and hospitality and any out of pocket expenses.

Francine was very happy with this arrangement and said she would put everything in hand upon her imminent return to Newfoundland.

Newfoundland has a raw beauty and bleakness about it and it was freezing cold when I arrived there in October 1989. Francine and her husband greeted me warmly at the tiny St John's airport - (in 2002 the airport underwent a multi -million extension) - and transported me in no time to the welcoming warmth of their home and after hot drinks and a good chat I was soon tucked up in my cosy bed where I spent a good night's restful sleep. The next morning became a guided tour of the local area and especially included the large, busy, sheltered part of St John's harbour which, historically. dates back to the 1500s. With its close proximity to Europe and fishing grounds it made it attractive to European fishermen.

Later, as the late Autumn sun peeked out of the dense cloud and temperatures rose a little higher, Francine and I walked, precariously, across flat rocks that sloped down to the North Sea and we sat for a while absorbing the vast and unfriendly waters below us, chilled by the strong wind that was blowing. Shivering I remarked:

"It must be quite challenging to live here as the environment seems so wild." She laughed and agreed it was, mentioning that she and her husband always headed somewhere exotic for their summer vacation in order to soak up the heat of the sun.

Arriving at the venue on the day of the weekend workshop 'Release the Inner Healer' to my surprise and apprehension, Francine had signed up 60 people and had arranged interviews with Canadian Broadcasting and TV networks, who put many questions to me about the NFSH and what I had come to teach. I spent a busy and extremely worthwhile two weeks in St John's and it is difficult to describe the overwhelming enthusiasm and appreciation the St John's students extended to me. They were thirsty for spiritual guidance and to be able to understand better the art and science of self-healing, distant healing, and how to be a healer.

The only blight on the proceedings came at the end when, the day before I was due to fly out to San Francisco, we watched the TV news reporting on the powerful earthquake that had occurred in San Francisco. With a sigh of relief I realised I had missed the earthquake by one day but rumours, fear, apprehension and speculation of another imminent 'quake' occurring began to negatively infiltrate my thoughts. I had to reassure myself by remembering that as a small child I had survived air raids and heavy bombing during World War II so what possibly could a 'little old earthquake' or two do to me. Nevertheless, I was somewhat relieved when I arrived safely back in Half Moon Bay, in California. Unfortunately, for my friends, the earthquake had shaken their home so violently all their crystal, crockery and ornaments had been smashed. Otherwise the house was fine.

During my time in Newfoundland I arranged some healing and counselling sessions in between classes and a young, single mother of a two-year-old girl, had asked to see me. Sally had been diagnosed with breast cancer and surgery had been recommended. All one can do, under such circumstances, is not to interfere with any medical diagnosis but to provide loving support and spiritual healing. As Sally had attended the 'Release the Inner Healing' workshops she intended putting into practise some of the supportive tools she had been taught, such as relaxation, meditation and self-healing. It was my intention to return to Newfoundland on my way back to England, six months hence, and Sally said she hoped to attend further workshops with me then.

Shockingly, another young woman suffering with acute spinal problems, confided in me that she had been consistently raped by her father and seven older brothers since the age of four. She was wearing a spinal corset and said she was in constant pain after several operations. It didn't take much intelligence to sum up the cause of such a miserable condition. One could only pray that in some way the explanation of self-healing would aid her future well being.

In March 1990 I visited Newfoundland again and temperatures were below freezing and, incredibly, I was able to walk out onto the frozen North Sea; heavy snowfalls had made travelling conditions extremely difficult and roads and houses were stacked with walls of snow. Even so, there was no lack of enthusiasm from the large numbers of students who had booked to attend the next stage of 'Release the Inner Healer' workshops. Francine asked if I could visit Sally in hospital before I left to travel back to England. Sally was quite ill and extremely disappointed that she would not be able to participate. Time was short, and I was only able to make two visits to the big ugly-looking hospital to do whatever I could to help her.

Sally was installed in a private, exceedingly gloomy room on the top floor of this rather ugly concrete hospital building, and when I entered there were three major items that caught my immediate attention and which disturbed me deeply: the room was grey and also windowless because the space for the original window had, unbelievably, been bricked up; the few flowers scattered about the room were not in vases but in formal arrangements like wreaths. Sally lay almost lifeless and nearly invisible in a cot bed with the sides up.

Smiling broadly I walked across to her and looking down said:

"Hello Sweetheart. It's so good to see you again. And I am so sorry you could not attend the weekend workshops. Never mind, though, I am here now and really pleased to see you."

Sally's pale face lit up immediately. "Oh! It's so good to see you Audrey. Thank you so much for coming. I was told your stay here was short and I wondered if you would have time to visit me."

I rolled down one of the cot rails and leaned down to give Sally a big hug.

"Of course I made time to come and see you and we have all been sending you lots of love and healing during the weekend and will continue to do so for as long as necessary."

Sally looked pleased and said "How kind of everyone. I am so lucky."

"All right Sally dear, this is what I propose to do. My first aim is to get this window opened so that you may have a view of whatever it is you would like to look out on."

Sally looked puzzled at my proposal and said: "That is not possible and I don't want to make any trouble. It would take ages to remove all those bricks and a lot of expense too."

"Don't worry Sally. There are other ways and means of opening the window but I do need your co-operation. Okay?" Sally tentatively nodded in the affirmative. I continued:

"All I need you to do for me now, is to make yourself comfortable, then breathe deeply and relax. Do this two or three times and relax and let go in the way we did when you came to the workshop last year. Now, allow yourself to be completely receptive to my voice and what I am saying. I know you can do this. Imagine for a moment that the window over there is wide open and the room is full of sunlight and that you can feel the warmth of the sun's rays bathing your face and body, filling your whole consciousness with a great sense of well being.

You are beginning to feel deeply relaxed, safe and comfortable. There is fresh, clear air flowing in now through the window. The air feels refreshing and uplifting. Gently take a deep inhalation of this purifying air and become aware of its calming and peaceful properties. As you breathe out, consciously relax and let go of all your fear. Become aware that all this emotion is being transmuted into the gentle breeze that sweeps it out of the window.

You are breathing in the universal life force of creation. So breathe in peace and love and breathe out any tension. The air in the room is glowing now with Angelic healing light, healing love, healing peace, sense the gentleness of this healing energy as it flows in and out of your consciousness on your breath. Every cell, every muscle, every organ, every system in your body consciousness is full of healing light.

Now become aware of how expansive and beautiful this room is becoming. It is full of healing light, it is full of creative energy, the view from the window is expansive now, you can create whatever you wish your view to be. There is no limit to your creativity. There are sunrises, sunsets, black velvet skies lit up by thousands of glittering stars, snow covered mountains, blue skies, lush forests, tranquil lakes, countryside full of colourful flowers, green hills, rocky paths leading to wherever you wish to be. A quiet sanctuary where you can meet your healing guides. There is no limit. You are in charge, you can change the view from your window to whatever you wish it to be. You now have a window on the world without restriction. Allow your mind and body to reap the therapeutic benefit of Mother Nature's creative healing vibration as they strengthen and support you on every level. Then, finally, come back into your room, now full of healing light, and give thanks for the blessings you have received until the next time you are ready to look out of your window on the world again."

Sally asked for a hug and said: "Thank you. That was a beautiful experience. I feel really happy. I was amazed at how easy it was to open the window and be able to look out on so many different places. I feel quite excited. That window is now a window on the world for me. It will never feel bricked up ever again."

Three days after I arrived home from Newfoundland I was fast asleep when the telephone woke me up. It was the middle of the night.

"Hello, who is calling?" I asked sleepily.

"Hi, Audrey, this is Sally. Oh dear. Did I wake you up? I forgot about the time difference."

"That's okay dear. Is everything all right?" I asked.

"Yes, everything is just wonderful. I am going home tomorrow for a few days respite, until my next round of treatments begin. I feel much stronger and have been walking round my room and down the corridor. I am so looking forward to being with my little girl again. My mum didn't want to bring her to the hospital in case it frightened her. She is only three. And thank you with all my heart for unblocking that window."

"Oh Sally, that is such wonderful news. I am delighted for you. Do keep in touch with me. Take care and have a happy time with your daughter and mother."

Act 8 Scene 5:

North Carolina and NFSHA Inc.

'We must accept finite disappointment but never lose infinite
Hope'
- Main Luther King Jr.

Undoubtedly in the 1990s there seemed to be a burgeoning interest across North America in spirituality, including a proliferation of New Age books, tapes, courses in channelling past lives, and even the possibility of living off just air by studying 'Breatharianism' or learning how to disappear and reappear! The prospect of which elicited a hostile reaction from the American Medical Association who resented any kind of alternative or complementary treatment that was being offered.

The time was ripe therefore in 1992 to establish an umbrella organisation in America and one such new establishment was claiming in a series of articles and advertisements that they were the National Federation of Spiritual Healers of America Inc, affiliated to the long established British NFSH, the New Zealand and Australian federations and others, and were seeking membership applications from not only spiritual healers but any kind of complementary therapist.

In my role as the British NFSH North American Liaison Officer in the USA at the time, I contacted the editor of a metaphysical magazine, an Englishman living in Atlanta, Georgia, who claimed to have incorporated the NFSHA, without bothering to seek permission from the British counterpart to use its title and then make false claims of their affiliation to us. He was unyielding to requests from our executive to publish a disclaimer, saying it was too late as his organisation had been incorporated as a non-profit business.

The legitimate concern we had was that it had taken years of dedication and responsibility for the British NFSH to make spiritual healing respectable and acceptable to the British medical profession and public alike and that it might be better to limit membership of NFSH America to spiritual healing or, preferably, consider using another title.

The NFSH America Inc launched its first Healer Conference in 1992 in North Carolina and invited me to attend as their Key Note Speaker. The conference attracted 175 people and a great deal of interest and enthusiasm for the British healer development programme, which I had explained in depth in my conference address, and requests were forthcoming that I should be invited to teach the training at future conferences.

During my visit I met a number of Reiki healers - a form of Oriental based healing about which, at the time, I was totally ignorant - who all agreed there was no comparison between the limited Reiki syllabus they had studied and the British NFSH syllabus. Consequently, over the next couple of years I travelled to different parts of America to teach spiritual healer development courses and was invited to become a member of the NFSH America Inc Board of Directors and to give public lectures and demonstrations of healing at the Atlanta EXPO Show at which I presented a two hour healer's workshop which 70 people signed up to. Subsequently, the same pattern was followed when I travelled to Florida, Houston, and California. Though tired at times by all the travelling it never ceased to be a joy and a blessing for me to share and exchange energy with so many lovely and loving students. The exchange of energy was a great blessing for me in my own continuous spiritual development.

In 1993 for legal purposes it became necessary for me to become an American Ordained Reverend and I studied healing and counselling correspondence courses with the Alliance of Divine Love organisation in Florida and received personal mentoring from other members as and when I could, including a religious session with my dear friend the Very Revd. Edward Carpenter, then Dean of Westminster Abbey, when back in England. You cannot legally practice or give demonstrations of spiritual healing in America unless you are an ordained Reverend. My ordination took place with others in 1993 at the end of one of the American conferences.

Sadly it was eventually discovered that NFSH America had not in fact been incorporated and was faced with numerous problems which were constantly discussed at their Board meetings which I attended. After three years of unlimited support from the British organisation and a great deal of personal Trans-Atlantic journeying by me to different venues to provide healer development training, the American organisation was disbanded and my association with it ended.

Act 8 Scene 6:

Florida

'It's not the years in your life that count it's the life in your years'
- Abe Lincoln

During one of my several brief visits to Florida in the 1990s to participate in Healing Conferences and teach healer development workshops, I was invited to attend an HIV/Aids centre in Miami and to work as a spiritual healer during afternoon and evening sessions there. This was my first encounter with sufferers of this serious illness and I was not quite sure what to expect. The venue was spacious and provided numerous kinds of support services that included hair and toe nail cutting, showers, therapeutic massage, communal areas for rest and relaxation, counselling, and a cafeteria.

In the large and lofty hall where the healing treatments were scheduled to take place, dozens of chairs were placed into a circle, for those able to sit, while the acutely sick were lying down on mattresses placed on the floor in the middle of the room. After a ten minute spoken relaxation and guided visualisation by the group leader, some ten healers, including myself, were allocated specific areas in the room in which we were to offer healing to those who wished to receive it. There must have been approximately a hundred sick people in total who were in various stages of this dreadful disease, all of whom requested our services. It was one of the most heart-rending situations in which I found myself placed and one of the most humbling and quite overwhelming experiences. The healthier clients were terrified to see how ill they might become, like the ones around them that were too sick to sit or stand.

An overwhelming feeling of inadequacy enveloped me. Never was I made more aware that I was only a channel for this divine healing energy and that it must be 'thy will be done, not my will be done' as I prepared to attune to my own and the client's Higher Self, asking for permission to connect to and be able to channel this energy of unconditional love to them. It was a healing experience like no other and I will never forget that despite their personal fears, grateful thanks and appreciation was graciously extended to me, in abundance, by those persons, some close to death, to whom I was privileged to offer healing.

When I left the Centre it was with a heavy heart and tears in my eyes. It is really hard to express what an amazing and privileged experience it was for me to witness such courage and appreciation by all those afflicted. There was an outpouring of such pure and unconditional love energy flowing in all directions around that vast room it seemed to reach into and touch the hearts and minds of everyone present at that time. Never had I felt so humbled in being able to channel spiritual healing.

Act 8 Scene 7:

Toronto

'Challenges are meant to be met and overcome'
- Liu Xiang

In March 1991 at the request of an NFSH English healer resident in Canada, who was setting up the Ontario Healers Network (OHN), I travelled to Toronto for the explicit purpose of teaching the healer development syllabus to some 50 of their members.

Travelling across North America was not always as glamorous as it may seem. One never quite knew, in advance, what kind of accommodation would be provided by the host. Accommodation in hotels was rare, except when being used as a venue for conferences. It was much more homely to be offered a guest room in the host's own residence but also sometimes very controlling.

The OHN organiser asked me, in advance, if I had any special requirements for my stay with him and his wife during my visit. I appreciated this gesture and explained I was a non-smoker and a vegetarian and preferred to be in a non-smoking environment.

Landing at Toronto airport in freezing rain the drive to my host's apartment was something of a nightmare as the windscreen constantly became a sheet of ice, despite having the heater blasting the glass and the windscreen wipers full on. After the long flight from England I was jet lagged and anxious to reach my final destination, have a warm drink and retire to bed for some much needed sleep. My host introduced me to his wife whom I was shocked and saddened to observe looked extremely ill and near to death; she was seated in an arm chair puffing away at a cigarette. A lighter and a pack of cigarettes rested on the arm of the chair. It was explained to me she had just come home from hospital having suffered an embolism in one lung, following surgery. I couldn't believe she was smoking! I was then informed there was nothing to eat or drink available so we would have to go to the store to buy something, which meant another car ride in the freezing rain and icy conditions, which we had just left behind!

Later, after some hot soup and feeling completely exhausted, I asked to be shown to my room so I could retire. This turned out to be a tiny box room full of all kinds of paraphernalia but no bed. To my surprise an old armchair was opened out and became a narrow bed which, unfortunately, stuck up at one end. My host sat on it and told me it would be all right once I laid down. There was no space to unpack or even hang up one item of clothing so everything remained in my suitcase. Some very tattered sheets were provided and here I was expected to sleep for the next week, and use the sitting room for private counselling sessions, in which his poor sick wife was chain smoking herself literally to death!

The following day embarrassed course attendees apologised to me, saying that many offers of comfortable accommodation had been forthcoming but were refused. After completion of the Toronto training two delegates, Richard Hayden and Howard Berry, invited me to Lakefield, eighty miles north of Toronto, for the purpose of leading some workshops for their local healing group members who were unable to travel to Toronto. Richard adamantly reassured me that his wife had prepared their comfortable and spacious guest room already in anticipation of my acceptance. My Toronto host offered to drive me to Lakefield a couple of days later, accompanied by his wife, but I put my foot down and insisted that if she came she could not smoke in the car. She stayed home.

My room at Lakefield was beautifully decorated with fitted wardrobes, a large comfortable bed and en-suite bathroom. It seemed like Buckingham Palace after what I had recently endured. Sadly, but not unexpectedly, my Toronto host lost his wife soon after I returned to the UK but he continued to dedicate his energy to making the Ontario Healers Association a great success.

One of the most spectacular highlights of my Lakefield visit was being able to attend a five tribes Native American Indian all day Pow-Wow with hundreds of natives colourfully dressed in their full regalia. Happily, I was able to dance for two hours to incredible drumming by these wonderful and colourful people and mingle to my hearts content. One tribe leader, employed as a social worker, explained to me that the unnatural conditions of reservation life for his people had caused many of them to become alcoholics and drug addicts. He invited me to his home on the reservation and blessed me by demonstrating the sacred Pipe Ceremony. He explained many of his people could not speak in their original tongue, and had forgotten their heritage, but his own grandmother had educated him in many of the ancient rituals and to understand and speak in his native language. He explained there were rehabilitation programmes in operation for anyone keen to overcome their problems and all kinds of support systems as well. The cruel conditions these people had suffered in the past and the virtual annihilation of their race, by subsequent American governments, was still inflicting deep and ongoing wounds even in this present generation.

Act 8 Scene 8:
Alaska

'Alaskan natives have healing practices that go back 10,000 years and today these practices are beginning to re-emerge'
- Stanford School of Medicine Ethnogeriatrics

Flying on Alaskan Airlines from San Francisco in October 1990 I peered out of the aircraft window that was taking me to Anchorage, in Alaska. Below lay the summit of my beloved Mount Shasta. My heart stirred with joy at such a sight knowing that it would have been impossible when hiking on the mountain for me ever to have reached the top. Now I was being afforded this stunning bird's eye view of the glistening snow capped twin peaks as the plane flew over them.

Although Audrey Sunnyboy's letter from Alaska took three months to arrive at the UK office it soon received prompt attention. Having found the former address of Head Office in the book she was reading 'We Are All Healers' by Sally Hammond, Audrey Sunnyboy - who is Athabascan Indian and Yupik Eskimo - wrote requesting distant healing for some of her family. She also enquired as to whether anyone from the NFSH could visit Anchorage as she was part of a 30 strong woman's healing group, the members of which flew hundreds of miles to be together in order to practise and discuss Native American Indian healing. Audrey's letter was forwarded to me in California to which an office colleague had cheekily added: "Fancy a trip to

Alaska?" I certainly did. One month later I was winging my way there with my face pressed hard to the aircraft window enjoying the moving spectacular landscape below of icebergs, snow capped mountains and ice fields.

Once owned by Russia, Alaska was sold to America for twelve million dollars in 1867, marking the end of Russia's efforts to expand trade and settlements to the Pacific coast of North America. This proved to have a devastating effect on the native Alaskan's lifestyle. With the influence of western materialism during three hundred years and the cruel disruption of both village and family life, sometimes by the forcible removal of children from their homes, to be 'westernised', the Alaskan Indians were systematically stripped of their heritage and culture and thus began to lose all sense of identity.

Angry, frustrated and abused, this gentle race of Inuit and Yupik people passed on their confusion and channelled their bitterness and pain into drug addiction, alcoholism, sexual abuse and suicide, all of which reached unprecedented levels in Alaska. At the time of my visit marijuana was still legal and the birth of babies to young teenagers was higher than in third world countries. Unsurprisingly, the Alaskan Native Health Board became heavily committed to fostering native self-determination in primary care, prevention and health promotion.

My host for my visit, Audrey Sunnyboy, was Programme Director for Traditional/Alternative Healing. Many of the professional women who attended my healer development workshops worked alongside teams of educated Native American Indians, travelling to remote villages to provide training in native heritage, history and self-survival. Sex abuse was chronic and some of the women I met during the course had, themselves, been abused and were recovering drug users and alcoholics. Their personal suffering and self-healing was nothing short of courageous and their transformation spurred them on to support other victims. Travelling to remote villages they set up 'Talking Circles' to hear what older people had to say about the situation, offering encouragement, love and support.

As part of a wide-ranging programme, some villagers adopted laws to restrict alcohol sale and assaults had fallen by 46 per cent and domestic violence by 56 per cent. The dramatic change among Iñupiat Eskimos was linked to a unique spiritual awareness programme designed by the Elders called 'Iñupiat Ilitqusiat' meaning 'going back to traditional ways'. Traditional dancing, drumming and chanting, proved to be very healing with people swaying to the rhythms echoing down the decades and centuries.

I found the environment of Alaska powerful and all-consuming along with the brave women I was privileged to share time with. One American lady had flown 800 miles from Barrow to participate in the workshops and broke down in tears at the conclusion as she didn't want to return there. She told me her husband worked on the oil pipe line and if they could tolerate the year-round twenty-four-hours of darkness and sub-zero temperatures for a couple of years, they would then be able to buy their own home outright. She felt she had gained so much from being in the group and also a much better understanding of the mechanics of healing.

Before my departure I was taken on some breathtaking scenic drives to see the huge icebergs and watch shoals of Beluga whales swimming and leaping out of the water, surrounded by breathtaking snow capped mountain ranges wherever we went. It intrigued me to discover that most of the icebergs were not white, as expected, but ice blue. Finally, I was invited by the women to participate in an evening of Shamanism in my honour, during which they drummed and chanted as they cleansed my aura by a smudging process. The Shaman (healer) took a blessed eagle's feather and wafted a smoky sage incense around my body and chakras, flicking away any negative disturbances and smoothing any ruffles. Then they drummed and chanted for me. Afterwards I was presented with a smudging kit which included the eagle's feather which I was instructed must never touch the ground and a beautiful Abalone shell in which to place the sage smudging stick of incense. It was such a blessed and memorable experience among natural healers.

When it was time to leave I left Alaska with a heavy heart but totally rejuvenated by the sheer power of the natural energy of nature and the beauty and courage of the wonderful women I had been privileged to share such a sacred time with. Yes, I thought, Sally Hammond's book which had inspired Audrey Sunnyboy's contact with the NFSH office in the first place was aptly named and, in my humble opinion, was completely accurate: 'We Are All Healers'.

Act 8 Scene 9:

Israel

'It isn't enough to talk about peace. One must believe in it.
One must work at it'
- Eleanor Roosevelt

In 1993 the MPH (Meditation for Peace, Harmony and Creative Living) organisation in Israel, formed a spiritual healing section which became affiliated to the NFSH. Many of their members had regularly attended our healing conferences and courses. On one of these occasions in 1996, Menhora, the President, invited me to speak and lead a healing workshop at a Peace Conference they were organising in Tel Aviv.

Menhora warned me not to mention 'Peace Conference' to anyone while travelling to Israel, so it was rather nerve racking being interrogated by Israeli airport security officials, on departure from London Heathrow Airport, who insisted upon knowing the purpose and duration of my visit and requested full details of where and with whom I would be staying. To all intents and purposes I was on a private visit. Upon my arrival in Tel Aviv, Menhora met me and then drove me to where I would be lodging with two of their members, a husband and wife, who had just moved in to a new apartment situated on a vast building site in the middle of nowhere. Noisy bulldozers, tractors and builders were scattered everywhere while a desert dust polluted the air which was unpleasant to breathe. It seemed like a wilderness; I knew I would never be able to find my way out of it without assistance and felt grateful that my hosts would be driving me to and from Tel Aviv.

The Peace Conference was a wonderful experience for me. I love and respect working with group energy, which is always special and challenging, mainly because we are all individuals until we begin to harmonise, blend and exchange our personal energy with one another and within the group's collective consciousness, when it is then amplified.

The spiritual healing workshop was enthusiastically received as it was an opportunity for novice healers to practise the act of healing on someone. Stepping into another person's aura is a huge responsibility and it is essential that the healer is well prepared beforehand in case, inadvertently, they pollute it in some way. The spiritual healer may have just finished smoking, or drinking, which negatively affects their out-breath, as they will be breathing out much darker colours. All of which weakens their ability to transmute any negative energy in the other person's aura.

These types of conferences usually generate a great deal of light, love, peace and healing energy; it is a blessing to be a part of it and to be able to send it out to places where it is most needed, especially Tel Aviv where the ongoing conflict between Arab and Jew was so rampant. Much as I wanted to it was impossible to visit nearby Bethlehem as it was an Arab area. Jewish cars had different licence plates to Arab ones so visitors ran the risk of their vehicle being shot at. Suicide bombers were active and generally speaking it was awful being so close to such hatred and conflict in the midst of a much needed Peace Conference.

It is always a blessing and a privilege to mix with other Speakers and delegates at these events. A Japanese Holy Buddhist

Monk, named Or Orlam, gave an impressive demonstration of energy work and we exchanged personal sessions with one another. Then, to my complete surprise, Or Orlam generously presented me with a brushed painting of a Japanese symbol of the 'Angel or Deity of Wisdom'. Or Orlam wrote these words on the back of it:

'Bodhisattva - Spiritual ideas of Mahayana Buddhism: A person who has attained Enlightenment, is motivated by Compassion, to remain within the cycle of re-birth and thereby to further the liberation of all living beings'

(On my return to the UK I carefully stored this precious gift in a drawer and some years later when I studied Reiki healing I realised how significant the symbol was to the Reiki system I was about to teach. I retrieved the scroll from the drawer in my bedroom, had it framed and hung it on the wall where I could view it from my bed. Then when I began to teach Spiritual Reiki I added this Angel or Deity of Wisdom symbol, at the appropriate student level, to the other Reiki symbols.)

Reiki is different from spiritual healing as it relies upon a system of ancient (holy) symbols to which the Reiki Master/ Teacher has previously been attuned and which affect brain waves. During a healing session the Reiki healer draws or mentally places these symbols into the client's physical, emotional and mental levels of consciousness.

During a lunchtime break from the conference I went for a quick stroll on a nearby beach, where I was approached by a lovely lady, who I shall call Grace, who had the most amazing head of rich golden hair which I likened to the mane of a lion. Grace was attending the conference and she gave me a warm and loving hug of appreciation and generously asked if she could show me around once the conference ended. I mentioned it had always been a dream of mine to visit the Qmran area where the Essene Brotherhood had dwelt by the shores of the Dead Sea and over periods of meticulous record keeping had scribed 'The Dead Sea Scrolls'. Generations later the sacred and hidden scrolls were fortuitously discovered by a shepherd boy when some of his flock had wandered into caves in the Qmran area. Grace informed me that coincidentally she was headed there with a young American visitor, Henry, and cordially invited me to join them and to stay overnight at her home in Jerusalem. It was a heaven sent opportunity that I could not refuse.

After informing my hosts and providing them with the details of Grace's offer it was arranged that following the Qmran visit Grace would make certain I caught the correct bus from Jerusalem to a designated destination where my hosts would be waiting to take me back to their home.

Grace introduced Henry and me to her larger-than-life flamboyant husband, Michael, a former actor until he lost a leg in an accident. He reminded me of Orson Welles. "Welcome home woman," he said in a very dramatic voice, "I am hungry and want to eat as soon as possible if you don't mind. And who are these people, may I ask, that you bring to our home?" Unfazed, Grace played his game, and introduced us. Later we enjoyed a happy meal together and retired soon after, knowing we would be leaving for Qmran at 3AM in the morning.

Driving out into the desert in the pre-dawn hours I seemed to be lost in time as I perceived the biblical-type scene of a shepherd in the distance tending his flock. The silence was profound and the desert seemed endless. Finally, we reached Mt. Mosada in time to climb up to the top to sit and look out across the Dead Sea waiting for the sun to rise. A memorable moment. It was hard to imagine that the Essenes had fled to this Mount for refuge from the Romans and had efficiently managed to create a habitable place with drainage, bathing areas, and other amenities for the community to live. Eventually, though, rather than be taken by the invading Romans they had preferred to end their lives by jumping to their deaths by flinging themselves off the Mount. Soon we were on our way to a Kibbutz where we rested and disrobed into bathing suits and hats in order to submerge into the sulphur filled water in the swimming pool. Easing myself into the pool I was immediately rendered into the horizontal position with an amazing feeling of complete weightlessness. After showering and dressing we were finally backtracking towards Qmran.

I was quite overcome with awe. I said to myself: "Am I really here, in this lonely and desolate place, surrounded by huge caves placed high in the chalky looking hills all around us, where the Essenes had lived, prayed, and communed with Angels on a daily basis through their seven fold peace meditations I had read about?"

The remains of parts of their dwelling places were laid out in a ground map of large stones and notices signifying the different areas. I made my way to the room of scribes and sat down cross legged leaning against an upright stone for support and closed my eyes in prayer and meditation. Afterwards I walked out across the stony rubble towards the caves while imagining I was the shepherd boy chasing after his sheep that had disappeared into these large cavernous hollows. It is impossible for me to describe what coming to Qmran meant to me. I stepped back into a timeless sequence of events. All I knew for absolute certainty was that I had been here before in another lifetime as an Essene.

Back once more in Jerusalem Grace and I took our leave of one another and I waved goodbye to her from the bus she had put me on. Unfortunately it was the wrong one and took me to the incredibly busy multi-levelled Tel Aviv bus station that looked more like an airport than the outlandish destination where my hosts would be waiting to collect me.

Attempting to keep calm and not panic I rummaged through my holdall for the piece of paper on which my host's telephone number and address were written. Realising I had no money I needed to find a bank. It was late and dark outside and hundreds of people were all making their way to different areas. There were lots of armed soldiers patrolling the terminal and I asked one of them to direct me to the nearest bank; it was situated three levels down in the basement and I ended up there in quite an agitated state in case the bank might be closed. Fortunately, I was able to draw some cash and then began to look for a public telephone booth which, of course, was up at the previous level.

The vastness of the terminal made it difficult to locate a phone booth and once more I asked an Israeli soldier for direction. Suddenly, I became overwhelmed with fear. I was all alone. It was late at night. I kept getting the answer phone when I called my hosts, realising they would be waiting - goodness knows where - for me to arrive. I decided to ask someone which bus I needed to take to get back home to where I was staying, One bus driver told me to get on his vehicle which I struggled to do as it was so crowded only to be told, intuitively, to get off the bus immediately. Pushing past alighting passengers I did manage to do so, only to wonder what on earth to do next?

Darkness having descended by now I was trying to gather myself together when I noticed a taxi area outside and decided to hire one to take me to the address I had written down on my piece of paper. Four or five taxi drivers starting peering at the paper and passing it around chatting in Yiddish and shaking their heads. Evidently because the address was in a new development area they had no idea where to find it. Suddenly, a rather robust taxi driver signalled for me to get into his cab which very reluctantly I did. He held the piece of paper in his hand and we drove off and out into the night. His English was very sparse so we were unable to have much conversation. Seated in the back of his cab I could hear him speaking on the telephone several times. Where on earth were we I wondered? We were out in the countryside: it was pitch black and there were no street lights. Suddenly the cab stopped at a deserted run-down petrol station and the driver started shouting at me. "You get out now. Get out now." I was terrified. With as much authority as I could muster, I told him, "No. I am not getting out here. Where are we anyway? I want you to take me to the address on that paper I gave you." Then he shouted again "get out now, get out now".

"Oh dear God, help me please" I silently uttered. Then, suddenly, I saw the headlights of a car driving towards the cab and stop. With great relief I saw my hosts get out of the car to pick me up. The taxi driver had apparently managed to speak to them in Yiddish on the phone, asking for directions, but instead they had chosen to meet up at this derelict petrol station. I have never experienced such relief. Back home in their apartment they asked if they could take me to Tel Aviv for dinner which I politely declined. I was stressed and dead tired and needed sleep as I was flying home the next day.

Six months later I was given the most appalling news. Grace and her husband had been found dead in bed at their apartment from carbon monoxide poisoning. I felt devastated.

Act 8 Scene 10:

Spain (Madrid)

'The aim of the wise is not to secure pleasure, but to avoid pain'

- Aristotle

Colin Bloy, who died in February 2010, was an eminent healer, dowser, author and founder of Fountain International. Colin invited me to teach some healing workshops in Madrid and said he would act as an interpreter as most of the people who would be attending spoke very little English and he spoke fluent Spanish.

To my everlasting joy I was introduced to Belen Ullastres, a talented artist and mother of three sons, who invited me to stay in her apartment where she lived in the ancient City of Madrid. Belen was also attending the healing workshops I was there to lead. She spoke a little English and we soon realised there was an inexplicable bond between us. It was as if we had known each other through many lifetimes. The course participants were mainly middle-aged ladies who all adored Colin and made no bones about it. I found him to be absolutely charming and could understand why he held such an attraction for the opposite sex. While teaching the workshops I found it quite challenging to be speaking in English and then having to pause while Colin interpreted the information into Spanish. It was a new experience for me but I soon got the hang of how to do it. For the subsequent healing workshops that took place Colin found other interpreters for me as he was in such demand himself to share his dowsing and healing expertise in various parts of Spain.

At the completion of another workshop just north of Madrid, Belen invited me to visit the country villa she owned, which was situated in a small farming community surrounded by lots of wide open countryside and farm animals. It seemed a real haven of peace and tranquility. To my surprise I found I was not the only guest at the villa. Gathered there to greet us upon arrival were three teenage boys who, with much love, flung themselves, one by one, into Belen's open arms as they greeted one another. Later I learned that these young men's parents had sent them off to lead a monastic life when they were aged around nine or ten. Each of the boys had harrowing stories to tell about the horrendous sexual abuse they had endured at the hands of the monks who were responsible for their welfare. Antonio, now aged eighteen, told me that aged nine he was destined to become a monk. Shortly after his parents had delivered him into the hands of one of the monks from the monastery he was to attend and he had waved a tearful goodbye to his parents, the monk ushered Antonio into his car, then drove off until they were in a fairly isolated area and stopped the car.

Antonio was then ordered by the monk to get out of the car which he did. It was then that the monk attempted to drag him into some woodland area. Terrified, Antonio said he struggled and ran back to the car where the monk then chased him round it until he could grab him. That was the first of many years of sexual abuse Antonio suffered at the hands of this and many other monks at the monastery. The two other teenage boys had similar horrific stories to relate. Belen was involved in socially rehabilitating victims of such appalling abuse and these young lads were to join us at her villa for some therapeutic relief. Needless to say I was pleased to be able to offer my services as a spiritual healer. The boys were keen to participate in the healing and meditation sessions and their English was quite good, which was a relief for me.

When Antonio was 20 he attended another one of my regular healing workshops in Madrid, accompanied by his beautiful girl friend Maria, who was studying art at university. At the conclusion of the three-day course, I was in the process of gathering up all my equipment when Antonio and Maria came to say farewell. Maria was smiling and started to thank me profusely saying how much she had enjoyed what she had been taught. Then, shyly, she handed over a picture she had felt compelled to draw while I was talking to the class, when she saw a golden ray of light in my aura and watched, spellbound, as the face of a Native American Indian guide appeared standing at my side, behind whom was an angel. The picture she had painted in water colour was really special and it is now in a frame hanging on my bedroom wall. What a beautiful gift I had been blessed with.

On my last visit to Madrid, Belen was very excited to be taking me to participate in an annual conference being held at the Valle de Los Caídos (Valley of the Fallen) commissioned by Franco in honour of the 1932-1936 Civil War. This vast complex, situated outside Madrid, had once been a monastery, which accounted for the long corridors of dismal cell like rooms, and also housed a small chapel. Hundreds of people were gathering excitedly in anticipation of the forthcoming psychic programme of Speakers and Workshops.

Looking out of the cell-like window in my bedroom I felt extremely depressed and began to develop a really unpleasant headache. The atmosphere around me seemed very heavy as if I was imprisoned. I felt fearful and apprehensive and wondered how a place that had once been a monastery could bear down upon me in such a manner. I lit a candle and recited 'The Great Invocation' and then cleansed the room with the incense I always carried with me. I wondered how I would survive having to sleep in this truly negative space for two nights.

Afterwards I found out that during the dictatorship of General Francisco Franco's reign in Spain this place had been built by condemned political prisoners, who were treated as slaves and subjected to much pain and torture. All of which seemed to be negatively trapped into the fabric of the building. My headache only cleared once I was back in Madrid in Belen's apartment and I was able to smudge my aura and carry out a self-healing and cleansing process.

Mallorca

Following a request from a British woman, Pamela Lyons de Arageo, living in Mallorca, for someone to come and teach healer development courses to her meditation group, myself and another tutor arrived at the Son Bono Convent, Genova, situated five miles from the cathedral city of Palma. The beautiful convent had amazing views of the sea from its terraces and was close to the Belvere Templars castle above the city. A Mother Superior and three Sisters ran the spotlessly clean convent with help from a local lady who cooked the specially requested vegetarian food, which was almost unheard of then. There was a small beautiful chapel on the premises.

The nuns could not speak any English but there were ways of communicating by sign language when a Spanish-speaking person was not around. Being elderly and suffering with arthritis they were keen to experience the laying-on-of-hands whenever possible and were sincerely grateful.

Some 40 English-speaking mixed nationality students signed up for the training programme, which was the first of many and which, subsequently, led to the establishment of a number of NFSH Support/Development groups on the Island over the period 1993-1998. Pamela became a very dear and close friend and I encouraged her to become a Tutor as I realised she had a lot to offer the healing movement. At first she needed convincing and a lot of persuasion but happily she took the plunge and eventually tutored the NFSH healer development programme for many successful years. Currently, she is now a Trustee member of the Board, responsible for assembling and editing 'Spiritus' the organisation's magazine. Pam is also a prolific and published writer in her own right.

Act 8 Scene 11:

Portugal

In 1998 I was teaching Spiritual Reiki for the first time at the Surrey Heath Adult Education Centre in Camberley, Surrey when, out of the blue, I received an invitation from Frederick Smith, a retired British funeral director, now living in the Algarve, to teach Reiki to members of the Portugal Healing Association of which he and his wife were a part. The chosen venue for the three day course was a wonderful residential Yoga complex, called 'School of Life', run by yoga teacher Sylta Kalmpath. There were acres of naturally lush habitat, where residential participants were housed in small cabins, which included the luxury of a bathroom and kitchenette. The main venue building was built entirely of polished pinewood the roof of which was dome shaped. It was pretty spectacular and could house near on one hundred people.

After flying into Faro airport where I was met by Frederick and his wife, I was somewhat shocked when he told me that some sixty people of mixed age groups and languages, had signed up for the three-day weekend. I was very mindful of the responsibility that would be mine and a little concerned that the number had exceeded my original recommendation of twenty. Two interpreters were on hand to relay the information I was to impart and, fortunately, there were volunteers to assist me with the practical work the students would be engaged in. There was nothing I could do about how challenging I felt it would be so

I asked 'Upstairs' for guidance and support and said to myself: "Oh well, in for a penny in for a pound."

The intense eagerness and commitment to learn about Reiki which the students portrayed during all the classes was really uplifting for me and I soon felt confident that the Portuguese translation of my English was flowing well. Especially evident when the students had to take turns to give each other Reiki treatments under my guidance. Incorporated into the Reiki system I also added all the additional subject matter which was part of the spiritual healer development training and which, in my humble opinion, rounded off the students' knowledge and ability much better than learning Reiki on its own.

Such was the enthusiasm of the Portuguese I returned a number of times to teach there and loved the fact that no matter what language we spoke or what country we were born or lived in, there remained this true potential to connect to and awaken the spirit within and a profound desire to share the gift of healing with other fellow humans. We certainly became as 'ONE' and I felt richly blessed and grateful to be meeting and exchanging energy with such lovely groups of people.

Act 9 Scene 1:

Adult Education

Surrey Heath Adult Education Centre in my previous home town of Camberley in Surrey promoted in their curriculum a number of alternative and complementary subjects and I was able to teach courses there for some ten years or more during the 1990s up to 2006 such was the public interest in spiritual development through studying and practising the art of relaxation, creative visualisation, meditation and self-healing. Eventually, in 1998, my course manager asked if I could teach Reiki because they were being asked for this kind of course.

Co-incidentally, I had already completed the Reiki Master/Teacher training. This system of energy healing was beginning to become immensely popular in the UK and, initially, also extremely expensive and I was disappointed by the lack of spiritual development included in the Reiki syllabus. In fact the content seemed really light-weight and not worthy of the exorbitant fees generally being charged at that time. The UK Reiki Federation had been set up to address this and I was invited to become one of their co-ordinators and contributed a series of articles for their magazine and taught some workshops at their conferences.

In agreeing to teach Reiki to students attending the Adult Education centre I emphatically decided it must be 'Spiritual' Reiki and to include much of what I had been taught and was teaching in connection with spiritual healer development such as:

The art of relaxation. Breath work. Essentials of grounding and protection. Understanding the function of the chakra system (energy body). The importance of personal attunement with the Higher Self. Meditation - A channel for healing. The different levels of consciousness.

(See section on 'If you want to be a Healer' in second part of this book).

Thus for the next six years an impressive flow of students, some of whom were from the medical and other professions, came to study Reiki and spiritual development with me at the Adult Education Centre.

Many students expressed their outrage at the very high prices some trainers were charging to learn Reiki. I had personally met a lady in Cornwall who was charging £10,000 for level one and two only. I queried how she could justify this outrageous sum but she was not at all deterred.

Adult Education charges were very reasonable. I received a modest £17.00 an hour fee for the weekend; not the huge sums of money that some other teachers were raking in privately which, to me, was very materialistic and unspiritual. The class number was set at twelve students and there was always a waiting list for places.

I embraced and taught the Usui Japanese system of Reiki, which is a very precise and structured healing technique, using certain symbols which represent a kind of tattoo on the sub-conscious body. My personal method of teaching Reiki included the spiritual mechanics of healing through the body's energy system. I extended each section for each Reiki level to ensure students fully understood and practised the Reiki hand positions on each other. Personally, I don't feel you can give someone a Reiki treatment without being spiritually developed yourself and able to understand the process of healing and the effects it will have on each other's energy body. Fortunately now there are some wonderful Reiki books available which address some of these most important issues.

One of my Adult Education students was intent on earning her living as soon as possible through offering Reiki treatments at a set fee but did not complete the full series of training sessions, which disturbed me. She began advertising for clients - prematurely in my opinion - and a few months later telephoned me.

"Hello Audrey. I do so wish now that I had listened to your advice and completed the full Reiki training before giving treatments to the public. I have been treating five or six clients a day for the last two months and I am feeling absolutely wiped out."

"Oh dear," I replied, "that is quite a lot of treatments for a beginner to be doing if they are not experienced in self-protection. The Reiki symbols cannot do everything for you in this respect. You must be in a state of spiritual or Reiki attunement before working in another person's energy field. If not you will be unable to transmute any of their negativity and find you are using your own magnetic energy which, over time, will deplete your energy system."

"Yes" she quietly agreed, "that is what must have happened to me. I feel totally 'burnt out'. I want to come back and start the Reiki training from the beginning, if you will agree to this. I have learnt my lesson the hard way and I am not afraid to admit it."

Over the six years of teaching and practising the Usui Reiki system of healing it was heartening for me to have been blessed with the realisation that most of the students who came to study Reiki were in the National Health Service working as nurses, radiographers and counsellors. There were also those who were counsellors, aromatherapists, reflexologists, massage therapists and dieticians. The Camberley Adult Education Centre was pioneering the introduction of complementary medicine and enabling those who came to my Reiki classes to have the opportunity to study the system in return for a moderate fee.

After completing Reiki 1 and 2 at the Adult Education a good number of students signed up with me privately to complete their Reiki 3 Practitioner level and, if invited to do so, the Teacher level. They were encouraged to attend my monthly Reiki support group where they gained more experience and confidence. Some of them became really good Reiki healers as well as teachers.

Act 10 Scene 1:

Retirement

In 2002 my daughter Ruth married and planned to make her home in California where her American husband lived and worked. Ruth loved England so much she felt the need to invest in buying a small studio flat we had found in Warminster to rent out. It made her feel she still owned a little place of her own in this country. While in Warminster I pointed out to Ruth that we were near to the town of Frome (pronounced Froom) in the county of Somerset which we had always bypassed on our regular early visits to Glastonbury and my curiosity peeked to go and check out the area. Frome is at the eastern end of the Mendip Hills and dates back to 685 when evidence of Saxon occupation was discovered there. As Ruth and I strolled along Frome high street my attention was drawn to a large notice in an estate agents window offering luxury apartments in the conversion of The Old Brewery, located in 6th century Gentle Street, which dated back to the Saxon period. Captivated by the prices and description of this new development, and the picturesque surrounding area, I made a mind-blowing instant decision to purchase, off-plan, an apartment on the top floor of The Old Brewery. Calculating on the difference between the sale of my Camberley flat, and the purchase price of the new one in Frome, would effectively gain me some much needed capital due to the price difference. At the age of seventy, this was just what

I needed as I wanted to finally wind down my work commitments and take life more leisurely.

My siblings, friends and students were all suitably shocked, for various reasons, when I informed them of my intentions, and I had to reassure them that I was only an hour and a half away by car.

Incredibly excited by what I had done I never in my wildest dreams could ever have imagined the three years of absolute hell that lay ahead of me after moving in to The Old Brewery. The sale of my old flat in Tudor Hall was stressfully completed just the day before I took possession of my new luxury home in Frome, which I couldn't wait to see furnished with the two new sofas and other items I had bought for the place. It was so much more spacious than the one I was vacating.

In retrospect, and being completely naïve, it did not occur to me that the builders were illegally requesting me to move into what was, essentially, still a building site. The lift wasn't functioning and my apartment was on the top floor. Carpenters, electricians, and painters were everywhere. There were cables spread all over the stairs, pots of paint, and all kinds of tools lying around everywhere. The site foreman convinced me into believing that two more apartments were soon to be occupied when I raised concern at being a lone occupant in such circumstances.

Suffice to say he lied to me, one of many lies that were to follow. Concerned by the situation Ruth postponed going to America for three months so as to offer her support in what was a frightening position for me to face alone. To all intents and purposes The Old Brewery was a building site and a work in progress, as well as proving to be an invitation to intruders, who carried out fourteen break-ins, due to the complete lack of any security. The builders were totally unconcerned for my safety and consistently pointed out that this kind of situation was normal when one bought off-plan, as I had. It was a perfectly miserable scenario which made me feel completely helpless. I repeated optimistically to myself that it couldn't get any worse, only better as time went on, but it did get so much worse.

One afternoon Ruth came whizzing into the apartment from town, where she had been shopping, urgently informing me that the roof was on fire just along from my bedroom, where I could see thick black smoke swirling around. She said the fire engine was already on site and we should go down to the main exit immediately. It appeared that some roofing contractors had been stripping the roof and burning all the bitumen and other rubbish, at roof level, which was totally illegal, after which they had left for the day. Residents with breathing problems alerted the fire service and police due to all the choking smoke spreading around the town. The police asked me if there was a Foreman or Caretaker on site they could talk to. Of course there wasn't. I gave them the name of the builders and they took it from there.

After all this drama Ruth and I returned to my apartment, made dinner, and settled down for the evening. Just before retiring at 11PM we noticed bright flames outside the sitting room window, shooting down from the roof, and telephoned the fire brigade urgently. Again we went down three flights of stairs, to the main exit, and were met by several firemen who were busily readying their hoses to, once again, extinguish the roof fire which had somehow self-ignited. This time they made a thorough job of it and, unfortunately, gallons of water entered the lower part of the building where the Master Carpenter had stored all his doors and other materials, which were now sodden.

Eventually, just after 1AM, with firemen crawling all over the inside of The Old Brewery, aghast that anyone could be in residence in such a building site, Ruth and I entertained a half-dozen of them in my flat distributing welcome cups of hot tea to them. The firemen were appalled that I had been forced into moving into an unfinished building which was unsafe and, in which no fire alarm system had yet been installed. They told me to expect their Fire Officer to call on me, as they were going to make a full report on the hazardous situation into which I had been placed.

The Fire Officer, accompanied by the Mendip Council's Building Inspector, called round the next day. He was embarrassed by what had occurred. I queried with him how it was that the flat had been signed off for occupancy. He said it was only signed off as having been completed, which was not entirely true, as my flat did not have its specified fire alarm system installed, and the lift wasn't functioning. He remained thunderingly silent.

After Ruth eventually left for California I felt really lonely and was made anxious by all the aggravation created by the builders on a day-to-day basis. Quite often some of the labourers were the worse for drink and one of them told me some were on drugs. I thought to myself if this was retirement I preferred to go on working. Stressed and depleted by the miserable circumstances I found myself in, my back succumbed agonizingly to a slipped disc and I could hardly stand up straight.

I was alone, with just a couple of new healer contacts I had made at a recent NFSH regional AGM, where a pleasant lady had approached me saying:

"I don't believe it is you Audrey. I did my healer training with you in Scotland twenty years ago, before moving down this way. How lovely to meet up with you."

After a lovely chat she gave me her telephone number which, under my present circumstances, turned out to be a life saver. Joan responded immediately to my cry for help and came round to see me. She administered a soothing back massage with lavender oil, after which she gave me some welcome spiritual healing. Joan was shocked at the unfinished state of The Old Brewery and made several supportive calls to keep my spirits up and continued the healing treatments. My back eventually improved and Joan and I became close friends which, at the time, was a God send.

To my dismay, I learned that almost all of the twenty-four other apartments in The Old Brewery were bought to let, so it was hard to get to know anyone really well or make any long-term friendships.

A young couple with a new baby moved into the apartment below mine which was owned by a British Airways pilot. Occasionally I would meet them in the lift and they seemed very pleasant but I was intrigued by a pungent aroma that seeped up into my kitchen around 6PM each day, emanating from their place below. I wondered what they could be cooking.

Another owner had let his large, luxury apartment to a youngish woman, apparently suffering from paranoid schizophrenia, her permanent resident female carer informed me.

Gradually more apartments were ready for occupancy and, like me, a lady on the ground floor actually purchased her place intent upon making it her permanent home. Wendy and I became good friends, jointly providing emotional support to one another when needed, against the total inconsideration of the builders, who were a complete law unto themselves.

Late one afternoon there was a terrible commotion taking place downstairs and police were forcing entry into the flat below mine, where the young couple were living. I had no idea what the problem might be. The next day the BA pilot who owned the flat invited me to come and observe the damage that this young couple had wreaked havoc upon. The young man had been growing cannabis in the bathroom which, when smoking same each afternoon after work, accounted for the pungent smell seeping into my place. The beautiful white carpet that had been laid throughout the pilot's flat, was now covered in burn marks from stubbed-out smokes, as were some of the walls. Someone had been ironing on the floor and there were singed iron marks all over the carpet. The police had been alerted by an outside neighbour that someone in The Old Brewery was shooting with a rifle from a window there taking pot shots. The young couple and their baby disappeared and never returned to The Old Brewery.

Meanwhile the female resident and her carer, who were now participating in a toxic lesbian relationship, were nearly killing one another with stab wounds on a regular basis. Police and ambulance crews were being called to The Old Brewery once or twice a week when these supposed 'lover's tiffs' took place. Blood from their injuries would drip down the carpeted staircase. What on earth was I doing living in such a place with such 'goings on' I asked myself? Summing up all my inner strength and faith that things could only improve now that the building was completed and the builders had left and most of the apartments were occupied, I breathed a huge sigh of relief.

Finally two-and-a-half-years on everything had settled down. The trouble-makers were gone and my friend Wendy and I sighed with relief. So it was particularly disappointing for me, when Wendy moved out into a stone built house with a garden. Fortunately she was just down the road so we could still meet up. Wendy was fed up with all the noisy 'night clubbers' that passed her ground floor flat at weekends. She also loved gardening, so her move made sense. The other residents of Gentle Street who lived in exquisite Grade II properties, were beginning to lose their patience when, each weekend, their peaceful environs were invaded by noisy and sometimes drunken persons using Gentle Street as a means of getting from one part of the town to another.

Fast asleep in my apartment one night, I was awakened at 2AM by the screeching fire alarm which seemed ear-splittingly loud. Staggering out of bed and donning a dressing gown, I opened my front door and peered over the balcony hoping to see other residents on the move. Everything seemed very quiet. It was the weekend when some residents usually took off somewhere or other at that time. At first I hesitated about going down the staircase to the ground floor. I was on the third level. Reason and sense prevailed though and I picked up my handbag and keys and ventured forth to the next floor below. Each floor had a corridor, the length of which was partitioned by a wall which contained the original Old Brewery windows inserted into it, behind which were other apartments. As I rounded the corner I noticed, with abject terror, that two strange men were viciously fighting one another using machetes. It seemed totally unreal, like a scene from a horror film, and in a split second I completely stopped breathing and my legs felt weak. Somehow I forced my feet to move and I made for the next set of stairs when, suddenly, the two men came violently crashing through the door, onto the landing, and were just about to fall on top of me, when one of the assailants pulled the other back. My legs buckled under me with shock and terror.

Upon finally reaching the ground floor I perceived an unknown man, very drunk, who was leaning up against the smashed fire alarm box and I noticed all the glass on the ground. He wore a yellow t-shirt covered in the blood that was pouring from his nose. Suddenly another resident appeared from his flat and I yelled at him to call the police.

In any event it wasn't necessary as the residents of Gentle Street had already done so. The Fire Brigade were also at the scene and rendered the screeching fire alarm silent. I informed the police of the machete fight taking place within the building and they radioed for a special squad who arrived some twenty minutes later with large reinforced perspex shields and they entered The Old Brewery to conduct a search. They found the machetes but not the two men who were long gone and who were part of a gang seeking some kind of retribution. The main entrance to The Old Brewery had been smashed open as those who were being chased sought refuge inside from the chasers who had, unwittingly, set off the fire alarm, creating shock, horror and havoc.

After being out on the street for nearly three hours, at 5AM the police said I could safely return to my apartment, which I vowed to put on the market and sell as soon as possible. My dream of having a lovely permanent home in Frome was well and truly shattered. I needed some peace and security. Where and how this could be achieved I knew not and I asked God to assist me in this endeavour.

Suffice it to say, Spirit intervened in a most fortuitous manner. I remembered the new independent living retirement homes that were now completed in nearby Glastonbury. Without delay I drove there and viewed about a dozen or so empty apartments before making my choice. My 'Old Brewery' flat was purchased by a company called 'Quick Move' at below the market price but my deal included no legal costs, free packing and unpacking of all contents plus free removal. In addition, a supplementary sum of money was paid towards the cost of my apartment by the building company, to enable me to afford the cost of the apartment I had chosen.

Beautiful, mystical, ancient Glastonbury situated in the legendary Isle of Avalon in Somerset already felt like home to me. I was familiar with the town due to all the healing courses I had taught there and the different spiritual events I had participated in at various times.

Communal living, however, initially proved to be a challenge for me due to the varying age groups and personalities of the other fellow residents. At times it appeared to be 'God's Waiting Room' when flat owners I hardly knew, 'passed away' in succession. It was a real lesson in understanding the weaknesses and strengths of everyone. Eventually I settled down and soon became involved in a full 'outside life' joining and leading meditation and healing groups, volunteering at Chalice Well Gatehouse, meeting and greeting visitors from all across the world. Chalice Well is describe as a 'Living Sanctuary' and one of Britain's most ancient wells, nestling in the Vale of Avalon, between The Tor and Chalice Hill.

Another bonus for me was to be situated just across the street from Glastonbury Abbey, which in 1086, when the Domesday Book was commissioned to provide records and a census of life in England, was named the richest monastery in Britain, until it was plundered and destroyed by King Henry VIII in the 16th century when virtually all the monasteries, friaries and nunneries, were destroyed in what was termed The Dissolution of the Monasteries. The Abbey is supposedly the burial place of the legendary King Arthur.

Now a haven of peace and tranquility, I feel really blessed in being able to walk the Abbey's thirty-three acres of magical grounds full of wonderful trees and to be able to sit, meditate and contemplate peacefully by the lake, looking across to Chalice Hill and the 500 foot Tor. Not forgetting as well, my project of writing this story of my life's journey and how Spirit brought me here to Glastonbury, a place both my daughter Ruth and I have always loved and admired.

Thousands of tourists from across the world visit Glastonbury every year to soak up and enjoy its history and all the incredible displays of colourful flowers that decorate the streets and buildings, for which the town has been given a silver award. Just about every kind of therapy is available from the plethora of therapists situated around the town and the cafe culture is prolific. I now feel very content to be settled in Glastonbury in what is described and accepted as this heartland of the 'Isle of Avalon'. It's like coming home.

I have often pondered the question of why I had to experience so much distress while living in Frome? Was it meant to be a stepping-stone to living in Glastonbury? Or was it from the perspective of 'shit happens' (as Alcoholics Anonymous puts it that something just happens and it is not our fault) or whether I was placed there for a reason? On reflection perhaps I was there to transmute some very negative energy from past and present situations. I accept too that the more your consciousness takes you towards the light it will also attract the darkness. And, thankfully, the light prevailed.

Act 10 Scene 2:

Conclusion

'The closer you come to God the more, surely, you will know him as Divine Love itself. The nearest of the near, the very dearest of the dear'
- Paramhansa Yogananda

In conclusion I truly believe that whatever role we may have been chosen to perform in this current stage show called 'Life, by the Head of Production, we should endeavour to determine our character's strengths and weaknesses as much as possible. Other fellow members of the cast will, by their performances, challenge our ability to express empathy, compassion and forgiveness wherever it is written into the script. If we put our heart and soul into this endeavour by rehearsing diligently until it becomes second nature, our heart will surely open and the energy of unconditional love will be able to flow.

While there may be much for us to pursue, ponder upon and achieve before defining who we really are meant to be portraying in this play called 'Life', I am now absolutely convinced that we can all be cast in the role of healer at one level or another. All we have to do is extend a happy smile to a stranger, embrace someone who needs a hug because they are lonely or lack love and make time to extend encouragement to a friend or family member where and when appropriate. Most importantly we must endeavour to always be open to embrace the Head of Production's continuing support, guidance and divine love, light, peace and healing by allowing time to 'go within' and listen to that 'still voice of the silence'.

And as the curtain slowly falls down upon this current production in which I have played a major role and you have (hopefully) been an attentive audience, I can positively look forward with eager anticipation to successfully auditioning for my new role in any other production that may be scheduled in the future.

Namaste.

Love and Blessings.

PART II

IF YOU WANT TO BE A HEALER

Introduction:

*'Pythagoras said that the most divine art was that of healing.
And as the healing is most divine it must occupy itself with
the soul as well as with the body; for no creature can be
sound so long as the higher part of it is sickly'*
- **Appollonius of Tyana d. (96AD)**

Paramhansa Yogananda explains there are three kinds of illness: Physical - Mental - Spiritual. Physical sickness is due to different forms of toxic conditions, infectious disease and accidents. Mental sickness is caused by fear, worry, anger and other emotional disharmonies. Soul sickness is caused due to our ignorance of our true relationship with God. Ignorance is the supreme disease. When one banishes ignorance one also banishes the cause of physical, mental and spiritual disease. Wisdom is the great cleanser.

My sincere aim and objective in Part II of Challenging Boundaries is to offer some encouraging guidance and support in understanding the art and science of 'spiritual' healing and to explain what it is we need to know and practise if we want to become any kind of healer of self or others. This guidance is based on a significant number of years of personal study and investigation with the renowned psychic energy researcher Lilla Bek and my subsequent tutoring of spiritual healer development courses to thousands of seekers from all persuasions, in many different countries over a period of thirty years.

This part of the book is a mini-course into the mechanics of healing through the body's energy system defining what we mean by using 'spiritual' energy and its importance when opening a channel for healing. A plethora of practical exercises are included covering the essential art of breathing, relaxation, meditation and visualisation all of which when practised regularly will enhance the body's ability to become stronger and more protective and make us a better healer.

Information about our etheric body and aura offers insight into the composition of consciousness and how our energy body functions through the chakra system. We will learn how to strengthen, protect and purify these vital, transforming energies through practising the appropriate exercises that are explained.

Spiritual development through the practise of conscious breath work, relaxation of both mind and body and creative visualisation and meditation exercises are all outlined in detail and will support our personal endeavour in attaining harmony and balance throughout the body consciousness. The art of attunement with the Higher Self, known as 'The Light of the Soul' incorporates the importance of earthing techniques, self protection and the expansion of consciousness.

Important guidelines on the use of hand positions during the act of healing and the difference between magnetic and spiritual healing are outlined as are distant or telepathic healing through the group consciousness which provide alternative methods of transmitting healing.

I suggest that you carefully read through and study the whole of part II before you attempt to practise any healing, even if it is only on family members or friends using the protocols I have laid down.

If, eventually, you feel encouraged to become a profession-al healer you will need full public liability insurance cover which is available as a student healer member of the NFSH Healing Trust whose healer development training courses I can fully recommend. They also have a professional Code of Conduct for their healer members and a national and inter-national healer referral service which is used by members of the public seeking the services of a well trained and certified 'spiritual' healer.

It is my earnest hope that, like me, you will aspire to becom-ing fulfilled in the knowledge that you are not just your body but that your body is in your consciousness which is infinite. Much Love and Light go with you on your healing journey.

Chapter 1:

Journey to the Light

'There is a Power that will lighten your way to Health, Happiness, Peace and Success, if you will but turn toward that Light'

- Paramhansa Yogananda

It is my belief that all 'spiritual' growth and practice has to come from deep within oneself and that when we are considering new information we must ensure that we are aligning with our own personal inner truth.

Basically, what this means is that whatever kind of alternative and holistic therapy we are practising on ourselves or someone else, whether it be Spiritual Healing, Reiki, Massage, Reflexology, Aromatherapy etc., it should be beholden upon us, initially, to know how to attune to and work through the Higher Self which resides in part of our higher consciousness and relates to the Soul energy. We will then be channelling the additional 'spiritual' healing power of unconditional love. Defining the word **'Spiritual'** in the dictionary it relates to **'affecting the human spirit or soul level as opposed to the materialistic or physical level. Being responsible for the spiritual well being.'**

Unconsciously we are learning to love and honour ourselves on a more 'spiritual' level. At such times it is not impossible for something quite remarkable to occur.

In my humble opinion there can be nothing more admirable or exciting than discovering your own innate ability to open a 'spiritual' channel for healing self, others and our Planet Mother Earth. Life is composed of highs and lows and we can all expect to experience our fair share of loss and disappointment as well as happiness in large or small doses, depending upon how spiritually asleep we are and what it might take to wake us up. I can personally testify that sometimes it is through the greatest emotional pain or trauma that something magical stirs deep inside of us and intuitively we find the courage, strength and support needed to survive and begin a self-healing journey to the light of understanding as to who-what-and-why we are.

My life took on a whole new concept after practising meditation when I was able to transcend from the Lower Self (the body) and connect to my Higher Self (Spirit) with the profound realisation that 'I am my body but I am not my body. My body is in my consciousness and my consciousness is infinite.' Meditation is a journey to the Light which, for me, shed new light upon the reality of knowing my 'True Self' or 'Divine Self' which is sometimes referred to as 'the light that we are' or 'the spirit within' - 'that part of us that is eternal: The 'I AM'. 'Divine Self' or 'Christ Consciousness' which Jesus embodied and practised as total unconditional love for all humanity without exception.

I felt I had awakened from a long sleep or had been let out of a prison of my own making only to discover there was so much more to me than just my body. Relentlessly I pursued the study of all the other parts of me that functioned despite my ignorance or intervention.

I became inspired and encouraged by the words of Frederic Lionel, a Teacher of the Ancient Wisdom who stated:

"Spiritual' Healing is the Highest form of Wisdom".

Chapter 2:
Spiritual Development

'As soon as you trust yourself you will know how to live'
- Goethe

There should be no limit to the way in which spiritual development allows us to fully realise our spiritual potential. Embracing ways in which we can awaken our senses and increase our sensitivity through the study of any form of healing therapy, meditation, relaxation and breathing properly, are true gifts of the spirit within. Each of us has our own range of sensitivities: a preference for music, art, or a greater affinity to the trees and flowers to name but a few. In spiritual practice, we are using our abilities to deepen our understanding, not by using the intellect but by using our intuition: the ability to pick up subtle feelings, to sense atmospheres, moods, tensions, harmony, and tranquility. We begin to sense ourselves more deeply. Subtle changes occur in the way we live our life and we begin to sense ourselves on different levels. We begin to sense other people observing their body language, the way they move, their eyes, their voice but, above all, we sense their presence, their vibrations.

As we become more attuned to the collective and creative power of unconditional love we become more consciously aware of the divine love and wisdom flowing through us, sensing how this energy changes us, relaxes the body and uplifts the mind and helps us to breathe more deeply, encouraging the release of toxins and opening us up to the divine power of 'spiritual' healing. We are also exchanging energy with the Cosmic universal intelligence - we call 'God'- and, according to our personal receptivity and sensitivity, will deepen our connection to all of the five senses and beyond. Conscious preparation before practising any kind of therapy requires self development and study of the art and science of relaxation and meditation which will increase our sensitivity.

We are all composed of different colours. Colour is light broken down into seven vibratory rates and we all vibrate differently. As our moods change so do our colours. If you were to look at the energy in a particular room you should be able to determine, intuitively, what colours the room is producing. For instance if the room in question was constantly used for intellectual purposes it would produce a lot of yellow colours and you would feel that. If the room was used for very negative purposes then it would produce a low-grade energy and darker colours which would make you feel heavy. When a number of healers or people interested in healing come together there is usually a lot of blue and a feeling of well-being. When we reach the point where our own field of energy is beginning to intuit and sense it is our intuition that guides us to certain places. And it will only be that area - the intuitive field - that will take you further. I can personally testify that as you do more healing the energy of intuition increases. Something very beautiful starts to happen. The right book or the right person appears in your life. The right ideas are given to you by someone and enormous changes begin to occur. Now, if you avoid coincidences, your life might fall apart because you are avoiding your development. If your life has already fallen apart then you can say yes you have been prepared already by having had to deal with such experiences. As this energy begins to evolve it will attract people to you and you may end up not just being a healer but also a teacher, which happened to me.

All of our bodies, physical, emotional, mental, causal, have energy centres, or chakras, also referred to as 'wheels of light', through which these 'bodies' must manifest. We are composed of minute, small, large and very large energy points; it is an electrical system. Although this system is invisible, with the progress of science we are able to manifest it more and more. For example, lasers being used in surgery and sound waves being used in food production to invisibly stir mayonnaise. These invisible levels do exist.

So what is the highest level of attunement and how do we know when we have reached it? We don't. We have to believe we can reach it by honouring and blessing our intention and accepting that the 'highest' within us is on different levels and will take us to the level to which we have spiritually developed through the practice of prayer and meditation. The key to the development of our gifts is relaxation. It is becoming an industry because there is so much tension in life. Relaxation 'opens' our energy centres. It enables the body to be supplied with more Cosmic energy, enough for us to 'see' colours. If you want to go on developing then you have to learn how to relax. Practical relaxation exercises are included later in the book.

As we progress, intuitively, self-healing will become more important to us. We will begin to understand that the body is the vehicle for the soul, a temple of light that provides safe sanctuary in which there is a centre of unconditional love. The human body is incredibly intelligent. It acts as a wonderful bio-feedback system. Informing us through pain or dis-ease that we need to change in some way or another. We must remember, though, when dealing with others, that we are only the catalyst and cannot force someone to change.

We will begin to honour and bless the body consciousness, its wisdom and intelligence. The more we understand how little we really know the more we will understand. If we are not aware we are nowhere.

'**Spiritual**' healing can only be undertaken when the healer/practitioner is able to attune to and channel energy from a '**spiritual**' level of consciousness. I believe we constantly have a choice. From which level do we want to function? This is vitally important. It has been claimed that we are all healers on one level or another. Which is true: comforting a child that has fallen over and comes to you crying with a bloody knee and holding them close and giving them love is one example of healing; caring for a sick person and offering them encouragement is another form of healing. There are so many loving and supportive ways in which one can offer kindness, support and understanding to another, whatever the problem may be or the occasion. These particular acts of love in action at the physical level, however, if constantly repeated, may eventually deplete one's physical well being. Hence we need to develop our potential from a 'spiritual' dimension within our true self and we need to take 'time out' for our own health and well-being and take the necessary steps to renew our personal energy body as often as we can through spiritual development.

Chapter 3:

Transforming Energy

'All healers should fully understand the mechanics of heal-ing and the energy system through which all healing is processed. If you want to build a beautiful cabinet without any idea of how to use the tools involved in carpentry, how would you succeed? If you want to become an optimum healer it is important that you become fully conversant with the energy body and the way in which healing works and your own part in the process'
- Lilla Bek

It is helpful to remember that whatever alternative therapy we practise on someone whether it be a massage technique, Reiki or spiritual healing, we must first understand the energy system involved before we can utilise and transform the per-sonal energy available to us on seven levels of consciousness. All therapies can be totally enhanced when we aim to prac-tise them from the highest possible level of attunement by en-deavouring to become more spiritually motivated to opening a channel for healing through the Higher Self. This requires us to practise deep relaxation and good breathing techniques in or-der for our physical energy to be transformed to a higher level. The creative life-force energy centre resides at the base of the spine where this energy is consciously or unconsciously trans-formed by us for whatever purpose we need it for, enabling that energy to move up the spine from the physical level into the other chakras that link into the emotional, mental, causal levels and eventually up to the top of the head and beyond, to the Higher Self, in order for the chakra system to 'open' fully and absorb more light.

If we are unable to control ourselves and do not have the ability to cope with the forces we are channelling then these forces are useless and could be destructive. We know from work on the Brain Mirror that chakras (energy centres) do change with the brain waves and experiments have proved that when the healer's eyes are closed and they concentrate on the energy centres certain kinds of brain waves appear. Brain Mirror tests have been carried out to determine how much a healer could 'open' and in some instances the Brain Mirror was unable to cope when the healer opened very widely.

As our auric space expands and we begin to link more effectively with our Higher Self aspect, our brain waves move into 'Alpha' and 'Theta' linking to the right hemisphere of the brain. These brain waves can only be achieved through deep relaxation of the body which then connects us to the levels of inspiration, creativity, tranquility, extra sensory perception and other amazing powers that exist at this level. We can usually recognise when our brain waves reach 'Alpha/Theta' and we may 'see' with the inner eye a deep blue or purple light or other colours, while meditating; another sensation may be a feeling of floating, expansion, or deep love and peacefulness. Sometimes we may feel a tight band around the forehead. This usually means the energy is becoming blocked so we need to relax more deeply and breathe better.

Essentially the first and foremost of the spiritual qualities we need to develop is attunement. At all levels of our being we are manifestations of the Creator, the Source; at our highest level we are 'One' with that Source. Attunement is becoming one with the Source itself. The more pure and perfect channel we become, the more we are then able to hold and radiate the divine light of unconditional love.

A spiritual or Reiki healer or therapist who is constantly engaged in a healing capacity with a plethora of sick clients needs to learn how to by-pass the physical level of endeavour and gain an understanding of the art and science of good breath work, relaxation of mind and body, meditation and attunement with the Higher Self, or higher levels of consciousness. When applying any form of spiritual healing the healer is acting as a catalyst, a support system, a 'release mechanism' for their client to 'let go' of all they no longer need or want to hold on to. When attuned to the Higher Self the healer will be protected and able to transmute any negative energy their client is releasing. This is spiritual love in action. No-one really heals anyone. We have to heal ourselves.

In other words an effective and developed spiritual therapist does not give of their own physical or magnetic energy and aims to channel spiritual energy that comes through them not from them. They accept it is 'Thy Will be Done - Not My Will Be Done'. They must understand that it is beholden upon them to 'cleanse' their personal energy levels as often as possible, both before and after a healing session.

Potentially we are all natural transformers of energy and are constantly utilising energy for everything we do in life, albeit to wash the floor, cook a meal, go for a jog, study science or the arts, become a doctor, nurse, teacher, therapist, counsellor or a spiritual healer. From where do we get this energy supply to keep us going? Quite unconsciously we are exchanging and transforming energy from everything and everyone around us: water, air, earth and, particularly, the creative and therapeutic life force energy of nature's trees, plants and flowers.

Essentially, we are 'Beings of Light' existing on seven levels. Light is a vibration which is commonly called an electromagnetic field and as spirit manifests into matter we are given a support system on earth so that we may function at the physical level during our lifetime. We do, however, remain connected to that part of us that is spiritual/divine and it is possible, through meditation and attunement, to connect to the Source of Light and rekindle our association with the part of us that is all-knowing, all intelligent. That part of us we call Spirit lives within us all. Even when spirit descends into matter it is still perfect. Spirit cannot be contaminated by anything that is imperfect. It is only at the physical level that we are able to contaminate ourselves. To heal the physical self, it is to spirit we must return in order to achieve balance and harmony at all levels.

Chapter 4:

Etheric (Vital) Body

'All things by law divine in one another's being mingle'
- Shelley

We must bear in mind that when we are working with 'spiritual' healing energy it will not only be penetrating and having a beneficial affect upon the dense physical body, but it will also affect the invisible ones as well, which make up our extended consciousness.

Circulating around our physical body we have an electromagnetic field of cosmic energy, invisible to most of us, composed of the aura within which is the etheric body which works in conjunction with and is the direct counterpart of the physical body. Some of us have a much larger etheric body than others, according to our evolution and our present lifestyle. The etheric body links internally to our chakra system and is an important part of the circuit of energy that is constantly functioning around us. Even if we have a leg or an arm amputated the etheric body remains intact. Hence the sensation amputees experience even though the missing limb is no longer there.

Without necessarily realising it when we sit in a room we are constantly exchanging energies with one another and changing the vibrations within that space. Our personal vibrations impregnate the chairs we sit on and the floor we walk on. These vibrations may be good or not so good according to how we are thinking, feeling and acting on any occasion. There may be times when certain people we encounter may inadvertently 'drain us dry' and we may wonder why? Quite unconsciously they have taken advantage of our abundance of energy and absorbed some of it for themselves. Or the situation could be reversed and we may for some reason begin to feel depleted. To avoid this situation we can personally renew our energy levels on a daily basis by making a conscious effort to boost it by a therapeutic routine of aura breathing exercises and meditation, examples of which are specifically outlined in other chapters.

If we make an effort to learn as much as possible about 'Who, What, and Why We Are' we can then begin to look at life in a more meaningful way and also from another dimension. The etheric body has been described by Alice Bailey as 'the archetype upon which the dense, physical form is built. It is through the etheric body that all energy flows, whether it is from the soul or from the sun or from a planet. The etheric body is the transmitter of 'prana'- life force energy.

The etheric body is also described as 'fundamentally the most important response apparatus which we possess.' It not only produces the right functioning of the five senses, providing five major points of contact with the tangible world, but it also enables us to register sensitively the subtler worlds when energised and controlled by the soul, the spiritual realms.

The etheric body is composed of interlocking and circulating lines of force and of points where these lines of force intersect, thus forming centres of energy. Where many such lines of force criss-cross each other we have larger energy transforming stations, known as chakras, or wheels of light, which monitor and regulate energy at the level it may be required by us at any one time. In addition, there are minor lines of force which create small and even smaller spiritual transforming points all over the body consciousness, such as acupuncture points.

It is vitally important for a spiritual healer/therapist to understand that we are composed of layers or levels of energy which are all part of an electrical field, known as the aura, around us. Our energy levels are composed of light particles, points of light, all over the body consciousness, which have been broken down into seven vibrations of light, akin to the colours of the rainbow, which create an energy transforming system. We all vibrate differently. Every person is different. As our moods change so do our colours/vibrations.

There are seven major energy transforming centres, known as chakras, which are rooted in to the spinal column (main circuit) in the physical body through the glandular and endocrine system which work very closely to the network of nerves. There are other major centres situated in the shoulders, knees, ears, hands and feet. Although the body is covered with minor energy centres and every pore of the skin has seven levels of consciousness, we concentrate mainly on the seven energy points situated down the spine from the top of the head to the sacrum. All these chakras, whether large or small, are transforming stations; they are like power points which transform energy from higher planes down to vibratory rates we are able to use on the physical body. Without these transformers we would not be able to exchange energy with one another or cope with all the different vibrations passing through our system e.g. tv, radio, satellite, computers, mobile phones, i-pads etc.

Quite naturally, throughout our lifetime – even before we become spiritually enlightened - this system is working for us. Without it we would be like a puppet on a string, limp and lifeless. Food, for example, is being transformed into usefulness for the body consciousness and, in particular, the brain. In our lungs we are able to transform prana (life-force energy) into the usefulness of breath – not just for the physical body but also for the etheric body. Cosmically speaking then, we have the permeating breath of God moving through us on every level.

Chapter 5:

The Chakra System and the Auric Field
Primary Colours: Red - Yellow - Blue

'We have all the levels of consciousness within us from the 'I Am' down to the physical and are already using the main rays'
- Lilla Bek

I AM - The Divine Self
INTUITION
WILL (Causal)
MENTAL
EMOTIONAL
ETHERIC
PHYSICAL

Situated down our spinal column are the seven major energy centres (chakras) from which we are constantly drawing and transforming energy at one level or another for whatever purpose we require. These main energy centres act like history books storing and recording all information from the moment we are conceived. In fact every spiritual point on the body is keeping a record of how we think, feel and act. All dis-ease is first registered in the etheric body hence, when giving spiritual healing, it is the etheric body we need to reach, as it is in that body wherein will lie the cause of the imbalance we are endeavouring to clear. Spiritual healing aims to balance and harmonise the body consciousness at all levels. We should always bless and honour this process.

COLOUR RED:

This chakra colour is linked to the Physical Body through the Gonads or base chakra, wherein lies the creative life force energy (or kundalini) from where we draw energy to raise our consciousness. Red feeds and strengthens the circulation of the physical body. It is an active energy which cleanses and purifies. It has the slowest vibration rate of 430–480 nanometres per second and its complementary centre is the green heart centre. As we draw life force energy from the red centre we must put our 'heart' into whatever it is we hope to achieve.

COLOUR ORANGE:

This chakra colour is linked to the Emotional Body associated with the abdomen and controls the adrenal glands, assimilation, and helps to strengthen the digestive system. Malfunction of the adrenals is registered here. The Essene community always blessed their food and ate it slowly in complete silence, believing whatever we are doing we will also be digesting. Orange helps to stimulate, balance and harmonise. It has a vibration rate of 500–510 nanometres per second and its complementary centre is the pale blue of the throat centre. Whatever we cannot stomach or digest in life needs to be expressed.

COLOUR YELLOW:

This chakra colour is linked to the Mental Body via the solar plexus and controls the pancreas. Physiologically it reflects the left side of the brain which specialises in logical/practical/analytical thinking. Medically it can indicate disharmonies in the organs such as the pancreas or the liver. Yellow is a refreshing colour, a natural tonic, which helps to activate and invigorate. It has a vibration rate of 520–530 nanometres per second and its complementary centre is the violet centre at the top of the head. The violet centre is linked to the right side of the brain which is more creative and can balance the intellect of the left brain through the practice of meditation and the creative arts.

COLOUR GREEN:

This chakra colour is linked to the Causal Body, also called the body of will, and the heart chakra, and controls the thymus gland – it is a bridge between physical and spiritual bodies – green is also linked to nature. The chakras below the heart connect to the 'Lower Self' and the chakras above the heart connect to the 'Higher Self'. Green is the Master ray of harmony and fusion. It is a building colour – a support for the heart. This centre is quite vulnerable. Over-emotional tendencies can affect the heart, also taking drugs, smoking, too much coffee or alcohol can have an adverse effect upon the heart and other chakras. A part of the soul resides in the heart. It has a vibration rate of 540–550 nanometres per second and its complementary centre is the red centre.

COLOUR BLUE:

This chakra colour links us to the thyroid gland in the throat. It is the centre of communication and how we express ourselves. It helps to activate and control metabolism. If the thyroid gland is out of balance it affects the whole body. The thyroid controls the lungs, bronchial and respiratory system and helps us to release properly. Blue is also a colour of natural healing for body-mind-spirit. It has a vibratory rate of 620–650 nanometres per second. Its complementary centre is the orange centre.

COLOUR INDIGO:

This chakra colour links us to the Brow and the pituitary gland which is the intuitive centre or the 'Third eye' which has been described as a computer storing all past, present and future events. It supports the right side of the brain which specialises in imagination, intuition and creative thoughts. It has a vibratory rate of 650–670 nanometres per second. It is the co-ordinator for the other centres.

COLOUR VIOLET:

This chakra colour is the seventh, final and outermost circuit and links us to the pineal gland and the seat of consciousness. The door to the Creator. It is the wisdom centre. Consciousness enters and leaves through this centre. It is the colour of realisation and links us to all possibilities. Through meditation this centre can rejuvenate the body for as long as it is beneficial to the soul. It has a vibratory rate of 740–750 nanometres per second. Its complementary centre is the yellow centre.

Working with the Chakras:

The 'Tibetan Master DK' through Alice Bailey says:

'Each of us is recognised by the brilliance of our light. The finer the grade of matter built into our bodies, the more brilliantly will shine forth the indwelling light. Hence nothing can prevent our progress forward if we but attend to the purification of our vehicle.'

Generally speaking different experiences and circumstances in life have a profound effect upon us and our chakras. We are multi-dimensional beings functioning simultaneously on different levels. So, if we want to be able to heal from the highest spiritual level, albeit utilising different therapies such as Reiki, therapeutic massage, acupuncture, aromatherapy, and reflexology, we first have to aim for the highest attunement possible to Spirit or to the 'Light' by '**opening**' the chakras. Energy can then be transformed from the base (red) centre, which has the lowest vibration, transforming energy up the spinal column, and 'opening' each chakra on the way, until the highest vibration at the top of the head is reached and we can then go beyond the physical level into deeper and more spiritual levels of consciousness. We are aiming to change our brain wave from the everyday, practical level of Beta into Theta which will then connect us to the divine level of consciousness.

The main chakra that must open, and is usually the last to 'open' fully, is the heart chakra, and this energy centre will only respond if we are very deeply relaxed and breathing consciously. Otherwise one is aiming to reach the higher levels of consciousness by opening and transforming energy from the base (red) chakra, up the spinal column, opening the other chakras, orange, yellow, green, blue, indigo and violet, in an endeavour to bring higher energy, over the crown, down through the chakra system. If the healer is not relaxed and not in a state of attunement, then the flow of energy may become blocked in the heart chakra and overcharge that centre. If the healer/therapist starts to feel sweaty or overheated, this may be a sign to desist from the healing act and focus more on relaxation before proceeding any further in order to protect the heart.

The 'I AM' consciousness, meaning the 'Divine Self', sometimes referred to as the 'Everlasting Self', the part of us that is eternal and 'The Light that we are' which is inside us – has to make us more aware of the possibility that exists for us to be able to change. All over the body are spiritual transformation points which are indestructible. If we think of the stars in the sky being a star system all over the body and that these star points have the means of being able to take energy higher, and we know that all over the body are higher points which awaken through deep relaxation and meditation, then no matter how sick we feel, no matter how negative we may become, there is within us a level so spiritual that we are still able to reach God or the

Christ consciousness of unconditional love. To reach these very high states may take time – aeons of it – but eventually we will make it. There may be many obstacles: the world is polluted by our thoughts, by bacteria, by dis-ease and disharmony. So part of our ability is to be able to transmute the negative forces into more positive ones.

The Auric Space:

The aura around us consists of a great cosmic fountain of energies coming from the Cosmos and from the earth linked with our own emanations and everything around us. The aura is different from moment to moment depending upon what is penetrating it and on the human level the exchange can be quite extraordinary. It is affected by how we think, feel and act, from moment to moment.

The auric space around us is constantly bombarded with negative energies and even more so when we work as therapists or healers as by so doing we expose ourselves to other people's pain, trauma, and misery. Fortunately, a more 'enlightened' soul has a stronger energy field or auric space with which to deal with these negative forces. No matter what kind of situation you know exists, negativity is usually a darker, heavier energy trying to take over a lighter and purer energy, and it has a profound effect upon the chakra system.

As the aura is composed of the emanations of the etheric body, it is very spiritual in its perfection. We are responsible for this space around us at all times. If we think or act negatively our aura becomes heavier. If we think or act positively, motivated by a desire to do and think good thoughts, then our auric space becomes lighter and purer. The aura is an incredible transformer and transmuter and responds as we, ourselves respond. The outer edge of the aura puts out 'feelers' and is the most sensitive part of all; the aura is never quite still. It can sense or feel what is going on around us and is a great protector or better still an efficient transmuter. We have to learn to expand our aura. Whatever we touch, wherever we sit, stand, or walk our footsteps are everywhere. We will have extended ourself.

The aura depends upon its strength and ability through our breath. If we are relaxed, healthy and well-balanced our aura can deal quite efficiently with any nasty thought forms or negativity which just hits the outer edges of the aura, where it is transmuted either by our own magnetism or the force of our energy. The negative energy falls away, useless, and earths itself into the ground. So, as healers we should be able to take all the negativity of another person and eventually be able to transmute it. We should aim to make our auric space strong and healthy and capable always of reflecting back Love, which is a very powerful force. You should then be able to transmute all the negativity of another person. It is important for us to strengthen the outer edges of the aura. As we offer ourselves for development and expansion of our awareness, and we begin to meditate and heal, we cannot avoid having to clear or transmute some of the more negative aspects of our own character. Ultimately we will have learnt how to automatically transmute any negativity because we have become a 'Reflector' rather than an 'Absorber'. The healthier we are the healthier are the vibrations we leave behind for others.

While visiting Atlanta, Georgia, I was asked to teach a class of some 20 massage therapists how to protect themselves while giving treatments to clients. To gain their State Licence they were required to carry out one hundred massage treatments, over a certain period of time. Unfortunately, this had resulted in most of them falling apart, feeling depressed and exhausted. Some therapists told me they were carrying out eight massages a day. Sadly, their training programme did not include self-healing, or self-preparation, nor had it cautioned them on how to protect themselves while working in such close proximity to the body consciousness of their client. They knew nothing about the etheric body or how to transform and protect their personal energy levels. Consequently, their auric field was absorbing whatever negativity their client wanted to release during the massage. They had become an 'Absorber' rather than a 'Light Reflector'. Ultimately, spiritual healing acts as a release mechanism and the healer has to be able to transmute whatever is being released by their client. The aura breathing exercise outlined in the next chapter strengthens, balances and cleanses the auric field. If practised regularly on a daily basis and before and after any spiritual treatments the aura will automatically transmute any negativity and act as a great protector. If possible try and breathe in and out through the nose while practising any breathing exercises.

Chapter 6:

How To Strengthen, Psychically Protect And Purify The Aura

We need to remember that the space around us is sacred. Correct breathing strengthens the whole of the auric field and helps us to release any tension from the physical body and pollution from the energy body that surrounds the physical body.

Weak breath = Weak aura

Strong breath = Strong aura

We breathe! Nature breathes! The Planet breathes! The permeating breath of God/universal consciousness is in everything! I should explain that the word 'God' for me means universal consciousness, or universal intelligence and the Light of the Soul'.

Weak breath = Contracted aura

Contracted aura = Negative thought forms

Penetration of any kind of negativity into our auric space becomes deeper and easier because the auric space becomes contracted and less vibrant. Negative people attract accidents and negative conditions. If we are agitated, exhausted, depleted or very unfit our energy body reflects this. It contracts, hardens, loses its reflective quality. It does this for protection. We must aim to make our auric space strong, healthy and always capable of reflecting back loving and positive energy, which is a powerful force. We should clear our aura and prevent others from polluting it. If we do this, we are also in a better position to clear other people's auras. In reality, if we do all the right things to maintain good health and well-being we should be able to deal with any negative energy and transmute it effectively.

THE AURA CLEANSING EGG BREATH:

The following breathing exercise is used to Centre, Balance and Earth higher energies flowing into the consciousness. It also clears, cleanses, strengthens and psychically protects the auric space by dissolving and releasing negative though forms. Used on a daily basis it will keep you strong and healthy.

It is recommended that you perform the cleansing breath three times: the first time to re-connect; the second time to re-lease and cleanse; the third time to recharge and radiate. Your thoughts should be focused on the specific purpose each time you do it.

Cautionary note: Anyone suffering with a heart condition or uncontrolled high blood pressure must not practise very deep breathing or breath retention.

Imagine that your body is in the centre of a cosmic egg and that you have seven of these expanding egg shapes around your body.

These represent the seven levels of the auric space from the physical, emotional, mental, causal to the spiritual levels.

The physical level is the first level and is the closest to the body. The other levels begin to expand further and further away from the body.

You will repeat the following breath seven times, commencing close to the body and expanding further away from the body with each new in- breath so as to be creating a wide circuit around the body.

Do not force the breath and breathe in and out through the nose. The in and out breath should be the same length. Really let go on each out breath to relax and release toxins from the body.

Conduct the exercise whilst stationery either standing, sitting or lying down.

Commence:-

You begin by breathing in Red up the back of the body from the feet to the top of the head and breathing out Red down the front of the body sweeping underneath the feet. Red is linked to the base chakra and to the physical body and strengthens circulation.

Next you breathe in Golden Orange up the back of the body from the feet to the top of the head and breathe out Golden Orange down the front of the body sweeping underneath the feet. Orange links to the abdomen and the emotional body and helps to stimulate and cleanse the organs around the abdomen.

Next you breathe in Golden Yellow up the back of the body from the feet to the top of the head and breathe out Golden Yellow down the front of the body sweeping underneath the feet. yellow links to the solar plexus and mental body and left-hemisphere of the brain. yellow is a refreshing colour, a natural tonic which helps to activate and invigorate that chakra.

Next you breathe in Green up the back of the body from the feet to the top of the head and breathe out Green down the front of the body sweeping underneath the feet. Green links to the heart chakra or causal body, also called the 'body of will', which is a bridge between your physical and spiritual bodies. Green also links to nature. Green is the master ray of harmony and balance.

Next you breathe in Blue up the back of the body from the feet to the top of the head and breathe out Blue down the front of the body sweeping underneath the feet. Blue links to the throat chakra, the lungs, and thyroid gland and helps to control metabolism. blue is also a colour of natural healing for mind, body and spirit.

Next you breathe in Indigo up the back of the body from the feet to the top of the head and breathe out Indigo down the front of the body sweeping underneath the feet. Indigo links to the 'third eye' chakra in the centre of the forehead. The 'third eye' acts as the co-ordinator for the chakra system and balances both right and left hemispheres of the brain. Breathing Indigo around the body is a pacifying experience which helps the mind to release the past and face the future calmly and confidently. Indigo is a supporting energy for imagination, intuition and creative thought. When connected to the highest source this chakra becomes a channel for light and insight.

Next you breathe in Violet up the back of the body from the feet to the top of the head and breathe out Violet down the front of the body sweeping underneath the feet. Violet is linked to the crown chakra at the top of the head, the outermost circuit and is an excellent cleanser for migraines and headaches. Violet is the colour of art and creativity which links us to our spiritual identity. Violet is also the colour of realisation which links us to all possibilities.

Next repeat this exercise by breathing in each of the seven individual colours up the right hand side of the body from

the feet to the top of the head and breathing out down the left hand side of the body sweeping underneath the feet.

Commencing and ending the day with this breathing exercise is highly recommended to ensure we are well balanced and grounded.

Chapter 7:

The Art of Attunement

Understanding and practising the art of attunement is of major importance to anyone wishing to open a safe spiritual channel for their healing therapy or when practising meditation, which requires entering into a higher state of consciousness. In part one of 'Challenging Boundaries' Act 3 Scene 10 under 'Spiritual Teachers' I referred to Max Cade's outstanding work on the Mind Mirror, which monitored the brain waves of healers while engaged in channelling healing to someone. The outcome would prove whether or not the healer was able to reach the 'fifth state of meditation' or the attunement level necessary in which to produce a Theta brain wave. At this level we can bypass the physical level of consciousness and reach a divine level enabling this higher energy to flow through us and into the person or situation we are engaged in. We need to practise and develop the levels of attunement regularly to become the best healing channel possible.

The following helpful guidelines and recommendations are outlined below:-

Stretching:

We should try to stretch as much as possible during the day and especially before commencing any kind of conscious breathing, relaxation, visualisation, meditation and healing.

Breathing for Relaxation and Preparation:

The aim of any breathing exercise is to remove tiredness and tension and to restore the balance of the physical, emotional, and mental bodies. Breathing well is important as is breathing correctly. Most people only oxygenate one fifth of their lung capacity through poor breathing. The deeper and longer the IN and OUT breath the more toxins are released from the body. We also release TENSION which means the body is not holding on to negativity.

Breathing Correctly:

There are two ways of breathing in, either by lifting the chest or by pushing down the diaphragm when the abdomen will expand – rather than the chest – as in the first method. Use the second method if you wish to remain relaxed. Practise that you are breathing by pushing down the diaphragm (breathe into the abdomen and expand it as if you were blowing up a small balloon and as you exhale the balloon deflates.) When this is automatic proceed with the following exercise.

The Exercise:

Close your eyes and 'listen' to your breath. Get in rhythm with the 'IN' and 'OUT' flow of your breath. As you breathe in and out through your nose count 'ONE'; you breathe in and let the breath flow and count 'TWO'. Continue until you reach 'TEN' and just before you let the breath 'OUT' count 'ONE' and start again. THINK OF NOTHING EXCEPT YOUR BREATH. KEEP WATCHING YOUR BREATH AND COUNTING. Gradually you will breathe more slowly and your hands, forearms, arms, shoulders and body will become heavier and heavier and LET GO! Any tiredness or negative energy will flow down and out through the feet into the ground where it will be transmuted.

Earthing Exercise:

Before we raise our consciousness we must focus on our feet, feeling them relaxed and heavy so that our physical body is properly grounded. Make the feet feel very strong. Imagine that underneath the feet there are golden rootlets of energy penetrating deeply into the earth. Imagine there is a flow of 'light' energy releasing from each of the toes, (each toe has a chakra point on the tip) lengthening the feet to twice their size. It cannot be emphasised enough that if we want to become a channel of divine consciousness, it is essential to 'earth' the physical body first, which is done through the feet. From the feet, move up and relax the legs, buttocks, abdomen, chest, heart, shoulders and neck. Linger over each place and breathe in healing light, healing love, relaxing and letting go of any tension. Then continue with the following:

Protection & Expansion:

Centre the physical body in an imaginative pure golden, protective, circle of light. Then gently breathe in the golden light and breathe out the golden light while visualising the circle of light expanding simultaneously above you, below you and all around you. We must remember that when we raise our consciousness the whole of our auric space has to breathe and expand. We fill it with this golden light as we breathe in this protective golden energy into our chakras. Our aura, or the space around us, has to be able to breathe and expand at all times so we should never place ourself into a sealed bubble as this would be constricting.

We then gently breathe into the red base chakra, filling it with golden light, then repeating this breath we work through the orange, yellow, green, blue, indigo and violet centres breathing golden light into each. As we move energy into the higher levels and the auric space begins to expand our circuit will become alive, vibrant, so it is essential we are safely 'earthed' beforehand. We all have an 'earthing' mechanism in the feet that grounds us. Just as any electrical apparatus, such as a toaster or an iron, can blow a fuse when switched on, if it does not have an earthing element, so too can we if we do not make our earthing as strong as possible.

When we are 'opening' up to higher parts of our being it is best to do so through our Higher Self. The Higher Self is linking us to all possibilities in accordance with our attunement and purpose. When we move energy up the spine to the top of the head or beyond we have to feel 'safe' and leave behind a landing stage in order for us to safely return back to a physical level of consciousness. By using our feet to ground the physical body we can bring the energies back down from the top of the head through each of the chakras:

Crown	-	**Violet**
Brow	-	**Indigo**
Throat	-	**Pale Blue**
Heart	-	**Green**
Solar Plexus	-	**Yellow**
Abdomen	-	**Orange**
Reproductive	-	**Red**

We then ground and root the energy through the feet into the earth. You may like to picture in your mind's eye, that each chakra is like the bud of a rose, which opens its petals fully when we 'open' each chakra, and closes down again to become a bud, when we close down each chakra. This process of closing down should always be used after giving a spiritual treatment or coming out of meditation.

Permission - Relaxation - Visualisation Exercise:

Find a quiet space within you and feel it becoming tranquil. Using conscious breathing begin a sequence of breaths. Commence by Breathing in Light... Breathing out Light... Breathe in Peace... Breathe out Peace... Breathe in Love... Breathe out Love... Bless and honour your body as you breathe in and out this feeling of light, peace and love. Sense your body letting go - not holding on, relaxing deeply and feeling at peace.

Sense your inner and outer space becoming tranquil. Fill your mind with the harmony of nature. Soft green grass, tall trees, a garden filled with flowers, shrubs and universal love. Visualise yourself walking in this garden, bathed in soft, warm rays of golden light from the sun, looking up to a clear blue sky above.

Feel the soft, warm rays of light as a loving energy that bathes your whole being. Sense the blueness of the sky as peace and tranquility. Feel yourself centred within the light with your feet touching the firm earth - grounding you.

Bless and honour your intent for the treatment you are to give whether it be self-healing, contact healing, or distant healing. Ask for permission from your Higher Self and the other person's Higher Self that through divine love and wisdom you may become a receptive vessel able to channel spiritual healing for the highest purpose and highest good of all concerned.

To return to the physical level we sense our body and especially our feet by stamping them. Bring your hands up in the prayer position over the head and gradually over the brow, throat, heart, solar plexus, abdomen, reproductive area. Then down the legs into the feet. We can then rub our hands briskly together followed by a really good stretch.

Chapter 8:
Creative Visualisation

Used properly creative visualisation can tap into Nature's therapeutic energy and is an important, if not essential, part of the healing process. Most healers I know, like myself, offer some form of relaxing imagery to help their client become more relaxed, attuned and receptive prior to the act of healing. A spiritual healer is endeavouring to open a channel, not only for themselves but for their client. Energy moves better through an open channel and can break down any tension or discord that might be present.

Creative visualisation has been likened to dreaming or imagining the kind of positive changes that may be supportive and transforming. It is an active exercise unlike meditation which is a passive one.

We all recognise that thought is very creative and lies at the back of everything we do from baking a cake, designing a new car, or creating new opportunities. Thought has to occur first. It holds the creative energy that sets everything into motion. Thus, if we look at our lives we should be able to recognise them as a projection or a product of our thoughts.

The idea that energy follows thought is recognised and is being used and explored in ever-increasing ways. In the field of psychology and psychotherapy many techniques are based on this fundamental premise. Creative visualisation is a programme for reprogramming the subconscious mind.

Nature's imagery is very powerful and has a deep, therapeutic effect upon the energy body. It is usually to nature that we physically turn when planning a vacation or need some 'time out', perhaps heading for the open countryside, full of lush green pastures, avenues of trees, rolling hills in the distance, above which the warm golden sun shines down from a clear blue sky; or, perhaps, walking on a sandy, white beach, scattered with sea shells, seaweed, drift wood, and tuning in to the power and strength of the ocean tides flowing in and out; or hiking through rugged terrain leading to mountain treks; or enjoying spending more time in the garden among the colourful flowers and plants. The choices are endless. I doubt there isn't a person alive who hasn't been deeply touched on one level or another simply by watching the sun set or the sun rise. Imagine, for a moment, the sky streaked with glorious colours of peach, apricot and golden hues as the sun sets into the night sky. Daylight with all the hustle and bustle has disappeared to be replaced by the passive, feminine energy of the night. A silvery moon against black velvet. Starlight. Rest. Peace.

A spiritual healer should never include anything aggressive in a visualisation and always focus on the beauty and colour of nature's healing impact upon a person's energy body. Utilising different symbols can move a person's consciousness to different levels. One can enter the garden of the creative mind and find everything in nature to relax and go deeper. Using nature in imagery takes one straight to the heart centre and the heart of creativity which utilises the intuitive right hemisphere of the brain. Keep the visualisation as natural as possible. I once witnessed a healer suggesting to a person that they should visualise the trunk of an elephant penetrating the top of their head and imagining that the elephant was sucking out all of their pain and misery! This is quite aggressive and much more left brain activity, which is not recommended.

Different symbols and colours in nature act as steps in the consciousness. A journey to the soul. The healer must be able to construct a visualisation that does not take a person too far, or that would make them feel unsafe. Their voice should be soothing and calming thereby instilling confidence and peacefulness in their client.

Ensure your client is warm and comfortable whether sitting or lying down. If they are lying down ensure their head is supported and their chin is downward tilted. Make suggestions like 'breathe a little deeper' - 'just relax and let go'.

Encourage your client to imagine their feet have lengthened and that they feel quite heavy. Suggest that underneath the feet they have roots (like a tree) that penetrate down deep into the earth that connect them to Mother Earth.

Focus their breathing on relaxing necessary parts of the body: feet, ankles, legs, buttocks, hands, arms, shoulders, neck, face and head. Use a soft voice. Do not rush.

Get the person who is to receive the visualisation 'centred' using their imagination. Suggest they are being bathed in sunlight, which is pleasantly warm, and which is creating a protective golden circle of light all around them in which they are totally centred.

When the person appears relaxed and happy the creative visualisation can begin. Keep the journey simple. Always commence the journey from a 'safe place' e.g. a small garden, a room near an open window, or a simple country scene sitting underneath a beautiful tree,

Remember you are connecting the person to their energy body, so start the journey using nature's warm colours such as red and orange, to 'earth/ground' their consciousness. Bring in yellow as the golden sun, which vitalises and protects, and nature's green mixtures to harmonise and balance and 'open' the heart. A pale blue sky connects to the throat centre of communication, use flowers or shrubs of indigo and violet for the top of the head.

The language of Symbols in Visualisation: (As taught to me by Lilla Bek).

Landscapes: Commencing a visualisation from a small garden, paved courtyard, or sitting in a room looking out through an open window creates a feeling of security. Never place a person in a wide open space as this can be very unsettling or at the top of a mountain which would move energy to the top of the head far too quickly.

Rocks: Including paths lined by rocks or rocky countryside can be very earthing and stabilising and also acts as a 'grounding' element for your client's consciousness.

Trees: Using trees creates stability and their roots help to ground the client's consciousness. The spine of the tree offers strength and support. Trees can also be used for expanding awareness, as the client is guided to 'reach up' and 'branch out'. This will also help their auric space to widen and become more protective.

Gates: At the beginning of a visualisation, gates can be used to 'open' the consciousness, as can doors; they need to be firmly closed at the end of the journey/visualisation.

Bridges: These will take you across to 'something new' such as 'new possibilities' or a new energy level. Don't make a bridge too steep or too high as this will bring in a feeling of insecurity.

Hills: Unlike mountains, hills will not 'lift' the consciousness too suddenly or too far. Make the hills appear soft and easy to climb.

Open Spaces: They may create feelings of insecurity, and space a person out or make them feel lost.

Cornfields: A symbol of harvesting. Never cut the corn down. It represents fulfilment. Suggest a walk alongside a field of golden corn.

Water: Using water takes the person away from solid matter. It can help things to flow more easily. Some people have a fear of being in or on water so to avoid any reaction, place them near a cascading fountain, creating myriads of swirling pools that reflect the sun's rays. Or sit them near a tranquil lake of calm blue water; watching the waves on the sea shore flowing in and out.

Mountains: For beginners, using mountains may take the consciousness too far. If used, it should be a gradual journey to the mountains. Never put a person at the top of a mountain to begin with. It will make them light-headed. You are taking them straight to the top of the head, the crown chakra too quickly.

Going Down: Caution should be exercised when going deeper, e.g. into underground caves or deep ravines, as these represent subterranean levels of the mind and/or going through into the person's psyche.

Spirals: Take care how you use spirals. Spiral staircases of wood are much more grounding, whereas silver staircases/spirals can take the person too far too soon.

Sky: This represents a womb for the world and is linked to the higher chakras and will take a person higher in consciousness. Before bringing in an expanse of blue sky you can stop someone from going too high too soon by adding a few fluffy white clouds or shield the sky with tall trees.

Rainbows: A complete rainbow from earth to sky will not only root the individual but will also take them higher and will help them to experience the colours within their consciousness.

Colours: These link to energy dimensions and to the energy centres: Red, Orange, Yellow, Green, Light Blue, Indigo and Violet.

Rose: Represents spiritual love. Also Mediumship.

Green: Neutralising and balancing.

Lighter Blues: Therapeutic, calming, cooling, very spiritual.

Darker Blues: Ray of inspiration. Links with Higher Self.

Silver: Takes one right across to the other side. Use warily and only in special situations such as terminal conditions.

Gold: Very protective. Links with wisdom. Undeveloped people prefer gold to silver when meditating or using creative visualisation.

Sound: Adding sounds adds sensitivity. Birds chirping. Water cascading from a fountain or waterfall. A soft breeze blowing. The rustle of trees. Crunchy pathways.

Below is a suggested creative visualisation that you can practise on someone. Or they can give it to you. Speak slowly. Don't rush. Give time for the person to sense and experience each stage of the journey.

Creative Visualisation Exercise.

NB: You can record this or have someone read it to you. Or you can read it to someone.

Make yourself comfortable and relax.

I want you to imagine you are sitting in a familiar house, in a pleasant, comfortable room, as you look out through an open window to the walled garden below. Dawn is just breaking. There is a peaceful stillness in the air, and the sounds of a happy chorus of birds welcoming the beginning of a new day.

Casting your eyes around the pleasant garden they are drawn to a cluster of luscious red flowers trailing down from a hanging basket, one of many, attached to the sandy coloured brickwork wall.

A gentle breeze flutters into the room, bathing your face and body in a refreshing uplifting manner. You stand up, breathing in the freshness of the day. You have a good stretch, and begin to make your way out of the room and down the small, wooden stair case to the garden below. You step outside onto a paved patio area while becoming aware of the warm, vitalising glow of the rising sun breaking through a cloud-swept sky. You take a deep, relaxing breath, and embrace the new day just beginning.

From the patio you step barefoot onto the lush green lawn which is still covered with some early morning dew, causing the soles of your feet and toes to tingle and feel connected to Mother Earth.

Walking round the garden you admire the many colourful plants, flowers, shrubs and trees that complement the hanging baskets on the wall. All the colours seem to blend so beautifully.

Red, orange, yellow, green, pale blue, deep blue and violet. You inhale nature's perfumery. Nature's beauty.

It is all so refreshing... So uplifting... So peaceful...

You follow the path to the centre of the garden where there is a circular paved area in the middle of which is a small fountain feature of cascading, sparkling water falling into a sunlit pool. Nearby, on the ground, are some brown sandals and you slip your feet into them now that your feet are dry. Sitting down on a white seat you observe and listen to the droplets of splashing water as each descends and creates an energetic whirlpool that reflects the colours of the rainbow.

The garden feels so peaceful. You soak up nature's beauty and uplifting vibrations, while listening to the sounds of birdsong filling you with joy and relaxation. The golden sun is shining brightly now and bathing you in a welcoming warmth as you gaze upward to the now clear blue sky above. A gentle breeze rustles the leaves on the branch of a nearby tree. You watch the leaves moving to and fro as the wind blows through the branches of the tree.

Rising from your garden seat you follow the path to the bottom of the garden and open the gate which leads into a leafy lane which takes you down a crunchy path, across a little stone bridge, under which a small stream gurgles happily along its way. From the bridge the path takes you alongside an inviting meadow. You open the gate and enter the meadow, which is full of green grasses mingled with wild flowers attracting a plethora of butterflies. The meadow path slopes gently upwards to the brow of a velvet green hill on which stands a great oak tree. You look all around taking in all the invigorating countryside spread out in every direction and alive with the healing energy of nature.

You seat yourself under the spreading, sheltering branches of this magnificent oak leaning backwards against its trunk so that your spine connects to the spine of the oak tree; you firmly place your own spine against the spine of the tree.

Spread all around you on the ground are the strong roots of this mighty oak which also penetrate deeply down into the earth below.

As you relax and rest with your back firmly supported against the tree's trunk you become aware of its great strength and power and the flow of vibrant energy flowing from the trunk and invigorating your whole body with new strength and support. You look upwards through the tree's branches observing the peaceful blue of the sky, and the warmth and company of the sun's descending rays enveloping you in a welcoming sensation of warmth and well being.

Relax, and absorb the peace and therapeutic healing energy of this special place. Remain here for a while now and enjoy the blessings of Mother Nature's love and healing light.

(*Give time for the person or yourself to enjoy the environment created. After a break end the visualisation with the following:*)

All is well. Be at peace. I am at peace.

You begin to stir a little now and in your mind's eye stand up and have a good stretch, then put your arms around the trunk of the oak tree, giving it all your love and blessings, while gaining more strength and support from it. Begin now to make your way back to where your journey commenced.

Then you make your way steadily down the hill towards the meadow gate, which you close firmly behind you. You cross over the small bridge, under which there is a shallow stream and walk back down the crunchy path of the lane that takes you to the gate that leads you back into the garden. You enter and close the gate firmly behind you and walk down the path past the sparkling fountain and make your way to the patio and into the house.

Your journey is complete. Your whole being feels refreshed, renewed, by the therapeutic and uplifting creative life force energy of Mother Nature by which you have been blessed. Slowly open your eyes and become aware of your physical body. Give your hands a brisk rub and have a good stretch.

Then stamp your feet on the ground to 'earth' all this new vital energy flowing within you.

Chapter 9:

Meditation - A Channel for Healing

'Meditation is not just an exercise in Silence. It is a meta-physical experience. As you connect to the 'Earthly Mother', and to the Source, of the Heavenly Father, you become a 'junction box' between Heaven and Earth'
- Frederic Lionel, French Mystic.

When we reach a point in our life where we are beginning to awaken to new possibilities and we feel the need to explore and experience our innermost thoughts and feelings at a much deeper level, the practice of meditation is paramount in this process. I like and quote what an anonymous American philosopher said:

*'What we are trying to do is **learn** enough to **change** enough to **grow** enough so that we can bring more **light** into the world. We have to do a lot of **changing** and a lot of **growing**.' He also said: 'What do we **gain** by crossing the **gulf** between the **earth** and the **moon** when we cannot cross the gulf that **exists within ourself.** That has to come first.'*

I firmly believe that meditation will assist us in crossing that gulf and inspires us to connect us more deeply to God, the Creator and Christ Consciousness. Meditation is a time for creating stillness in the mind-body-soul and will expand our spiritual awareness and is the key we are given to unlock the door to our inner sanctum, the indwelling part of us called the 'I Am' – the

Temple of the Soul. Written over the temples of ancient man were these vital words:

'Man know thyself and though shalt know God and the universe'

Practising meditation helps us to experience inner peace, self-awareness, and a change of brain wave as most of the time we function from the Beta level of consciousness, which is the rational, logical, thinking mind. In meditation we lift our consciousness to higher thoughts and feelings and can then 'open' a spiritual channel to our Higher Self for the purpose of healing ourselves and others.

Meditation is a passive exercise in gathering and focusing energy for spiritual healing, and to move into Alpha/Theta levels of consciousness, known as the fifth state of meditation, or the healing state. At this level we are more intuitive and can deepen our connection with the source of universal and unconditional love, which flows into our energy body and begins to transmute any disharmony or dis-ease that we need to release.

Through practising meditation we will become more centred and balanced within our personal energy body and more in harmony within all the levels of our Being. Meditation cleanses and purifies the chakra system and supports our endeavours to become a clearer channel for the healing energy to flow through us.

In meditation we will be gathering the creative life-force energy that resides in the base chakra, allowing that kundalini energy to 'open' the major chakras situated up the spinal column to the top of the head. The three chakras below the heart chakra, constitute the 'Lower Self' but once we have reached the heart chakra, and 'opened' it, through deep relaxation, we are then able to connect to our Higher Self. The level from which healing takes place.

A Practical Explanation:

The chakra system is similar to the gears in a car. We get into our vehicle with the intention of relaxing and taking a pleasant journey away from any hustle and bustle. We turn on the ignition, to start the engine, and then begin to move off slowly, placing the vehicle into first, then second and third gear so as to keep control as we increase the vehicle's speed. When the vehicle is running smoothly we move up a gear into fourth. Ultimately, we will find the fifth gear and be able to move into cruise control. In cruise control, we relax deeply and begin to enjoy the peace and beauty of the surrounding vistas. We experience a complete sense of freedom plus a desire to gather in as much of nature's creative life force available to us on this journey wherever it is taking us. We switch off the ignition and take time out to enjoy for a while the heightened feelings of inner peace and harmony.

When it is time to return from our journey we gradually take it out of cruise control, changing down into fifth, fourth, third, second and finally first gear. We then switch off the engine taking our time to check all is well with our vehicle. We have a good stretch and place our feet firmly on the ground. The journey is then over until the next time.

Dedication:

Meditation puts us into touch with the Higher Self, the 'Inner Teacher', the God consciousness within the part of us that is all-knowing and all-wise. When we meditate it is important to dedicate the energy we will be gathering. An example of how to do this is as follows:

Light a candle saying the Lamplighter Prayer which came out of the Lamplighter Movement and Network of Light, now linked to the Chalice Well in Glastonbury.

LAMPLIGHTER PRAYER

I kindle this little light on the earth plane

I dedicate it to the Service of the Spirit

I guard and cherish this flame as a living symbol

And an act of faith in the reality of the powers of light

May this ethereal light be a channel for the inflow of the

Healing powers of the Spirit

May the love of Christ permeate this building

Healing, protecting and warming the hearts of

all those who live in it or enter it

May the Being whom we know as Michael, Standard

Bearer of

The Christ, Wielder of the Sword of Light

Use this offering linking with all those who have lit the light

May the peace and the healing spread throughout the world

And the regions of the borderland.

So Be It!

Or you can choose one of the following dedications:

"I dedicate this light to a greater light and invoke its

presence here and now."

"I dedicate this meditation to open my consciousness to

Divine Love and Wisdom"

"I dedicate this meditation to becoming a better person,

a better Healer, or a better Teacher."

Meditation is also an opportunity to:

Look at relationships

Look at attitudes

Look at criticism, judgement, resentment

Learn to be reflective

Look at faults.

We are also learning to 'stand' what we cannot stand by becoming understanding.

There are many and varied ways to meditate.

You need to explore to discover what suits you, such as:

- Mental repetition of a prayer, mantra, words, or phrase
- Listening to calm music
- Watching the breath
- Concentrating on an object, a lighted candle (either within the mind or visually)
- Guided meditation

Suggested Healing Meditation

(This can be recorded and then listened to. Or you may wish to read it to someone or have them read it to you).

The following meditation exercise will open a channel for healing. Find somewhere quiet and peaceful. With your back well supported, hands gently resting in your lap with legs uncrossed and your feet flat on the floor.

Bless and honour the meditation asking that through divine love and wisdom you can open a healing channel to the angelic realms of love, light, and peace, and be connected and supported by your spiritual guides and teachers.

Repeat several times, silently, to yourself: "I AM A DIVINE BEING"

Bless and honour your body as you breathe in and out through the nose. Focus on your breath and feel your body relaxing and letting go.

Breathe in and out through the nose and relax. Breathe into any areas of the body that are tense, relaxing and letting go of any stress. Repeat this several times – watching the gentle inflow and outflow of your breath.

Breathe into the mind… relaxing and letting go of all unwanted thoughts, repeating this several times – watching the inflow and outflow of breath. Relax and feel at peace.

Repeat the mantra 'I Am A Divine Being'.

Sense your inner and outer space becoming tranquil.

Breathe in the 'breath of life' and new beginnings.

Breathe out all that you want to let go.

Breathe in the breath of creation, the life-force energy.

Feel it re-charging and replenishing every cell, every muscle, every organ, every system in your body consciousness.

Breathe in and connect your breath to the universal concepts of love and peace, repeating: "I breathe in Love… I breathe out Love… I breathe in Peace… I breathe out peace… I breathe in Love… I breathe out Love."

Send a blessing to your feet and sense the golden rootlets of energy beneath them deeply penetrating into the depths of the earth. Sense your feet lengthening, growing stronger and heavier.

Bless the 'Earthly Mother' and feel the connections to the earth as you go higher.

Bless the 'Heavenly Father' and feel the power of Universal Love enveloping you.

Breathe in the Light – Universal Light.

Breathe in the Love – Universal Love.

Breathe in the Angelic Healing Rays of Love, Light, and Peace.

Feel safely centred in a Circle of Golden Light which is creating a sacred space around you.

Breathe… Relax… Release… and Let Go!

Sense the healing love and light enveloping you.

Create and enter a quiet Sanctuary of Peace and Love.

Here is a place to contemplate…

Sense the Love… Sense the Peace…

This is the Sanctuary of the Higher Self.

Acknowledge this 'Presence' and ask that you will be guided and supported in all your endeavours as a Spiritual Healing channel.

Stay in the Silence. Invite your Healing Guides or Teachers to come forward… Seek any guidance and support. Listen to the voice of the Silence.

At the conclusion of your meditation come back slowly into your physical space. Sense your body, sense the physical space around you. Become aware of your feet. Stamp them on the ground. Rub your hands together.

Finally stand up and place your hands in the prayer position over your head, and bring them down slowly over the crown, the brow, the throat, the heart, the solar plexus, the abdomen and the reproductive centres. Closing down.

Then continue down the legs to the feet.

Finish off by having a good stretch.

Personally, I always light a candle prior to meditation and recite the 'Lamplighter Prayer'.

To develop an effective healing channel, it is beneficial to meditate as much as possible, as and when you can.

Chapter 10:

The Healing Room Environment

Raising the energy vibration of the healing space

It is well for us to remember that not only is it important in the healing process for us to personally reach a higher state of consciousness but we have to consider the environment of the room in which any kind of 'spiritual' healing or therapy is to take place. It should be clean and welcoming. If the room is a public one in use for many different purposes, then it will be more difficult to raise the energy vibration of that space unless it happens to be in a Quaker hall or some other such spiritual venue.

I was fortunate in that for a number of years I was able to use a room in my home set aside specifically for healing and meditation which made it easier to keep the room peaceful as opposed to a general purpose space that may have a larger degree of pollution.

Cleansing can be achieved by lighting a candle, smudging the room with sage or other incense, opening a window. Or just sit quietly and bless and honour the space/room and ask the Angels of Love, Light Peace and Healing to fill the room with their radiance.

Be aware that while most people don't object to the smell of incense some might have allergies or breathing problems. It may be advisable to limit this procedure to some time before and after a healing session takes place. The lighting of a candle is sacred as you are invoking the light. Bless, honour and dedicate the candle to invoke the light of the divine consciousness. I like to use the Lamplighter Prayer as mentioned previously in Chapter 9. It is a good idea to include some living plants in a healing room as they act as natural transformers of negative energy and also cleanse and clear the environment.

Lighting is important in the healing room and should not be too harsh as it makes it harder to relax. Appropriate soft and gentle music is an optional feature but may not always be suitable for some clients.

If healing is to take place with the person sitting on a chair then the chair should be comfortable to sit on and support the client's back.

If using a couch that is not adjustable make certain there is a firm and stable stool available to assist the other person in getting on and off the couch safely if it is at a higher level for them.

We are aiming to make the environment as safe and welcoming as possible to all concerned.

Chapter 11:

Conducting a Spiritual Healing Session for Practise, or Professionally, Using the Laying-on-of-Hands

Healer's Personal Hygiene and Preparation

Normally when an experienced spiritual healer is about to begin contact healing on someone it is usually because a request has been forthcoming and the person concerned has given their permission. A professionally trained healer member of the NFSH Healing Trust, for instance, will be insured and must conform to the organisation's Code of Conduct. Confidentiality between client and healer is essential. Ideally the healer should be clean, refreshed and relaxed and not a smoker, as smoking is an unhealthy habit. If the healer does still smoke then it is advisable that they refrain from doing so for at least two hours prior to the healing session. Not only will the healer be breathing out darker or dirtier colours into the client's aura, but if the client is a non-smoker they may find the smell of nicotine on the healer's breath to be unpleasant. Similarly it is best to avoid eating strong smelling foods, and eating in general, close to a healing session. This allows the breath to be fresh. It is also preferable not to give healing on a full stomach.

If, for any reason, the spiritual healer is very tired, unwell, or has not had time to prepare their own channel for healing, then it would be much better to refrain, unless it is an emergency or an unavoidable situation. Sadly, I have experienced receiving healing from unhealthy healers who, unwittingly, have taken my energy to heal themselves. Such a circumstance left me feeling absolutely depleted and as I got off the healing couch I felt as if I had aged a hundred years. Remember we owe it to ourselves to be as healthy as possible because the healthier we are the healthier and more vibrant are the energies we leave behind for others to experience.

Prior to beginning the healing session the healer should take a moment inwardly to request that through their own and the recipient's Higher Self the healing may proceed for the recipient's highest good and highest purpose.

Whether the client is seated in a chair, or resting on a couch, or in a hospital bed, the healer will be stepping into the client's auric space and there will be a unification of both auras. This is an extraordinary and intimate connection between the healer's and recipient's energy fields so it is really important that the healer's aura is vibrant, healthy, and full of light, able to radiate and stimulate the client's auric field and transmute any kind of negative energy that might be present. It is important to remember that the Healer is in a position of complete trust and must take this very seriously even if only working on a family member or friend.

Engaging with the Client

Welcome your client and put them at their ease. There is no need to ask them to remove any indoor clothing, other than shoes. Below are some suggestions for engagement and also to assist the healer in keeping a personal record card.

1. Ask them for their name and to explain very briefly why they wish to receive spiritual healing and whether they have seen a doctor and if so what was the diagnosis?

2. Reassure them that anything they may wish to tell you will be treated in the strictest confidence. Be sure to act empathetically and not sympathetically.

3. Explain to them that the physical body is an intelligent bio-feedback system which alerts us through pain and malfunction of any kind that we are out of balance or unconsciously holding on to something either at the physical, emotional, mental or spiritual level that seeks release.

4. Ask them what if anything they understand about spiritual healing and whether they believe in the power of unconditional love?

5. Explain to them that healing is very relaxing and that it is perfectly safe and that you will attune to a source of divine energy while carrying out the laying-on-hands working by gentle touch both on and off the body. Ask them if they have any objection to their body being touched in appropriate places? If they do then reassure them that healing still works if you don't touch. **(Touching the body means the healing energy is addressing any dis-ease at the physical level. When working off the body the healing energy is seeking out the cause of the problem in the etheric body at different levels)**.

6. Mention that the spiritual healer requests permission from them and acts as a transformer of divine energy through both the client's and the healer's Higher Self, which then flows into the client's energy field helping to balance and harmonise their personal life-force at all levels of body-mind-soul.

7. Reassure them that they will feel totally safe, relaxed and peaceful as the healing energy of unconditional love begins to flow into their consciousness.

8. Emphasise that as a healer they will never offer up a diagnosis of any kind if they are not medically qualified to do so.

In the past I have been asked whether a dead person might be doing the healing through me as they have known some healers who work with discarnate entities or guides during the session. Personally I emphasise that healing is universal and non-denominational and that it takes place through the intelligence of the Higher Self utilising the energy of unconditional love. It is common knowledge, however, that some healers do receive guidance from discarnate spirits who wish only to assist if possible and may in a previous life have had medical knowledge.

Relaxation is the key:

The first and essential aim of the healer is to help their client feel as comfortable and as relaxed as possible after explaining why they require a healing session. Put them at their ease and appear patient and understanding of their situation. We must remember to only be empathetic not sympathetic to avoid any longstanding attachment on either side.

My own preferred method of preparation always includes speaking an intuitive guided visualisation simultaneously to the initial channelling of the healing ray. The voice is such an amazing instrument for healing when you are in an altered state of consciousness. It can produce a higher vibration of soothing sounds and colours. For example if you guide your client into taking a peaceful, journey into the creative and therapeutic forces of nature, simply by suggesting they imagine they are sitting in or walking around a healing garden filled with lush green grass, colourful plants, flowers and trees, sensing the warmth of the sun shining down upon them from a blue sky, and being bathed in a feeling of warmth and well being, they will begin to relax, release and let go. This will ensure that their chakras will open and be able to more readily absorb the healing rays the healer is channelling.

These are only guidelines to assist beginners and/or to offer support to other healers.

Chapter 12:

The Laying-on-of-Hands

Prior to the Act of Healing:

1. Centre yourself into a circle of golden protective light.

2. Focus on your feet. Feel them heavy and grounding you.

3. 'Open' your chakras by visualising a beautiful rainbow inside you. (Opening means quickening or speeding up as you move into a higher vibration.)

4. Imagine your energy centres are being flooded with a sphere of pure cleansing light.

5. Breathe in rose pink – the ray of spiritual love – into the main chakras: red (base), orange (emotional), yellow (mental), green (causal), pale blue (communication), indigo (intuitive), up to the violet chakra (top of the head) sensing the energy in each centre glowing with unconditional love.

Let go! Let all thoughts pass through you! Let Go and Let God!

6. Ask to be used, through the Higher Self, as a channel for unconditional love and healing, e.g.

'Divine Love and Wisdom, guide, heal, empower and protect me as a channel of healing light and healing love. May this healing energy be for this person's highest good and highest purpose at this time. So be it.'

Experience the flow of unconditional love coming in over your head and moving down into your heart and into your hands.

Open the palms of your hands and visualise the palm chakras as little rose pink hearts, or a lotus flower opening its petals, as the hands fill with universal energy transforming the hands into hands of healing love – hands of healing light.

Sequence of Hand Positions for Chair Healing:

Step into your client's auric space and gently place both your hands onto their shoulders to indicate you are about to begin.

1. Crown Chakra: Violet. Seat of Higher Consciousness.

Without touching the crown raise both your hands up and over the top of your client's head for any further attunement with the Higher Self.

In some people the chakras may open very easily and in others they stick – like concrete! Commencing healing at the top of the head downwards activates the top chakra, which is vibrating faster, and these faster vibrations then activate in turn the lower chakras and assist them to 'open'. Starting the attunement at the top of the head not only means that you are working on the top chalice, which is a faster vibration and opens the lower (slower) centres/vibrations, but the crown and brow chakras are the co-ordinating energies for the whole of the chakra system.

I do know some healers start healing from the feet upwards which is not a good idea as not only have you not invoked the spiritual energy at the top of the head but when the client is releasing any negative energy during the session, it will be through their feet or through their breath.

Step to the right-hand side of your client and using both hands opposite each other continue scanning.

2. Brow Centre: Indigo, Intuitive Centre.

Working a little distance away from the body place one hand over the brow centre and the other hand opposite at the back of the head.

As this is the intuitive centre you can silently ask if there is any way you can be of help and whether there is anything you need to know.

Continue to scan down with hands placed front and back.

3. Throat Centre: Pale Blue, Centre of Communication and Clearing House for the Body.

4. Heart Centre: Green, Master Ray of Harmony.

(Also the bridge between Higher and Lower Self).

5. Solar Plexus: Yellow, Mental body.

6. Abdomen: Orange, Emotional body.

7. Base Centre: Red, Physical/Reproductive/Physical.

After this scanning down the body go back to the shoulders and affirm, for example, 'Divine Love and Wisdom. Guide, heal and empower me as a channel for healing,'

RIGHT-HAND SIDE OF THE BODY:

Next proceed to scan and strengthen the flow of energy between the following minor chakras:

1. Shoulder to Elbow

Place one hand on tip of shoulder and the other hand under the elbow.

2. Elbow to Wrist

One hand under the elbow and one hand on the wrist.

Move down the body.

3. Hip to Knee

Place one hand on the outer edge of the hip and one hand on the front of knee.

4. Knee to Ankle

Place one hand on the front of the knee and one hand on the ankle.

5. Right Foot

Place both hands on the right foot to 'earth' the energy.

LEFT-HAND SIDE OF THE BODY:

Repeat the same process now down the left hand side of the body. During this process the healer should be 'sensing' whether the flow of energy between these dual points of contact, is strong or weak. If weak then wait until the flow improves before proceeding to the next sequence. The reason for commencing on the right-hand side of the body is because it reflects the left-side of the brain which may be reflecting worries or concerns.

THE BACK OF THE BODY:

6. The Spine: Main Circuit.

Using both hands scan down the whole of the spinal column placing hands over each of the main chakras from shoulders down to the base of the spine. Sensing and checking for any overcharging or lack of energy in these centres.

THE AURIC FIELD:

7. Channel healing into the whole of the auric field around your client by moving away from their body both in front and behind.

COMPLETION:

Proceed now to complete the healing session by raising your hands over the client's crown centre. Give thanks to your Higher Self and ask that the healing process will continue to work for the client's highest good and highest purpose at this time.

Standing in front of your client gently stroke your hand across the shoulders and simultaneously down the arms, the hips, the legs, ankles and feet. Earth the feet by pressing down on them both. Repeat this procedure three times.

Then suggest to your client the following procedure:

1. Slowly open their eyes.

2. Rub their hands briskly together and have a good stretch.

3. Drink some water.

The same procedure can be replicated if you are doing couch healing. The only difference in the process being that instead of working sideways while using both hands when the client is seated, the healer will work down the front of the client's body using one or both hands simultaneously. (I sometimes keep one hand on the brow centre while scanning the other chakras). The main chakras down the spine flow from the front to the back of the body and vice versa. The front of the body being more connected to the physical consciousness and the back of the body more to the unconscious or collective level. **It is not necessary to ask the client to turn over on the couch.** As in chair healing you then address the right hand side of your client, starting at the shoulder to elbow, elbow to wrist, wrist to hand, then hip to knee and knee to ankle, ankle to foot on the right hand side of the body, then repeating the same procedure on the left hand side of the body.

During the healing session the healer will be guided by the Higher Self to sense, intuit, and generally receive some feedback, or otherwise, as balance and harmony is being restored to the whole of the client's body consciousness.

Remember that touching the body should always be gentle and appropriate. In my experience the client usually welcomes this part of the healing act if it is soothing and comforting. When you touch the body it is the physical level that is being addressed whereas when you work off the body you are working on all the different levels, physical, emotional, mental and causal.

On completion the client might want to share with the healer how they felt and ask the healer to share anything relevant. Only a medical practitioner can make a medical diagnosis.

It is possible for a healer to use earth energies in conjunction with their own electro-magnetic force, but the highest healing comes from drawing down and processing cosmic energy. If the healer is only using their own physical or magnetic energy they will probably become very tired and depleted.

The healer has to work on both the physical and etheric body and the first essential is that the healer should know how to 'open' their own chakras so that they can bring down cosmic light into the appropriate rays/colours/vibrations and then channel. In other words, the healer must be able to 'open' at the top of the head first to bring these energies through. To do this effectively we have to relax, release and let go of all tension, especially from the shoulders and from the heart. It is also vital that we breathe well.

We are supposed to be beautiful streams of energy. Regretfully, because of the daily pressures of living and the pollution and negativity in the atmosphere, we sometimes experience blockages in the energy flow which then creates an imbalance in the system. It doesn't take too long before this imbalance manifests at the physical level and is reflected in our state of health. Whether you are treating someone with migraine, skin problems, depression, or anxiety the dis-ease has originated first of all in the etheric body.

A healer ought to be able to sense intuitively where these imbalances occur through scanning with the hands the major energy centres and determining if a centre is depleted or over-energised.

While carrying out this procedure it is entirely up to the healer's intuition whether they want to touch the body or work slightly away from the body. It is good to include the auric space around the body so that the healing reaches the etheric and other levels. My personal experience is that the further away from the body I place my hands, the stronger the flow of energy emanating from them. Of course the body does like to be touched as in massage, reflexology and aromatherapy, and can reach a relaxed and meditative state. In healing, however, every movement should be gentle, especially over the head, and you may become aware that the Higher Self is bringing through warmer or cooler energies into your hands according to what is needed at the time. Cooler vibrations will soothe and calm, especially if someone is presenting a burn or unpleasant rash or wound. Warmer vibrations will stimulate and activate where necessary. A competent healer trusts in the Higher Self who is really in charge. The healer is only the channel for this divine energy. If, for any reason, either the healer or the client starts to feel too hot or sweaty during the healing session, this might mean that the energy centres are not fully open and there is a blockage in the flow. Take some time to relax and breathe well before continuing the act of healing.

If the healer is unable to bend easily while scanning the various chakras they could use a stool to sit on for this purpose. A recommended time-scale for a healing session depends upon the healer. If a client needs to talk and more time is required to relax them prior to the healing act then one hour would not be unreasonable. The healing act itself usually takes between 20 and 30 minutes. Nothing should ever be rushed which might cause stress or tension to either one of you. How many individual sessions of healing someone might need depends upon the healer and client's availability. The number of sessions would also depend on the client's wishes and the nature of their issue.

COMPLETION:

It is important to recognise that during the act of healing a synchronicity of alpha/theta brain waves will have occurred between the healer and the client. It will take time for the healer to 'earth' back into the physical level of being before bringing the session to a close. I bring my hands up over the head in the prayer position and then, slowly, bring them down the front of the body, over each chakra, proceeding right down the legs and then stamp my feet and rub my hands together and have a good stretch. Then I take a sip of water. After which the healer should first place their hands on each side of the client's shoulder area, which gives them an indication that you are finished, and which also transfers energy into the feet. On completion of a treatment the healer must bring the client's energy back down through the chakras and then ground and root the energies through the feet and into the earth. Then, working off the body, do a downward sweep with the hands, commencing over the client's head, and over the body to the feet. Give the feet a good rub. Ask the client to feel the weight of their body on the couch/chair and to slowly open their eyes. If seated on a chair the client should briskly rub their hands together, pat their knees and stamp their feet.

If couch healing then gently assist the client to sit up with their legs over the side of the couch. Ask them to have a good stretch and to briskly rub their hands together, pat their knees and sweep their hands down their legs and then rotate their feet moving and stretching their toes. Make certain they feel completely connected to their physical body. It is always a good practice to offer the client a glass of water.

After the session has ended let the client share with you how they felt during the healing and welcome their questions or comments. Before they leave the healing room be absolutely certain that they are steady on their feet and back into their physical level of consciousness especially if they are going to drive a vehicle.

NB: I sincerely recommend contacting the NFSH - Healing Trust Website for information about their healer development training programme. Their professional courses and ongoing mentoring and support provide the necessary guidance and development needed to practise healing.

Chapter 13:

Distant or Telepathic Healing

This is a powerful and very effective process to continue a client's healing from a distance, should they be hospitalised, or going away, or you have been asked to intercede on someone else's behalf. Distant healing can be sent individually by the healer, or in a group situation which, of course, amplifies the healing energy being transmitted. Distant healing should be carried out on a regular basis and should be considered part of a healer's spiritual healing practice. The healer uses the same channel and preparation as for contact healing when conducting distant healing.

In 1978 I was newly employed as a Secretary to the NFSH Administrator and when opening the daily incoming correspondence noted there were many letters from members of the public, both here and abroad, seeking a recommendation to one of our healer members. This concerned me because unfortunately at that time the NFSH did not offer distant healing as an alternative when a healer could not be found. So I requested and received permission to create a weekly distant healing/prayer group, using the Sanctuary at the office in Sunbury-on-Thames for this purpose.

Subsequently, every request for healing arriving at the office by post or by telephone was acknowledged by me and appropriate action taken. In the case of distant healing, each person's name or that of their pet cat, dog, or other animal would be recorded in a specially dedicated Distant Healing Book. The client was advised that distant healing would be carried out at a certain time and day each week for one month, after which a progress report was expected and a further new request to continue the distant healing for another month. There would not be a charge for this service but any donations to the NFSH Healing Trust would be very welcome.

I must stress here that any distant healing group or individual should refrain from listing any kind of illness against any names recorded. Only read out loud each named person. Repeating descriptions of an illness will create unwelcome negative vibrations which will affect the healing transmission.

Initially Don, myself and five colleagues formed this first official NFSH distant healing group meeting on a weekly basis. Using prayer and meditation, the seven of us aimed to amplify and project telepathically a flow of healing love and healing light to the individuals concerned. We could never have imagined that in the future thousands of names would regularly find their way onto an NFSH network of computerised distant healing group lists.

Working on the premise that 'thought' travels at the speed of light and encircles the planet three times per second, the collective healing prayers of the distant healing group members were transmitted telepathically to each person as only their name was read out from the healing book. At the end of each meeting we 'sent out the light' to the whole of humanity and Mother Earth using the prayer of 'The Great Invocation', details of which are given at the end of this section.

We must never underestimate the power and efficacy of distant/telepathic healing or consider it as being unfashionable or unrewarding compared with hands-on-healing. The renowned healer, Harry Edwards, (now deceased) stated that 'distance healing is the science of the future' as it can reach thousands in minutes.

In most instances the transmission of healing energy will, initially, be received into the recipient's auric field and the strength of this projection will largely depend upon what that individual is doing at the time it is being transmitted. If the receiver is 'tuned in' and more consciously aware at the time the distant healing transmission is taking place, their auric space will be more likely to instantly receive and filter the healing energy to the level where it is most needed. Due to the different time zones around the world, the recipient, for example, may be in a car driving to work or in their garden mowing their lawn. In these situations the healing energy will probably take a longer time to filter through and may be less effective, resulting in a weaker response. That is why telepathic healing should take place for each person on a regular basis to allow for this.

Distant healing requires the same spiritual attunement as contact healing in order to 'open' a spiritual channel through the healer and the client's Higher Self. In cases where the request for distant healing is made with or without the knowledge of the client, distant healing should be sent through that person's Higher Self for the highest good and highest purpose at that time; in which case the healing can then be accepted or rejected. It is helpful to remember that there is always a greater intelligence operating and this way it is more like a prayer – Thy will be done' – not 'My will be done.' I believe that distance healing opens a magical doorway to higher levels of consciousness and that the spiritual healer has the capacity to open these doors to love, compassion and inner peace. Unconditional Love is the greatest and purest energy and can only heal not harm.

One might query which is the most effective way for a healer to carry out a healing session either by the laying-on-of-hands or by distant healing? As previously mentioned in the chapter 'The Healing Room Environment' the professionally trained healer can take steps through meditation and preparation to raise their own consciousness and that of the room in which the healing will take place in advance of greeting their client. The mechanics of healing can then be conducted in the most efficacious way to personally balance and harmonise the body's energy system. Distant healing does not have this advantage.

The following Distant Healing Prayer was received by me in meditation.

Dear Father Mother God
Divine Source of all Love and Light
We ask that
As we gather here together
We may truly be receptive to
That wonderful emanation of your Love.
May we be able to link with your Golden Light
And draw it deep within our hearts;
And experience the Peace,
the Joy, and the Harmony
So that we may become true channels
Able to radiate this Light as a Healing Ray
To all those in need all over the World.
We ask for help and understanding
for all humankind
So that we may truly learn the lesson of Life
And unfold the Wisdom.
Help us to overcome greed and selfishness,
Corruption and cruelty.
Make us more aware of our responsibilities,
Particularly to our Animal and Plant Kingdom.
And may we ask for illumination
For all Human kind
In order to cleanse our planet
And draw to it the Light
And the Love and the Power necessary.
We especially ask for your Healing Rays to reach out to the
following people...
So now may we
Please make ourselves a Channel of Light...
A Channel of Love...
And radiate this Healing Force
to all whom we now mention.
AMC

THE GREAT INVOCATION

From the point of Light within the Mind of God
Let Light stream forth into the minds of human kind
Let Light descend on Earth.
From the Point of Love within the Heart of God
Let Love stream forth into the hearts of human kind
May Love return to Earth.
From the centre where the Will of God is known
Let purpose guide the little wills of human kind
The purpose which the Masters know and serve.
From the centre which we call the race of human kind
Let the Plan of Love and Light work out
And may it seal the door where evil dwells.
Let Light and Love and Power restore the Plan on Earth
So be it.

NB: For more details about this prayer, which was given out in 1945 and translated into 80 languages, contact the Lucis Trust web site and the link to The Great Invocation. Originally the prayer had been given to humanity by the Spiritual Hierarchy. From the writings of Alice Bailey she wrote:

'Light is the substance of things hoped for, the evidence of things not seen. The heart of the world is light and in that light we shall see God. In that light we find ourselves. In that light all things are revealed.'

The Great Invocation is simultaneously a prayer, an alignment technique, a meditation formula and a mantric invocation for Light and Love, evoking response. It embodies divine intent and summarises the purpose of the Plan for humanity. Concentrated, meditative thinking can reveal the underlying abstract idea in invocation. It can lead to new levels and dimensions of thought.

This invocation does not belong to any person or group but to humanity. Its beauty and strength lie in its simplicity and in the expression of certain central truths which all people, innately and normally, accept: the truth in the existence of a basic intelligence to whom we give the name of "God"; the truth that a great individuality, called by Christians the 'Christ', embodied that love so that we could understand; the truth that both love and intelligence are effects of what is called the Will of God; and the self-evident truth that only through humanity itself can the Divine Plan work out.

I first heard this prayer being spoken by Sir George Trevelyan at a Light Festival in Cheltenham, England, in the 1980s. Such was its effect upon me I have used it every day, ever since. Just a thought – where there is light there can never be darkness!

With the permission of the Lucis Trust they have agreed that the word 'man' may be replaced by the words 'humanity' or 'human kind'.

Chapter 14:

Group Soul Consciousness

There has never been a more exciting time than now and a greater opportunity in the history of our Planet and humanity's current evolutionary progress for any interested person to awaken more spiritually and manifest their soul's full potential through the group consciousness. So why not take the first steps towards developing a telepathic channel for healing through the group soul and join others around the Planet in networking the Angelic levels of Light, Love, Peace and Harmony in a true spirit of unification?

Everything in our world is changing rapidly around us. Time seems to be speeding up. We can feel ourselves being stretched on every level during our daily life as we endeavour to fit everything in. This is because our planet is moving into a higher or faster vibration – a more enlightened state of consciousness – and wants to take us with it.

This means we will experience a much more heightened state of awareness producing increased sensitivity and perception. According to the teachings of Alice Bailey expansion of consciousness is governed under natural law and comes in due course of time to every soul without exception. This brings with it a sense of purpose and a more insightful approach to self-discovery and a need to lovingly share and exchange this energy with others on a similar quest.

Never before has there been such an awakened interest in spiritual development and the collective realisation of giving life more meaning through service and honouring the path of the soul. **The soul is the vehicle for the descent of spirit into matter. The body is the vehicle for the soul and the bridge between soul and spirit.** We now have more direct and instant communication on many different levels. We can also develop telepathic communication on a soul-to-soul level. The Group Soul is drawing us into sharing and exchanging spiritual energy with one another by fusing the souls of the group into a unity of purpose and endeavour. It was a natural outcome of my spiritual development to become a group leader for spiritual development groups, using meditation, self-healing and distant healing.

All small groups of people naturally and inevitably arrive at some form of telepathic relationship between themselves and between personnel of similar groups. This is to be desired and fostered and should rightly increase. Mother Earth and all her Kingdoms are out of balance. To heal the planet we must first heal ourselves. We can participate and play an exciting role in the planetary preparation for this big shift in consciousness through the group soul. We are, after all, a microcosm of the macrocosm and act as universal mirrors for one another. Through spiritual development groups we can learn how to become telepathic healers and Light transformers; we can learn to heal ourselves and others; we can heal our Planet; we can connect more telepathically through the group consciousness by invoking the Divine Light of Unconditional Love. We can create a new world order.

It is so important now for everyone to boost their energy levels and raise their consciousness to a more ascended level.

Already this is beginning to take place through inner development. Inherently we want to become more in tune with personal offering and to create more balance and harmony in our lives. There was never a greater opportunity for the group soul to dedicate and bless that intent and motivation to improve our Higher Will. So many of us are already looking at ways to balance and harmonise our thoughts, feelings and actions. There is a new humanity emerging with a new sense of purpose, inner power and intuition.

Networking the Light

To create new pathways for the soul we must look at the path we are on now. Through inner attunement with the group soul we can create harmony where there is disharmony. To create a gateway to a new sense of purpose and intent we have to bless and honour our new thoughts, feelings and actions. How so?

From my long experience I believe that one effective way of speeding up this process is to consciously harness and amplify the combined energy of the group soul and take on the role of a spiritual group leader and become an Ambassador for Global Healing. What an exciting thought! Just think for a moment. By forming a spiritual development group to 'network the Light' on the earth plane we will, effectively, be creating a link to the great collective consciousness and universal flow of unconditional love. We can personally amplify and enhance our own spiritual intent utilising the combined and supportive energy of the group soul.

Through the group consciousness we can develop a telepathic channel able to receive, radiate and reflect the Cosmic Light of Healing to Humanity and Mother Earth.

There is nothing to prevent us from telepathically linking to a Global Network of Light Groups, on the conscious and unconscious planes, using them effectively to harness and generate the collective energy of Divine Love and Wisdom. We can invoke a healing vibration that will constantly surround and protect our 'Earth Mother' and all her Kingdoms. There is a great need for more spiritual development groups. There are so many seekers looking for fellow guidance through spiritual group endeavour. We can all serve humanity and this planet by responding positively to this 'wake-up' call from our Earth Mother. Undoubtedly, working through the group consciousness amplifies our intent and purpose.

Acquiring Leadership Skills

Forming a spiritual development group and becoming a group leader is an honourable and empowering process. Acquiring leadership skills requires a personal commitment and devotion to the call of service. It is not an easy task to point the way for others but a compelling and very worthwhile one. If one is guided then it is easier to guide. We have to be 'open' to the manifestation of inner truth to become a true example of the truth. It means we are acting as a catalyst for others to awaken to the true meaning of life. Life itself is the greatest lesson in leadership. It most certainly is true in my experience.

We are being led in so many directions through so many experiences. Someone has to lead those who do not know how to follow, who lack purpose, who deny their multi-dimensional consciousness. A spiritual group leader has to be true to Self, connect with the Higher Self – the true Leader – and then submit to that Leadership.

In becoming a spiritual group leader focused on telepathic healing and spreading the Light we can initiate a worldwide network of Light Groups. We all need healing so if we heal our self we can heal the Planet Earth. It will take courage and quite a lot of creative input and responsibility to begin to nurture and spiritually nourish a group of individuals. Fear not. As long as you are coming from your heart and your motivation is to strive for more spiritual understanding and to give life more meaning you cannot fail. It is essential for the spiritual group leader to blend and harmonise with the whole group, encouraging each member to open their own heart and share their strengths, weaknesses and aspirations.

A spiritual group leader will begin to develop a personal devotion to the call of service and be able to release the lower ego and work totally from the **Heart on the Love Ray**. It will be inspiring, uplifting as well as challenging.

It is quite surprising how quickly intuition develops and how much support we will ultimately receive from our own Higher Self, our **Inner Teacher**, and from the Angelic dimensions. If you are willing to serve humanity and accept this challenge you will find it immensely rewarding. There are so many seekers worldwide searching for such guidance and support and who want to share and exchange energy with one another. It is a special kind of privilege to undertake and encourage different kinds of people to develop and manifest their own, innate, potential to become a telepathic healing channel for the **Light of the Soul** which is the highest form of Wisdom and Service.

Leading spiritual and healer development groups in many different places and countries, I have been astonished by the empowering love, guidance and support of the group soul consciousness and how it teaches us to heal on a soul-to-soul level. One of the greatest advantages of a spiritual group leader is the fact that people are able to more quickly develop and amplify their inner potential on a regular basis in a loving and supportive environment.

Creating Group Harmony and Balance

The group soul consciousness is based on the principles of **Love - Harmony - Dedication** – and a desire to serve humanity.

It is the task of the spiritual group leader to create a good balance within the group consciousness so that no one should feel more important than any other person or feel they are in any way competing with their colleagues. The spiritual group leader also provides a backing system for anything that might crop up and which may be of concern to an individual person. Members should be invited to share what it is they are bringing to the group and what it is they want to take away. This should always be done in the spirit of loving support.

A group is really like a choir of singers. Without a Conductor they may all be 'out of tune'. The Conductor and Principal singer is the spiritual group leader whose voice, occasionally, can be heard above the others. Achieving harmony within the group may take a little time and practise but the ultimate results and spiritual work are well worth the effort.

Remember, each member of the group is a combination of seven different levels of awareness, seven different vibratory rates, forming one beautiful rainbow. They each bring their own particular colours to the group environment. There is no question of anyone claiming more importance than any other. Some may be more experienced but this will only enhance the advancement of the group if there is a completely harmonious sharing and exchange of energy in a loving and healing atmosphere.

The first aim of the spiritual group leader is to harmonise and balance these different colours and help everyone to safely reach the intuitive levels of consciousness through meditative practises. Each group member needs to be guided and supported to be able to develop a balance on a mental level and everyone should be encouraged to spiritually cleanse and purify themselves as a part of their own self-healing and spiritual growth. As you gain in experience as a spiritual group leader you will be able to sense how people feel, what kind of mood they are in, when they attend the group meeting. The creative input and energy generated by the whole group at these spiritual development meetings boosts and supports the spiritual group leader in a dynamic way. It is a complete offering and sharing of unconditional love and group endeavour to amplify one's own spiritual purpose to network the Light for our own self-healing and the healing of Humanity.

As the spiritual development group settles down and each member's awareness increases we should be able to sense when our consciousness is expanded to a higher level of awareness and perception. We should be able to feel the beneficial changes manifesting in our physical life.

Personal Contribution

Every group member makes a personal contribution of their own through the energy they bring to the group and which they are capable of transmuting. Personal and group harmony is the aim. There is no room for disruption from someone feeling more important than another. We all have something special to share with one another. Some members of the group may be able to 'see' colours or be naturally clairvoyant or clairaudient. This is good because their personal contribution may possibly help to boost other members in the group who lack these gifts and so they too can gain some of this energy for themselves. It is good to remember that the highest level is the humblest level. Nobody in the group should be allowed to 'show-off'. The spiritual group leader has to develop tact and sensitivity.

So, we may ask, does it matter if the spiritual group leader is not clairvoyant or clairaudient? This does not really matter so long as the spiritual group leader is capable of intuiting or sensing or feeling what is happening most of the time. The aim of the spiritual group leader is to be able to create the possibility for the combined group energy to reach the intuitive level of consciousness and to be able to safely 'open' everyone's potential for transformation. By being able to harmonise all the colours or vibrations available and working towards the 'highest', and reaching for white light the spiritual development group will then be able to work more effectively.

Working in Close Mental and Spiritual Co-operation

Leading groups has enhanced every aspect of my life and also been a wonderful Teacher for me. We are all mirrors for one another and what we see in someone else is there in us too. In a group situation there is much to reflect upon. Everyone helps one another by caring and sharing. We are learning to work in close mental and spiritual co-operation. We have to be willing to learn to subordinate our own personal ideas, personal growth, to the group quest. I am proud to call myself a spiritual development group leader. In my opinion being a member of a Spiritual Group is about the best thing that can happen to us though it is not always 'a piece of cake'. It is a challenge. It is an initiation. It is transformational.

Although spiritual growth will differ from person to person and must remain a personal quest, belonging to a spiritual development group will definitely accelerate and amplify one's own spiritual potential. Being able to relax and meditate, share and exchange healing energy within the context of the group soul can be a nurturing and positive expression of self-love and self-support.

Over the years many unsolicited progress reports from group members have reached me and feedback is always extremely useful to a Group Leader.

Here is an edited version of one such letter.

"The meeting last night was very special. I wanted to say so many things to you, to thank you. You have been one of the most influential people in my life and I feel very blessed to have known you. Through your Group Leadership I have met wonderful friends. I have opened up to Spirit and I have gained confidence in my abilities. I have gained true meaning in my life.

Prior to joining the Group, there was a void in my life and I didn't know how to fill it. All I knew was that "there was something else" – you and the group facilitated my finding that. I know there is still more out there or within me and I am excited about developing into other areas.

I hope to become the Leader of a Group. What is important is that you believed in me and encouraged me to believe in me. As you know my childhood was difficult, sometimes violent. I was discouraged from believing in myself. As a young child I just 'knew' things and my God was loving and inspirational and would hold me when I cried. Through your Leadership and the group support I started to heal my inner child and bring her back to me. I have worked on my Ego and my feelings of never being good enough. Ambition was a dirty word in my upbringing. I feel 'alive' now and my personal quest is to be the best I can possibly be. I hope, when I become a Group Leader, myself, I will be able to empower others as you and the Group have empowered me."

Through the regular practice of meditation and healing the spiritual group leader will be able to transform the group consciousness to higher levels of Mind and utilise this Divine energy for the good of humanity and the Planet. Go to it!

Chapter 15:

Suggested Format for Spiritual Group Meetings

NB: Drawing upon the previous spiritual attunement procedures covering breathing, relaxation, visualisation and meditation already outlined in the preceding chapters in part two of my book, here are some further helpful guidelines:-

Opening the Group Meeting

If possible place chairs in a circle around a small table on which a candle has been placed.

Then each member of the group stands in a circle around the table and hold hands with the right palm facing down in preparation later to 'send' loving energy around the group and then receive this energy into their left palm which is facing upwards.

The group leader lights the candle and dedicates the light to a greater light and invokes that light into the group endeavour. (*The Lamplighter Prayer and/or 'The Great Invocation' may be spoken individually or collectively*).

Each member is encouraged to focus on the candlelight for a few minutes and to breathe in the light purposely and slowly into every cell, every muscle, every organ, every system in their body consciousness. As they do so they should 'earth' this energy by consciously sending rootlets of golden energy from underneath their feet making them feel heavy and connected to the ground.

Still holding hands the group leader asks each group member to tune into the power of unconditional love and consciously breathe in this universal energy into their heart centre and again 'earth' this energy through their feet.

Still holding hands each group member is asked to release from the palm of their right hand a purposeful flow of love, light and peace to each group member and which will then be received by them into the palm of their left hand. Allow time for each member to sense, receive and exchange this circuit of spiritual energy. Then each group member should place both their hands over their heart centre to personally absorb this energy. This is a very bonding process and helps also to create a point of light within the centre of the group.

Next ask them to bring their hands up over their head in the prayer position and gradually bring their hands slowly down the front of their body and down to their feet. Then they should briskly rub their hands together. This 'grounds' their personal energy field. A group hug should then be encouraged.

Next ask the members to be be seated.

Group Sharing, Conversation and Preparation

The group leader welcomes everyone and asks them to consider these two questions:

"What do you feel you are bringing to the group session?"

"What would you like to take away from the group session?"

This allows everyone to ponder more deeply upon what can be exchanged within the group and to share any concerns, comments and suggestions.

The Group Leader should then explain the **'Aura Cleansing Egg Breath'** reminding everyone that this breathing exercise balances and harmonises the body consciousness on all levels. Each person then does this cleansing exercise.

Grounding, Relaxing & Centring

Sitting comfortably and with legs uncrossed and back supported the group leader will offer a spoken procedure for relaxation of both mind and body. Everyone is encouraged to let go of any stress or tension in their body by relaxing deeply and breathing in LOVE and breathing out PEACE as the body and mind respond. The group leader must now ensure that each member is able to ground their physical energy by asking them to tune in to their feet. They have to imagine that each foot is relaxing and lengthening to twice its size and as they tune in to the soles of their feet they should imagine strong, golden roots penetrating from them deep into the earth and grounding them securely in readiness for opening into a higher level or consciousness during meditation.

Next each member should then imagine they are **centred** in a pure circle of golden, protective Light which expands all around them on the in and out breath and creates a circle of protection in readiness for a change of consciousness. The group leader then leads the members into meditation and attunement for self-healing, distant healing, and sending out the light to Mother Earth, our Planet and all the Kingdoms.

Closing Down

The group leader will then adopt a 'closing down' procedure by making the group members consciously aware once more of their physical body seated in the chair and, particularly, to sense their feet firmly placed on the ground.

Finally, in conclusion, the Group Leader will ask the members to gently open their eyes and have a good stretch of both arms and legs and then briskly rub their hands together and stamp their feet.

The group can then feed back anything useful to the whole group.

When it is time to conclude the session each member should be invited to once again stand in a circle around the candle.

The group leader will then hold the candle and make a dedication in order to 'send out' the light, for example:

I dedicate this light to the healing of our planet.

I dedicate this light to the healing of humanity.

I dedicate this light to world peace.

The candle will then be passed around the group so that each member may also dedicate the light in whatever way they wish to do so.

After the light has been extinguished invite the members to share in a group hug before dispersing.

Chapter 16:

Some Questions and Answers

'God's love is either a miracle speeded up or slowed
down'
- Lilla Bek.

Below are a selection of questions put forward by healers
or student healers to my column in the 'Healing Review', an
NFSH publication.

Question: Does Spiritual Healing Cure?

Answer: Spiritual Healing is divine and works on many different levels, mostly invisible, and the healing energy definitely
disperses to where it is most needed and will always be beneficial in one way or another but not always at the physical level.
The reason being that at a cellular level there will be both positive and negative energies stored from this life and past lives
that need to be balanced and harmonised. As every cell has its
own brain and nervous system it is nothing short of a miracle
that healing reaches all parts of our body consciousness, ultimately at soul level.

I am reminded of a little song I heard and happily shared
with students attending courses, it is a very powerful affirma-
tion:

*'Every little cell in my body is happy. Every little cell in my
body is well. I'm so glad every little cell in my body is happy
and well'.*

Dedicated spiritual healers work with the power of unconditional love knowing that:

'It is thy will be done – not my will be done'.

All healing is self-healing and works for the highest good and highest purpose for the person who is seeking it. Most definitely is not 'my' will be done'.

There is also a question of karma – the law of cause and effect – which may mean that the illness of the person you are healing is providing some kind of karmic wisdom and might possibly be a life-transforming situation that brings with it specific lessons not only for the client but also for the spiritual healer.

Question: What are the main qualities of a spiritual healer?

Answer: Love is the most important quality followed by compassion and spiritual motivation. Love – unconditional love – is the highest vibration a healer endeavours to channel in a healing situation. Another quality is a sense of responsibility to one's self to improve their own health and wellbeing. In addition they won't be constantly seeking results but their focus will be to act as a beautiful reflector of divine love, light and peace in order for the act of healing to be 'Thy will be done – not my will be done.'

Question: How does spiritual healing work?

Answer: The spiritual healer attunes to and acts as a transformer of divine energy, which when introduced into the recipient's energy field acts as a release mechanism for the client to 'let go' of whatever negative energy they might consciously or unconsciously be holding on to. Spiritual healing helps to balance and harmonise the client's personal life-force at all levels of body, mind and soul. No healer really 'cures' anyone. Ultimately we have to heal ourselves. When we experience illness it is the body's way of telling us that we are dis-eased, out of balance and not in harmony. Spiritual healing helps a person to 'go beyond' the physical level and attain a heightened state of consciousness. It is at this point that the client's own self-healing process can be activated and a mechanism set in motion which boosts the client's own potential for releasing negative patterns and to make changes in their life which will assist them in restoring peace, harmony and health at all levels.

Question: What process is involved in trying to develop a personal healing channel and in becoming a confident spiritual healer?

Answer: Ideally we should be guided and supported by a reputable organisation such as the National Federation of Spiritual Healers, now re-named The NFSH Trust, who run excellent training and development courses in spiritual healing and who have gained public acclaim and respect for the high standards of professional healer-ship their members represent. More than anything a student healer needs encouragement and advice from someone more experienced to whom they can turn to. It is very commendable when someone feels spiritually motivated to develop their own healing potential. The development period is usually a time for transformation on all levels. Sometimes it feels as if it may take forever because these levels from which we can draw spiritual wellbeing are infinite but with love and humility we can begin to discover our own pathway to our Higher Self and connect to that part of our divinity which links us at a soul level to Spirit. As we discover how to relax, breathe well, meditate and attune to that highest aspect within each of us we will be able to connect to a higher source of energy. During the development period we should never force change or become impatient; everything should be allowed to unfold in a natural, gentle manner.

Question: Can any harm be done to someone if they are unaware that they are the recipient of distant healing from either an individual or a group?

Answer: The simple answer is 'No'. How can the energy of pure love harm anyone. That is what is being transmitted by a spiritual healer through their own and the client's Higher Self. In this way the energy can be accepted or rejected without interfering with a person's free-will. Ideally it is helpful if the person whose name is on the distant healing list is aware that they are receiving healing by this method but not essential. See my section on distant or telepathic healing which covers this point in depth.

Question: Is it wrong to accept money for healing?

Answer: This is an old-age and particularly thorny question. Some spiritual healers have 'conscientious objections' to accepting money on any pretext, even it if is only to cover expenses or is intended as a donation to a healing charity such as The NFSH Trust. Some feel they will have their healing gift taken away from them if they accept money. Conversely we each of us are worth our hire. Spiritual healing is always free but one's time and effort in providing this service is not. Most people prefer to exchange energy in some way either by knowing in advance what fee the spiritual healer charges, or what kind of donation they can make. Money is only an energy and no well-meaning, dedicated healer should ever feel unable to accept financial payment for work well done with the right intent. There is no spiritual law that says a person cannot give to receive. To prevent such an exchange taking place may actually create a karmic link between the spiritual healer and their client which will have to be cleared at some point.

Question: Are there any special symptoms that respond to healing more than others?

Answer: The main purpose of spiritual healing is not in treating any particular symptom but the whole person at all levels of their mind-body-soul. As it is now accepted that spiritual healing takes place on many levels of consciousness the intent of the spiritual healer is to reach the highest level possible, the Higher Self. At this level 'Thy Will' not 'My Will' be done.

RESOURCES

Helpful resource information

The NFSH Charitable Trust (Working name The Healing Trust)
Office email: office@thehealingtust.org.uk
www.thehealingtrust.org.uk

Lilla Bek
Details of her books and Unique Wisdom Teachings.
www.lillabek.com

Ananda
Offers free on-line copies of Paramhansa Yogananda's
Autobiography Of A Yogi - the world's best seller.
www.ananda.org

Self-Realization Fellowship World-Wide Spiritual Organization.
Founded by Paramahansa Yogananda in 1920.
www.yogananda.org

Creative visualisation and self-healing guided audio healing meditations with music

The Temple Meditation

Meditation - A Channel for Healing

Healing Light

Relax - Release, Let Go!

Angel Power

Reiki - Pathway to the Soul

Reiki - The Sacred Shrine

www.audreymurrcopland.com

Printed by Amazon Italia Logistica S.r.l.
Torrazza Piemonte (TO), Italy

11695228R00257